Dedication

To Christina Marie,
my one and only HKEY

The Windows 95 Registry

A Survival Guide for Users

John Woram

A Subsidiary of
Henry Holt and Co., Inc.

MIS:Press
a subsidiary of Henry Holt and Company, Inc.
115 West 18th Street
New York, NY 10011
http://www.mispress.com

First Edition—1996

Printed in the United States of America.

Library of Congress Cataloging-in-Publication Data
ISBN 1-55828-494-X

10 9 8 7 6 5 4 3

MIS:Press books are available at special discounts for bulk purchases for sales promotions, premiums, and fundraising. Special editions or book excerpts can also be created to specification.

For details contact: Special Sales Director
                         MIS:Press
                         a subsidiary of Henry Holt and Company, Inc.
                         115 West 18th Street
                         New York, New York 10011

Associate Publisher: *Paul Farrell*

Executive Editor: *Cary Sullivan*   **Production Editor:** *Stephanie Doyle*
Editor: *Michael Sprague*   **Copy Edit Manager:** *Shari Chappell*

CONTENTS

v

Chapter 3: The Windows 95 Registry Structure, Part II 73

Chapter 6: Backup, Restore, and Compare 261

Chapter 7: Troubleshooting the Registry 287

Chapter 8: Registry Error Messages 323

Index 345

Acknowledgments

This is the part nobody ever reads where, under the guise of profuse thanks, the author publicly identifies those who can later be implicated for whatever is wrong with the manuscript. Fortunately, my list is indeed short, for when most people of good sense heard this was to be a book about the Windows 95 Registry, they recalled pressing engagements elsewhere and departed with the assurance of getting back in touch "real soon now."

Of those who hung in there, Senior Technical Editor Dave Methvin at *Windows* magazine was always willing (or if not, he hid it well) to discuss some of the thornier points that kept sticking me. Likewise, Technical Editor John Yacono was a friendly guide through the mists surrounding a few network keys.

I should also extend a group thanks to the Windows SIG members of the Long Island PC Users Group, who could always be counted on to come up with inquiries about how—and sometimes why—the Registry does whatever it does. It's always helpful to know what the questions are before offering answers.

Closer to the scene of the crime, I mustn't forget to thank Publisher Paul Farrell at MIS:Press for thinking a guide book to the Windows 95 Registry would be a "good idea." He may or may not want to acknowledge that the idea was in fact his, but that will probably depend on the reviews. And down in the trenches, a special thank you to Editor Michael Sprague, who when the going got tough could always be counted on to lie about the real deadline and to assure Paul that everything was "right on track." Little does Michael know (unless he reads acknowledgment pages) that at least some of his work was done in advance by Nancy Lang at *Windows* magazine, who is in charge of making sure my monthly "Optimizing Windows" column—which often touches the Registry—bore at least a passing resemblance to reality. Or, as Nancy once put it: "So tell me, outside of the Registry, what else do you do?"

Last, and by all means least, thanks to the powers that be at Microsoft for inviting me to get in touch whenever a particularly difficult problem came up, and to acknowledge that my questions were always received with polite interest. I have no doubt their answers will be received here with the same interest, on the off-chance I live long enough to get any. In the meantime, I've devised my own, which are laid out in the chapters that follow. I'll keep my fingers crossed that what has worked well here on a variety of machines will work elsewhere too.

Just don't forget those backups (Chapter 6).

John Woram
Rockville Centre, NY
September 1996

PREFACE

Using Registry Editor incorrectly can cause serious problems that may require you to re-install Windows 95. Microsoft cannot guarantee that problems resulting from the incorrect use of Registry Editor can be solved. Use Registry Editor at your own risk.

WARNING

This cheery little greeting appears in more than 100 Microsoft technical papers, which might give one the impression that the company does not encourage its customers to mess around with the Registry—an impression reinforced by the almost-complete absence of useful information about it. The "Introducing Microsoft Windows 95" booklet that accompanies the product makes no mention of a Registry, other than a single page that describes how to restore it—whatever *it* is.

But, of course, there is online help: just click the Start menu's **Help** icon, look up **Registry**, and you'll be invited to click a check box if you want your Registry restored, assuming, of course, that your network administrator has set up a backup agent on the server and that you actually have 1) a network, 2) an administrator, 3) a backup agent, and 4) a server. What more could anyone *possibly* want to know about the Registry?

Well, there's also the Windows 95 Resource Kit, in whose 1348 pages you'll find about 20 on the Registry—barely enough to let you know that it exists and that you might need to restore it and to offer a few pages about five of its six keys. If you read it all (it doesn't take long), you'll discover there's an otherwise-undocumented Registry Editor utility in the **C:\Windows** folder, although this is included only with the CD-ROM version of Windows 95. The utility includes a help file, which, at about 18 Kbytes, is less than half the size of the average Windows 95 help file.

In short, the Windows 95 Registry is not entirely undocumented, but it comes close. Take away the restoration warnings, and it comes even closer. Hence this book, whose premise is that the Registry is right up there with death and taxes—unavoidable, rarely pleasant, but always something one wants to know a bit more about, if only to better cope with its mysteries. Like it or not, the Registry is about as inconsequential to the Windows 95 system as the human brain is to the Windows 95 user. Fortunately, further analysis of the relationship between Windows 95 and brains is beyond the scope of this book, which will have quite enough to do explaining the basic mechanics of the Registry, how to tune it, and what to do when it breaks down.

Although one should never underestimate the power of the Registry to bring the system down, it is actually quite clever about curing itself whenever something—or someone—makes it sick. In the course of preparing this book, it was subjected to just about every indignity imaginable, often just to see what would happen if it got kicked really hard here, and here, and there too. Often enough, it would just bounce back without complaining, at least until even more elegant tortures were devised. But—Microsoft's repeated warning notwithstanding—it was never necessary to execute the ultimate restoration technique: that of completely re-installing Windows 95 to recover from a Registry indiscretion.

From the point of view of the typical user, it is often possible to edit the Registry by indirect means; that is, to make some configuration change via the Control Panel or elsewhere, and just let Windows 95 attend to the Registry on its own. If you find yourself wondering, "Wouldn't it be easier to just ..., " the answer may very well be *yes*. But this is a book about the Registry and how it handles the road, regardless of who's driving. Sometimes the easier path is mentioned; other times it's not. Still other times, there *is* no easier path: either you edit the Registry or you do without. Regardless of who, or what, does the edit, it always helps to know a little something about how it all comes together. And in the Registry, it is sometimes a wonder that it comes together at all.

Describing the Registry is not unlike describing a bowl of spaghetti. Where do all the strands begin, and where do they end? No doubt, there are beginnings and ends, but they're not always easy to find. Which brings us (or at least, me) to the first problem: how to unravel the Registry and lay it out for viewing and dissection. For better or worse, here's how it was done.

Chapter 1 offers a general introduction to the Registry and the Registry Editor utility, which is then used in Chapters 2 and 3 as a magnifying glass through which to view each of the Registry's six keys, one at a time. Because the user will no doubt spend a lot of time in the key known as **HKEY_CLASSES_ROOT**, all of Chapter 2 is devoted to its subkey structure, and Chapter 3 covers the everything-else of the Registry. Given the internal relationships between one key and almost any other, a certain amount of back-and-forth work is required, so it may be best to do a quick skim of both chapters and then go back for a closer read.

The serious work begins in Chapter 4, where the Registry Editor is actually put to use as an editing tool. This is followed by Chapter 5, on using the Registry Editor and other means to customize the Registry.

Perhaps Chapter 6 belongs earlier in the book, because it covers the backup work that should be done before trying any of the techniques described in the previous chapters. But one needs to have read Chapter 4 (at least) in order to do that work, and Chapter 4 leads logically into Chapter 5, and... well, you get the idea.

The last two chapters are probably in the right sequence. Chapter 7 describes—if not all, at least some of—the things that can go wrong while getting through the previous chapters. The perceptive reader may detect a striking resemblance to the things that can go wrong while not wading through the previous chapters. So, whenever bad things happen and the Registry is a prime suspect, this is the place to start the search for evidence. However, if a problem is polite enough to announce itself by laying a message across the screen, try Chapter 8, where such messages are lined up for inspection. With luck, you'll find the one you're looking for or perhaps one that's close enough.

And now, a few words about the general organization of what follows, beginning with a question. When is a folder not a folder? To anyone who has already typed **REGEDIT.EXE** in the Run box, there's only one answer: when it's a Registry key. There are who knows how many icons in the Windows 95 universe—perhaps not millions and billions (heavy emphasis on the first syllables), but certainly more than a few. Yet to represent a Registry key, Microsoft has selected one of the few icons in its universe that may be easily confused with something else—the folder icon. Thus, a Windows 95 Registry window can sometimes look like a Windows 95 Explorer window, as shown here in Figure 1. Without looking at the Title and Menu Bars, can you tell which is the Registry and which is not?

The rest of this book contains many views of the Registry Editor window, not a few of which have been doctored a bit to present the most useful information with the least useless white space. In other words, many figures offer a composite view of several keys' worth of data, although the Registry itself will only divulge its contents one subkey at a time. The first figure of Chapter 1 is as good an example as any. If this had been a real Registry window, only one of the open keys would have been visible at a time. A line and arrow often leads from an open key to its contents, which is not really necessary in this one-line-per-key illustration, but which may be helpful elsewhere (the first figure in Chapter 4, for example), when several keys each lead to multiple lines of data. In other figures, a line runs from one key to another, as a visual aid in tracking the relationship between two or more keys.

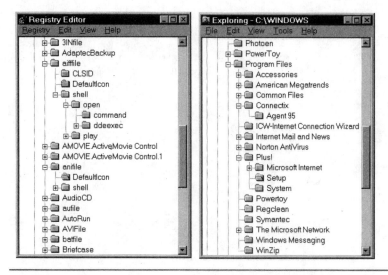

Figure 1 *At first glance, the Registry Editor window's Key Pane bears a close resemblance to a conventional Windows 95 Explorer window. Despite appearances, those icons are keys, not folders. Each one can be opened, closed, renamed, or deleted but not moved.*

Because the same illustration often shows Registry sections that are actually at some distance from each other, a double-tilde (≈) indicates a point where intervening keys are omitted. A single tilde (~) indicates a line that leads to additional keys that are all omitted.

If the Registry Editor's Status Bar is enabled, it gives the identity of the currently open key, which leads to a potential problem in those illustrations that show more than one open key. Accordingly, an ellipsis (...) at the end of any Status Bar line is a clue that the line has been edited to include only that segment of the complete path common to all displayed keys.

And now, let the confusion begin.

Chapter 1

Introduction to the Windows 95 Registry

The Registry simplifies the operating system by eliminating the need for AUTOEXEC.BAT, CONFIG.SYS, and INI files (except when legacy applications require them).

—*Microsoft Windows 95 Resource Kit*

"The check is in the mail."

—*American folklore*

If you believe either of these proverbs, you may believe the other one as well, and this book may not be the right one for you! Fortunately, one of them is a bit beyond the scope of this little book, which deals exclusively with the other one.

In fact, the first proverb is almost true, because quite often the Registry does make it possible to do away with **CONFIG.SYS** and **AUTOEXEC.BAT** files. However, you may be sure that the **INI** file will be with us for a long time. Although much information formerly found in various **INI** files is now stored in the Registry, other information remains in its traditional **INI** file location, for the benefit of those legacy applications that don't recognize the Registry. In still other cases, Windows 95 creates new **INI** files that did not exist in earlier versions of Windows.

As a result of all this, it is not unusual to find 25 or more **INI** files, even on a machine that had no previous version of Windows installed. Some of these files are installed by Windows 95 itself, others by applications designed to run under Windows 95 only. If you need hard proof, just open the Windows 95 Explorer's Tools menu and use the **Find** option to search for all **INI** files on drive **C**. You'll soon discover that the **INI** file is very much a part of the Windows 95 operating system. We therefore begin with a brief summary of its traditional use, in order to better understand its relationship with the new Windows 95 Registry.

In the discussion that follows, some information is valid for all versions of Windows, while some applies only to certain versions. Therefore, the following distinctions are made, as required:

Windows	All Windows and Windows for Work- groups versions, from 3.0 through Windows 95
Windows 3.*x*	All versions 3.0 through 3.11 only
Windows 95	Windows 95 only

An INI File Overview

The ubiquitous Windows initialization file is recognizable to one and all by its distinctive **INI** extension, as in **SYSTEM.INI**, **WIN.INI**, and countless other **WHATEVER.INI** files. Most such files are written into the **C:\WINDOWS** directory, although some may be found in other locations after this or that Windows application is installed. In any case, these **INI** files contain the configuration information that Windows needs to run both itself and the assortment of Windows applications and applets that are installed on the system.

INI File Format and Structure

With very few exceptions, such as the old **WINWORD.INI** (in Word for Windows, version 2), the **INI** file was—and still is—an ASCII file that can be edited via the DOS Edit utility, from the Windows Notepad applet, or from any word processor that can save a file in straight ASCII (text) format. The file is divided into sections, and information must be entered into the appropriate section in order to be recognized and implemented, as shown in these brief examples of typical **INI** file structure:

```
[SectionName]
item=filename.ext
driver=filename.drv
otheritem=C:\UTILITY\CUSTOM\whatever.ext

[AnotherSectionName]
Workgroup=ROCKVILLE
AutoLogon=Yes
EnableSharing=0

[YetAnotherName]
dma=1
irq=7
port=220
```

As these examples show, an **INI** file specifies many items that will vary from one system to another and therefore cannot be "hard-coded" into Windows itself. Such items might include the following:

- name of—and if necessary, path to—a specific file required by Windows

- a user-defined configuration (AutoLogon=Yes, Enable Sharing=0)

- hardware and/or software configuration (dma=1, irq=7, port=220)

In the final example, the DMA, IRQ, and port settings transmit information in one direction only; that is, the **INI** file informs Windows that a certain device requires the use of the indicated resources. If some other device requires one or more of the same resources, neither Windows itself nor its **INI** files can inform the device that the resource is unavailable and that it should therefore pick some other setting for itself.

The SYSTEM.INI File

As its name implies, this system initialization file contains system-specific information that Windows requires in order to open successfully. The [boot] section was, and still is, especially critical, in that it specifies various drivers that Windows needs. In Windows 95, the [386Enh] (Enhanced) section is typically much smaller than in previous versions, because many of the virtual device drivers formerly listed here are now found in the **C:\Windows\System\Iosubsys** folder and no longer need to be specified by a device= line in this section. Windows 95 automatically loads every **VXD** file it finds in the **Iosubsys** and **Vmm32** folders, so these files no longer need to be listed in the [386Enh] section of **SYSTEM.INI**.

Some other familiar sections are now conspicuous by their absence. For example, if Windows 95 recognizes an installed sound card, the **SYSTEM.INI** section that formerly specified the card's resources (that is, IRQ, DMA, and I/O settings) may be completely deleted, with some resource settings stored in the

Registry and others dynamically set each time Windows 95 opens. If, however, Windows 95 does *not* recognize the sound card or some other hardware device, then that device's resource settings will remain in **SYSTEM.INI**.

The WIN.INI File

In Windows 3.*x*, this file contained much of the data that the user might customize to suit personal preference, such as color schemes, some Desktop items (pattern, wallpaper, icon spacing, etc.), port settings, and fonts. Windows 95 stores much of this information in the Registry—in some cases actually deleting it from **WIN.INI** after making the necessary entries in the Registry. In other cases, Windows 95 maintains the same information in both **WIN.INI** and the Registry, and if for some reason the Registry data is missing, it will refer to **WIN.INI** for the needed information. For example, Windows 95 removes font information from **WIN.INI** after it has been written into the Registry. By contrast, the same Desktop pattern and wallpaper specifications are now found (and maintained) in both **WIN.INI** and the Registry.

Other INI Files

Windows 95 retains many other **INI** files, and there doesn't seem to be much consistency in how these are treated. In **CONTROL.INI**, for example, the [drivers.desc] and [Patterns] sections remain, while the color scheme's [current] and [color schemes] sections are transplanted to the Registry. Therefore, if you discover that an old familiar **INI** file is now only partially intact, it's quite likely that the missing information now resides in the Registry. As for what remains, some of that may be duplicated in the Registry.

The Rationale Behind the Registry

In addition to the **INI** files just described, Windows 3.1 introduced us to the Registration Database, whose **REG.DAT** file contained information on how various applications would open and how some of them would print documents. The database excerpt in Figure 1.1 shows how this data would look if the Windows 3.1 **REGEDIT.EXE** utility was executed in its so-called *verbose* mode. The figure shows three registered applications (Pbrush, regedit, wrifile), and under each one a *shell* branch leads to commands (open and print, in these examples) appropriate to the application. The figure also shows how the same information is stored in the Windows 95 Registry.

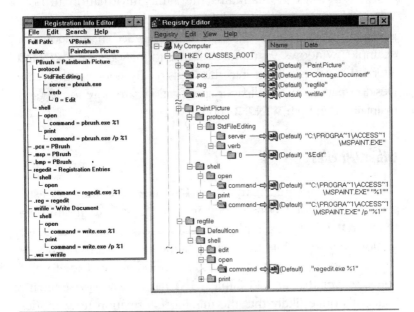

Figure 1.1 *This comparison of the Windows 3.1 Registration Info Editor and the Windows 95 Registry Editor windows shows how the same information is displayed by each editor.*

A Brief Introduction to the Windows 95 Registry Editor

Although detailed use of the Windows 95 Registry Editor is not discussed until Chapter 4, some minimal familiarity with the applet is necessary in order to survive the remaining sections of this Chapter and those that follow. Therefore, this section describes how to immediately access the Registry Editor so that you can better understand the definitions and description that follow. For the moment (that is, until Chapter 4), the Registry Editor will be used *only* as a passive viewing device.

The Registry Editor utility (**REGEDIT.EXE**) is copied to the **C:\Windows** folder on the hard disk during the Windows 95 setup procedure, but an icon is not made available as part of that procedure. For occasional use, simply select the Start menu's **Run** option, type **REGEDIT** in the Open: box, and either click the **OK** button or press the **Enter** key. For more extensive use, place a shortcut to the utility on the Desktop or in any other convenient location. In either case, the Registry Editor window should appear on the Windows 95 Desktop when the **REGEDIT.EXE** file is executed. The Registry Editor's component parts are described later in this chapter.

MS Plus! and the Registry

The Microsoft Plus! Companion for Windows 95 is a supplementary CD-ROM disc that adds additional features to Windows 95. In a few cases, a feature is already a part of Windows 95 alone, and MS Plus! simply adds a section to the Registry to enable that feature. The same feature can be enabled without installing MS Plus! by editing the Registry as described in various sections of Chapter 5.

OEM Versions of Windows 95

In the fourth quarter of 1996, Microsoft revised the version of Windows 95 supplied to various manufacturers for installation on computers sold to the general public. Among other things, the Registry in one of these OEM (Original Equipment Manufacturer) versions of Windows 95 may differ from that found on the software purchased separately from a retail outlet. In several places throughout this book, the term *OEM version* is used to specifically identify a Registry key or subkey that differs from the equivalent key in the conventional retail product.

In many cases, new features made available since the introduction of the original retail version of the Windows 95 CD-ROM disc may be downloaded from the Microsoft Web site (*www.microsoft.com*). Therefore, if a Registry component described here is not currently supported in your version of Windows 95, you may be able to find the necessary add-ons at that Web site.

MS Plus! and OEM Versions of Windows 95

Even if MS Plus! itself is not installed, some OEM versions add a **Plus!** subfolder beneath the **Program Files** folder, and this folder may lead to additional subfolders (**Microsoft Internet** or **System**, for example) that may be viewed via the Explorer applet. Because of this, a **Plus!** subkey may be found in the Registry, and various Data columns (described later) may contain numerous references to **Plus!** folders, even though the complete MS Plus! is not installed on the system.

Definitions

This section offers definitions of a few terms unique to the Registry. Because there are not that many of them, the definitions are listed here in the order in which they are likely to be encountered, rather than in the usual alphabetical sequence. Additional terms are defined in the chapters in which they are first used.

The Registry: Windows 95 writes much of its configuration information into the hidden **SYSTEM.DAT** and **USER.DAT** files, which are found in the **C:\Windows** folder. If the system is configured for multiple users, a separate **USER.DAT** file is created for each user, and each such file is found in the user's own custom Profiles area, as described in more detail in the "Custom Profiles" section of Chapter 4. These **DAT** files are referred to collectively as *The Registry*.

Registry Editor: The *Registry Editor* is the Windows 95 utility used to edit the Registry's **SYSTEM.DAT** and **USER.DAT** files. For routine configuration changes, the Registry is automatically edited whenever the user makes changes via the Control Panel or from some other Windows 95 applet or application. Alternatively, the Registry may be directly edited as described in Chapters 3 and 4.

In conventional **INI** file viewing, it is always clear which file is open, because the user must load that file into an Edit utility, where its name appears in the editor's Title Bar. By contrast, the Registry Editor loads data contained in the two **DAT** files but does not identify either file by name.

Any change made via the Registry Editor takes place immediately, and the new information is written into SYSTEM.DAT or USER.DAT, as appropriate. The usual Save File operation is not required, and in fact is not possible. In order to undo a change, the appropriate line must be re-edited.

N O T E

HKEY: The Registry is divided into six sections, each identified as HKEY_*SectionName*, which immediately raises the question, what's an HKEY? In Microspeak, it is the programming *handle* to a *key* (hence, *HKEY*) in which configuration information is stored.

Key: A *key* is the Registry analog to the folder (formerly, directory) seen in the Windows 95 Explorer. In fact, a folder icon appears next to each of the six HKEYs in the Registry.

Subkey: Again following the Explorer model, a boxed plus sign to the immediate left of a Registry key indicates there are one or more *subkeys* (analogous to subfolders) contained within the adjacent key. Each subkey may contain its own subkeys, and so on for several levels. Like the six HKEYs, each subkey is represented by a folder icon.

Key vs. Subkey: Because every HKEY and many subkeys lead to one or more additional subkeys, a tendency to describe the subkey, subsubkey, subsubsubkey, and so on must be avoided if at all possible. Accordingly, after any subkey has been introduced, it may subsequently be referred to as a *key*, while a key immediately below it is referred to as a *subkey*, until it becomes the focus of the discussion.

Subkey Level: In a few cases, a key leads to a subkey with the same name, which may in turn lead to another subkey—again with the same name, as shown by the example in Figure 1.2. If it is necessary to clearly differentiate one such key from another, it may be necessary to refer to the level at which it appears in the key\subkey structure. The figure illustrates a worst-case example, in which a level-5 **.Default** key leads to a level-6 **.Default** key, which leads to a level-7 **.Default** key. As shown in the figure, *My Computer* is at level 0, the six HKEYs are at level 1, and the subkeys are at level 2 or greater.

Refer to "A .Default Subkey Note" and Figure 3.3 in Chapter 3 for another example of multiple **.Default** keys.

Verb: For reasons that are not entirely clear, the Microspeak Dictionary defines the type of action that can be performed on an object as a *verb*. Two common verbs are play and edit. The typical use for an object is called the *primary verb*. Double-clicking an object usually executes the action specified by the primary verb. Other verbs are *secondary verbs*. Many objects support only one verb.

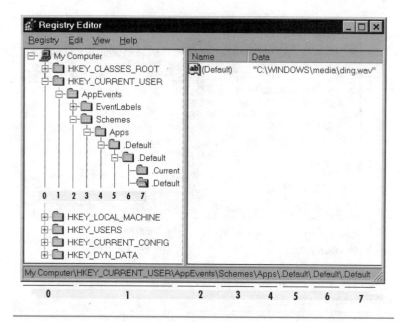

Figure 1.2 *This Registry Editor window shows three subkeys with the same name (.****Default****) at levels 5, 6, and 7 of the key structure. The Status Bar at the bottom of the window reports the complete Registry path to the open .****Default**** subkey at level 7.*

The Registry Editor Window

This section offers an overview of the Registry Editor window and its component parts. Like the Windows 95 Explorer, the window is divided into two panes, as illustrated in Figure 1.3. Items common to most other Windows 95 applications, and therefore already familiar to the user, are cited here for the sake of completeness, with description kept to a minimum for the sake of saving a few trees.

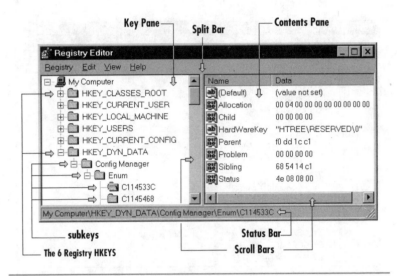

Key Pane ─ Split Bar ─ Contents Pane

subkeys
The 6 Registry HKEYS
Status Bar
Scroll Bars

Figure 1.3 *The component parts of the Windows 95 Registry Editor window.*

NOTE

The phrases Key Pane and Contents Pane are introduced in Figure 1.3 and are used throughout the book to distinguish one side of the Registry Editor window from the other. Both terms are the invention of the author and probably don't exist other than in these pages.

Title Bar

The *Title Bar* at the top of the window contains the conventional Windows 95 components: a Control menu icon, the title of the application, and the usual three buttons for minimize, restore, and close. No further explanation is needed here.

Menu Bar

As with most other Windows applets and applications, the *Menu Bar* appears directly under the Title Bar. As a central cross-reference

Although it is not possible to delete the six HKEY keys that appear directly beneath the My Computer icon, the subkeys beneath each HKEY may be deleted or renamed, and additional keys may be added, as will be described in Chapter 4.

Contents Pane

The Contents Pane on the right-hand side of the window is divided into a series of rows and columns, as described here.

Value

Forget everything you learned about the English language: in Microspeak, each horizontal row in the Contents Pane is referred to as a *value*. Thus, the information in the two columns is referred to elsewhere as the *value name* and the *value data*, even though the word *value* does not appear here in the Contents Pane.

Data Type Icon

In each row, the icon at the left side of the Name column indicates the format of the information in the Data column, as shown here:

Icon Text	Data Format
🔤	String (ASCII text) data
🔢	Binary data

Name

The Data Type icon is immediately followed by a descriptive name for the data that follows. The Registry Editor treats the icon and Name as a single entity under the Name column.

---

guide, each menu and menu option is listed here, even if it is described elsewhere (in that case, a reference to the appropriate chapter and section is provided). The menus and menu options are listed here in the sequence in which they appear; Figure 1.4 shows the options that appear on each menu.

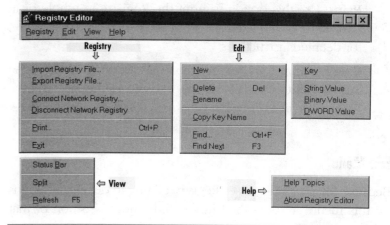

Figure 1.4 *The Registry Editor menus. The Edit menu's Copy Key Name option is available on Windows 95 OEM versions only.*

Control Menu

Click the icon at the extreme left-hand side of the Title Bar to access this menu. Its **Move**, **Size**, and other options are no different from those found on any other Control menu and are not discussed here.

Registry Menu

This menu is the Registry's equivalent to the File menu found on most other Menu Bars.

> **Import**, **Export Registry File**: These options are used to save (*export*) all or part of the registry into a separate file or

to write (*import*) a previously exported file back into the Registry, as described in detail in the "Registry Menu" section of Chapter 4.

Connect, **Disconnect Network Registry**: These options are also described in the "Registry Menu" section of Chapter 4.

Print: Use this option to print the Registry in whole or in part. Refer to the "Registry Print Jobs" section in Chapter 4 for detailed instructions.

Exit: For those torn between the Control menu's **Close** option and the **Exit** button at the opposite end of the Title Bar, the **Exit** option does just what you think it does.

Edit Menu

Because Chapter 4 discusses Registry editing in detail, all options on this menu are described in the "Edit Menu" section of that chapter.

View Menu

This menu offers the following three options, which are probably easier to access via keyboard or mouse.

Status Bar: If a check mark does not already appear to the left of this menu option, highlight it and click the primary mouse button to display the Status Bar at the bottom of the Registry Editor window. Better yet, press **Alt+V+B** to toggle the Status Bar on and off, as needed.

Split: Select this option to place a double-arrow pointer on the vertical Split bar that separates the Key Pane from the Contents Pane. Then drag the mouse or use the left and right arrow keys to move the bar.

Refresh: Select this option to refresh th Panes, as might be convenient if you've in either pane. The **Refresh** option will (if necessary) and remove highlighting f Pane, if there is any. If a key is highligh option does *not* remove that highlight. usually faster to press **F5**, which accomp task.

Help Menu

The Help menu provides only two options, as listed

Help Topics: Select this option to access Editor's help system.

About Registry Editor: Following the styl other Windows 95 *About* screens, this one is the Registry Editor at all. In case you need the it informs you of the Microsoft copyright and license and lists available memory and system re

The Key Pane

Again following the Windows 95 Explorer example, th Pane on the left-hand side of the window shows the R "folders," which are here referred to as *keys*. The "My Com designation next to the computer icon at the top of the Key is embedded in the **REGEDIT.EXE** file. Therefore, and u the equivalent icon in Explorer, it does not change if Desktop icon of the same name is renamed. Refer to " Computer window" in Chapter 5 if you really must change t to something else.

The first item in every key's Name column is always "(Default)" and the accompanying Data column usually—but not always—is "(value not set)" as shown in Figure 1.3.

NOTE

Data

The information presented in this column is the data associated with the value whose name appears in the Name column. Its format is as indicated by the Data Type icon at the beginning of the row; the data may take one of the following formats:

> **String Data**: This describes any data in human-readable format, such as the following examples:

```
"0"                               "1"
"apartment"                       (value not set)
"C:\WINDOWS\SYSTEM\cool.dll,41"   ""  (two quotation marks, no space)
"ROOT\PRINTER\0000"               "vxdfile"
```

> Note that string data is always enclosed in quotation marks, with the exception of the (value not set) data and other parenthetical remarks that indicate an empty data block or null value.

> **Binary Data**: In true Microspeak tradition, data defined as binary does not appear in binary format. Instead, it is given in hexadecimal format, as shown by these examples:

Name	Data
EditFlags	d8 07 00 00
Settings	60 00 00 00 00 01 ... 04 ... ff ff ff ... 00 00

> If a section of the Registry containing lines such as these were exported to a file (as described in Chapter 4), the same information would appear in the following format:

```
"EditFlags"=hex:d8,07,00,00
"Settings"=hex:60,00,00,00,00,01,… 04, … ff,ff,ff, … 00,00
```

Note that here the hex: label correctly identifies the data format. In any case, "binary" data displayed in the Registry can be recognized by the distinctive format *xx* space *yy* space *zz* space, where *xx*, *yy*, and *zz* are hexadecimal numbers.

DWORD Data: As a final variation, hexadecimal data may be presented in *DWORD* (double-word) format; that is, as a four-byte sequence such as in the following examples:

Name	Data
Height	0x00000240 (576)
Width	0x00000300 (768)

Although the DWORD format uses the same icon as the just-described binary data, it is easily recognized by *0x* followed by an unspaced four-byte hexadecimal sequence, followed by the decimal equivalent in parentheses. In an exported file, the same information would appear in the following format:

```
"Width"=dword:00000300
"Height"=dword:00000240
```

Data Format Comparisons

Don't waste a lot of time trying to make sense out of the various data formats. For example, the Registry Editor always displays true binary data—that is, a simple 0 or 1—in the *String* format, in which a single binary digit is enclosed in quotation marks. A decimal quantity in the Data column may also be designated as string data. As a rule-of-thumb, forget common sense and just realize that anything enclosed in quotes qualifies as string data. Any number *not* enclosed in quotes is binary or DWORD data, even though it is never shown in binary format.

In case of format anxiety, double-click on any Contents Pane icon: the Edit window's Title Bar will show one of the following legends, thus revealing the format of the data in that row:

Edit Binary value

Edit DWORD value

Edit String

Edit String

If you decide to edit the data, just make sure the revision remains in the same format. The edit procedure itself is described in detail in Chapter 4. For another example of format variations, see Figure 3.14 in Chapter 3.

Contents Pane—INI File Comparisons

To get an idea of the basic difference between how the Registry handles data formerly found in a typical **INI** file, the following examples show font and desktop information as stored in **WIN.INI** and as it now appears when viewed in the Registry Editor. Refer to "INI Files and the Registry" in Chapter 4 for additional details about how information may be moved from an **INI** file into the Registry.

FONT DATA

Every time Windows 95 opens, the [fonts] section of **WIN.INI** is checked to see if any legacy application installed fonts there during the previous session. If it did, the lines are written into the Registry and removed from **WIN.INI**. In the case of TrueType fonts, the matching *filename*.**FOT** file is deleted, because

The following example shows how a few TrueType fonts appear in **WIN.INI** and in the Registry:

WIN.INI File	Windows 95 Registry Fonts Subkey	
	Name	Data
[fonts]		
Arial(TrueType)=ARIAL.FOT	Arial (TrueType)	"ARIAL.TTF"
Courier New(TrueType)=COUR.FOT	Courier New (TrueType)	"COUR.TTF"
SYMBOL(TrueType)=SYMBOL.FOT	Symbol (TrueType)	"SYMBOL.TTF"
Times New Roman (TrueType)=TIMES.FOT	Times New Roman (TrueType)	"TIMES.TTF"
Wingdings(TrueType)= WINGDING.FOT	WingDings (TrueType)	"WINGDING.TTF"

Note that the Registry Editor gives no indication of the actual source of the displayed data. In this case, the font data shown is stored in **SYSTEM.DAT**, but the Registry Editor does not directly provide this information to the user. To determine the actual file location of any information displayed by the Registry Editor, refer to the "SYSTEM.DAT" and "USER.DAT" sections of Chapter 4.

DESKTOP DATA

This example shows how wallpaper was—and still is—specified in the **WIN.INI** file:

```
[Desktop]
Wallpaper=C:\WINDOWS\PLUS!.BMP
```

In the Registry, the [Desktop] section header becomes a **desktop** (usually, lowercase *d*) subkey under the **HKEY_CURRENT_USER\ Control Panel** subkey. If the **desktop** subkey is highlighted, the Contents Pane shows the following information:

Name	Data
Wallpaper	"C:\WINDOWS\PLUS!.BMP"

For the sake of legacy applications that are not aware of the Registry, this and other wallpaper specifications remain in **WIN.INI** as well.

Split Bar

This vertical bar separates the Key and Contents Panes and can be dragged horizontally in either direction. To do so, slowly move the mouse pointer toward the bar. When the pointer changes to a double-arrow, hold down the primary mouse button and drag the bar as desired. Or if you need to waste time, use the View menu's **Split** option, as described in the "Menu Bar" section earlier.

Scroll Bars

As in any other window, a Registry Editor window pane may display *scroll bars* if the pane size is not sufficient to display all the information it contains.

Status Bar

The Status Bar at the bottom of the Registry Editor window lists the full path to the highlighted subkey, whose contents are shown in the Contents Pane on the right-hand side of the Split bar. The Status Bar is enabled or disabled via the View menu or by pressing **Ctrl+V+B**, as previously described in the "Menu Bar" section.

CHAPTER 2

The Windows 95 Registry Structure, Part I

An HKEY Overview

As noted in Chapter 1, there are six HKEYs in the Registry. For the purposes of this overview, two of these keys are defined as Master HKEYs, and each derives its contents from its own hidden Registry file. Although these Master HKEYs may contain data for several hardware configurations and one or two users, only one of each configuration can be enabled at a time. Therefore, the Master HKEYs write the appropriate data into three other HKEYs every time Windows 95 opens. The choice of which hardware data to write into a derived key is decided as Windows 95 detects the current hardware configuration as it opens. The configuration for the current user is determined as the user enters a name and password as part of the opening procedure. However, if the system is not set up to require a user name, or if the user presses the **Escape** key in response to the opening name and password prompt, then data for a ".Default" user is selected. In any case, data for unneeded hardware configurations and an alternate user is ignored.

The contents of the sixth and final HKEY are dynamically derived from system RAM each time the system is powered on, and are neither copied from, not written to, any other key.

Figure 2.1 summarizes the procedure just described. The shaded areas represent the two master HKEYs, both of which are shown open. Within each master HKEY, a line with an arrow leads from one of its subkeys to the HKEY key that duplicates that subkey's contents.

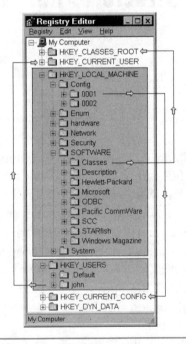

Figure 2.1 *The six Registry HKEYs. The contents of subkeys within the two shaded keys are duplicated by three of the other HKEYs, as indicated by the lines and arrows.*

To summarize this unique system, the two master HKEYs contain global data pertaining to various possible hardware and user configurations, while the three derived subkeys pertain only to the active hardware and current user configurations. For programming convenience, an application need not try to deduce which of several configurations within a Master HKEY is currently enabled. Instead, the application reads and writes data in the three derived keys, and that data is immediately recorded in the appropriate subkey within one of the master HKEYs.

For future reference, the HKEY headings in this and the next chapter begin with the abbreviation commonly used by Microsoft and others to identify the key whose full name immediately follows. This is followed by an [HKEY*subkey(s)*] in brackets to identify the Master key source from which the HKEY is derived. In the case of a Master key itself, a bracketed filename [SYSTEM.DAT *or* USER.DAT] indicates the Registry file in which the data is stored. Refer to the "SYSTEM.DAT" and "USER.DAT" sections of Chapter 4 for detailed information about these files and possible multiple copies of the **USER.DAT** file.

Because the **HKEY_CLASSES_ROOT** key alone requires about as much explanation as the other five keys combined, it is the only key described in this chapter. The other keys are described in Chapter 3.

HKCR: HKEY_CLASSES_ROOT key [HKLM\SOFTWARE\Classes]

As shown in Figure 2.2, the entire HKCR key structure is nothing more than a duplicate version of all subkeys found under the **HKEY_LOCAL_MACHINE\SOFTWARE\Classes** key. Created every time Windows opens, its primary purpose is to provide backward compatibility with the Windows 3.1 registration database. But of more interest to the user, this key provides convenient access to the **Classes** set of subkeys, which in their actual physical location are several levels below the HKLM key (described in the next chapter). In this section however, they are all immediately below the HKCR key, which makes it that much easier to find—and possibly edit—them.

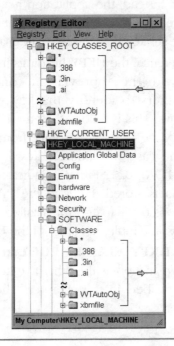

Figure 2.2 *This detail view shows how the entire contents of the* ***HKEY_LOCAL_MACHINE*** *key's* ***SOFTWARE\Classes*** *section is written into the* ***HKEY_CLASSES_ROOT*** *key.*

The Windows 95 Resource Kit places all these subkeys in two categories, *Filename-Extension* subkeys and *Class-Definition* keys, both of which are described as *subkeys* in this chapter. In addition, a third category (*Other HKCR subkeys*) is added here as a convenient place to describe a few subkeys that really don't fit comfortably under the Filename-Extension or Class-Definition category.

In any case, all such subkeys appear in alphabetical (ASCII code) order under the HKCR key, and therefore also under **HKLM\SOFTWARE\Classes** (see Chapter 3). As long as any subkey format matches one of those descriptions, its content should be quite similar to the examples given here.

NOTE

*Remember that **HKCR** is used for the convenience of users and programmers, but its subkey contents are really stored under the **HKLM\SOFTWARE\Classes** section.*

The Filename-Extension Subkey

Most such subkeys are identified by a leading period, usually followed by the three characters of a conventional filename extension, such as **.386**, **.bmp**, **.doc**, or **.txt**. A few applications add subkeys with one, two, or more than three characters, such as **.z**, **.ps**, **.ra**, or **.theme**).

Two subkeys that do not begin with a leading period but can be placed within the Filename-Extension category, are also described here.

Asterisk ("*")

This subkey is the first to appear under the **HKCR** key, and as elsewhere in the operating system, an asterisk signifies a wild card. It might be better thought of as a **.*** subkey, because the information found under it is applied to all files regardless of their extension. As shown by the composite illustration in Figure 2.3, the **Asterisk** key leads to a **Shellex** subkey, which leads to **ContextMenuHandlers** and **PropertySheetHandlers** subkeys, and these in turn are followed by still other subkeys.

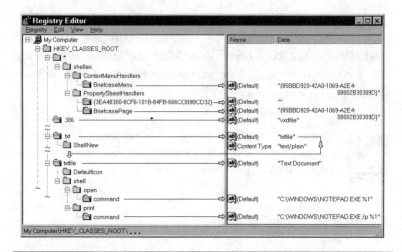

Figure 2.3 *This composite Registry Editor window shows the* ***Asterisk*** *key's subkey structure and illustrates how the* ***.txt*** *key's Contents Pane refers to the* ***txtfile*** *key. The latter's* ***shell*** *keys support the* ***Open*** *and* ***Print*** *commands on any text file's Context menu.*

For future reference, the specific relationship between the **Asterisk** key and its subkeys is discussed here. If any details given here describe subkeys that are unfamiliar, you may prefer to skim this section now and return to it after you read the rest of the chapter.

SHELLEX

As elsewhere in the Registry, the **Shellex** key leads to the subkeys described here.

> **ContextMenuHandlers and BriefcaseMenu:** The latter key's Contents Pane points to the **{85BBD920... CLSID** key for the Briefcase. Because this specific reference appears under the **Asterisk** key, the cited **CLSID** key is applied to

all files regardless of their extension. If any file is moved into the Briefcase, the key places an **Update** option on the file's Context menu. The same option does not appear on the Context menu of the file in its original location.

PropertySheetHandlers and {3EA48300...: Here, the key structure does not directly reveal the purpose of the **{3EA48300...** key, but if that subkey is opened under the **CLSID** key (not shown in the figure), its Contents Pane identifies it as an "OLE Docfile Property Page." Note that in this case, the conventional * = all files definition should be interpreted as * = all OLE files.

If the Context menu for any OLE document is open and its **Properties** option is selected, the Properties sheet will show three tabs labeled **General**, **Summary**, and **Statistics**. The latter two tabs are handled via the CLSID key discussed earlier. Because OLE documents can have a variety of extensions (Word **DOC** file, Excel **XLS** file, and so on), the presence of a subkey with this number under the **Asterisk** key makes these Property sheet tabs available to any OLE document, regardless of its extension. Note that the **{3EA48300...** subkey here under the **Asterisk** key is simply a pointer to the key with the same name in the **CLSID** section. At that location, the **InProcServer32** subkey indicates the file (**docprop.dll**) that actually handles the **Summary** and **Statistics** tabs. If that file were missing, these tabs would also be missing.

PropertySheetHandlers and BriefcasePage: Similar in concept to the **BriefcaseMenu** subkey described earlier, the **BriefcasePage** subkey supports the **Update Status** tab, which appears on the Properties sheet of any file located in a Briefcase. This tab does not appear if the **Properties** option for the equivalent file outside the Briefcase is selected, because this particular property is appropriate only to a file located in the Briefcase.

Asterisk vs. Folder Subkeys: Just as the **Asterisk** key pertains to all files without regard for their extension, a **Folder** key performs similar functions for all folders. Refer to "Folder" in the "Other HKCR Subkeys" section later in this chapter for further details.

Filename Extension (*.ext*): The *.ext* label will be used here to signify any **Filename-Extension** subkey that begins with a leading period followed (usually) by a three-character extension. At its simplest, the Contents Pane for each such key contains a single (Default) line, as shown in Figure 2.3 for the **.386** subkey. Here, the Contents Pane Data entry specifies the **Class-definition** subkey for any file with a **386** extension. This convention indicates that additional information about this file type will be found under a **Class-Definition** subkey, which in this case is labeled **vxdfile** (virtual driver file).

In a few **Extension** subkeys, the (Default) entry shows (value not set) in the Data column, which indicates there is no associated Class-Definition subkey. In this case, the **Extension** subkey itself may lead directly to a **Shell\Open\Command** subkey set, and the **Command** subkey specifies the application that launches any file with the extension specified by the **Extension** subkey. In still other cases, the **Extension** key leads instead to a **ShellNew** subkey, which is described later in the "Shell, Shellex, and ShellNew Key Structures" section.

MIME Contents Pane Modifications: Some Contents Panes list a Content Type entry, as shown in Figure 2.3 for the **.txt** subkey. This additional information is the *MIME* (Multipurpose Internet Mail Extension) equivalent of the subkey file extension, and it may be written into the

Registry by MS Plus! or some OEM versions of Windows 95. Table 2.1 lists some of the **Extension** subkeys in which a Content Type entry may be found.

Table 2.1 *MIME data added to various* **HKCR \ File Extension** *Subkeys* *

HKCR subkey(s)	— —Contents Pane— — (Default)	Content Type	Explorer\View\Options, †Registered File Types
.aif, .aifc, .aiff	aiffile	audio/aiff	AIFF format sound
.au	aufile	audio/basic	AU format sound
.avi	ActiveMovie	video/avi	Movie clip (ActiveMovie)
.gif	giffile	image/gif	GIF image
.htm, .html	htmfile	text/html	Internet document (HTML)
.jpe, .jpeg, .jpg	jpegfile	image/jpeg	JPEG image
.mov	ActiveMovie	video/QuickTime	Movie clip (ActiveMovie)
.mpeg, .mpg	ActiveMovie	video/mpeg	Movie clip (ActiveMovie)
.ra, .ram	ramfile	audio/x-pn-realaudio	RealAudio
.snd	aufile	audio/basic	AU format sound
.tif, .tiff	TIFImage. Document	image/tiff	TIF image document
.txt	txtfile	text/plain	Text document
.wav	SoundRec	audio/wav	Wave sound
.xbm	xbmfile	image/x-xbitmap	XBM image

* MIME data may be added by MS Plus!, or by an OEM version of Windows 95.

† Indicated MIME data also appears as **Content Type (MIME)** on **File Types** tab.

The Content Type information may be viewed one item at a time via Explorer's View menu. Select **Options** and click on the **File Types** tab to display the Options sheet in Figure 2.4. The top of the figure shows the default Options sheet, while the bottom shows that a new "Content Type (MIME)" line has been inserted in the File Type details section, followed by "text/plain" from the **.txt** subkey's Contents Pane (see Figure 2.3).

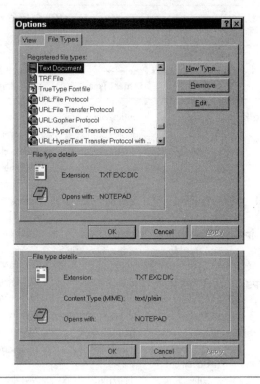

Figure 2.4 *On the Options sheet, the **File Types** tab lists Registered file types, with details about the highlighted file type appearing beneath the File Types window. The bottom of the illustration shows the "Content Type (MIME):" insertion installed by MS Plus! and some OEM versions of Windows 95.*

Refer to A "Property Sheet Handler for a Dialog Box" in the "PropertySheetHandlers" section later in this chapter for an explanation of how this specific property sheet handler is written into the Registry. See also the **MIME** subkey description under "Miscellaneous Other Subkeys" near the end of the "HKCR" section of this chapter.

Unknown: If the Registry does not contain a **Filename-Extension** key for a file with a certain extension (**.xyz**, for example), then Windows 95 has no idea what actions are appropriate to the file; it therefore refers to this **Unknown** subkey for instructions. Specifically, an unknown file's Context menu will show an **Open with** option. If selected, an Open With dialog box prompts the user to choose the program that should be used to open the file. Refer to **openas** in the **Shell** section of "Shell, Shellex, and ShellNew Key Structures" for additional details.

The Class-Definition Subkey

Although this subkey type is supposed to define all subkeys other than the **Filename-Extension** subkeys described earlier, this book divides these keys into several subclasses, as described here.

FileType

The names of many subkeys that follow the final **Filename-Extension** subkey describe various file types, such as **AVIFile, batfile,** and **txtfile**. Each such key is described here as a **FileType** subkey because it provides additional information about a file type whose filename extension appeared in the alphabetical list of **Filename-Extension** subkeys described earlier. For every **FileType** subkey in the Registry, there is a related **Filename-Extension** subkey, whose Contents Pane's (Default) line lists the associated **FileType** in the Data column. That data serves as a pointer to the **FileType** subkey being discussed.

FileType Subkeys

Because most of these subkeys are common to both **FileType** and other keys, they too are described separately later in this section. If the subkey appears under a **Shell, Shellex**, or **ShellNew** key, refer to the "Shell, Shellex, and ShellNew Key

Structures" section. Otherwise, consult "Miscellaneous Other Subkeys" for further details.

CLSID (Class Identification)

Briefly stated, a CLSID number identifies a Windows 95 object for OLE automation purposes, and there is a subkey here for every such device registered on the system. Every CLSID label takes the following form:

```
{aa bb cc dd—ee ff—gg hh—ii jj—kk ll mm nn oo pp}
```

Each double-letter pair is a one-byte hexadecimal number, and there are always 16 such numbers (bytes) in a 4-2-2-2-6 sequence enclosed by braces. A long hexadecimal string that conforms to this format is randomly generated by a software supplier for every Windows 95 application, and the chance that any two CLSID numbers would be identical is unlikely, to say the least. (Refer to "CLSID Generator Utility" in Chapter 4 for information on how to generate a unique CLSID number.)

If almost any **CLSID** subkey is opened, the Contents Pane's (Default) entry identifies the object associated with that CLSID number, as shown by the following examples:

CLSID Subkey Name	Data Column
{21EC2020-3AEA-1069-A2DD-08002B30309D}	"Control Panel"
{645FF040-5081-101B-9F08-00AA002F954D}	"Recycle Bin"
{73FDDC80-AEA9-101A-98A7-00AA00374959}	"WordPad Document"
{00028BA1-0000-0000-C000-000000000046}	(value not set)

There are a few subkeys in which the Data column does not identify the object, as shown by the last example. In a case such as this, a search for another subkey with the same name may help. In this specific example, the subkey shows up beneath a

ContextMenuHandlers key, which in turn is a subkey for another **CLSID** key. That key's Contents Pane identifies it as **The Microsoft Network**, so we may conclude that this "(value not set)" subkey is also part of the Microsoft Network.

In still other cases, there may be a **ProgID** (described later) subkey below the **CLSID** key, and that key's Contents Pane may identify the object.

{CLSID}

Although no subkey under the **CLSID** key is so labeled, this generic designation is used here and elsewhere in this book in discussions that refer to all subkeys under the **CLSID** key. If such a subkey requires specific identification, then the first four bytes are given, followed by an ellipsis, as in {**21EC2020....** If necessary, the full 16-character number is given.

Refer to "Editing the Start Menu" in Chapter 4 for information on using a **CLSID** to place a new item on the Start menu.

*If a {**CLSID**} subkey is found elsewhere in the Registry, it usually serves as a pointer to a key with the same number found here.*

NOTE

SERVER AND HANDLER SUBKEYS

One or more of the subkeys listed here will be found under each {**CLSID**} key in this section of the Registry:

InprocHandler, **InprocHandler32**   In-process handler

InprocServer, **InprocServer32**   In-process server

LocalServer, **LocalServer32**   Local server

The *32* suffix indicates a 32-bit device. Although not described in detail here, each key's Contents Pane gives the path and filename for the server file that supports the function specified by the **{CLSID}** key. In most cases, if that file is damaged or missing, an error message will appear if the function is accessed. For example, the **C:\Windows\System\Viewer\sccview.dll** file supports the Context menu's **Quick View** option. If the file is missing, a There is no viewer... message appears if that option is selected.

By contrast, a key listed earlier may cite a file that does not exist. In this case, the function is for the moment supported by other means, but it may be handled by this subkey if some application installs a file with the specified name in the future. See "{D3B1DE00..." in the "HKCR\Drive" section later in the chapter for a specific example.

PROGID (PROGRAMMATIC IDENTIFIER)

This subkey is found under many—but not all—**{CLSID}** keys, but it might be better labeled **DocID,** because its Contents Pane Data column identifies not a program, but rather specifies the name of a **Document.Identifier** subkey, which is described in the next section.

THE DOCUMENT.IDENTIFIER SUBKEY

There's a bit of jargon confusion here: Microsoft documentation refers to this subkey as a **ProgID** key. But as just noted, there is a subkey under many **{CLSID}** keys whose name actually is **ProgID**. Also, this subkey is *not* a program identifier; it is instead a description of a specific document type. Therefore, for the purposes of this explanation, **ProgID** is reserved for the specific **{CLSID}** subkey that bears that name, while **Document.Identifier** is used here to identify the key we are discussing now. A period may appear in the name, just as it does in an actual key name. Thus, the key may be labeled as **MS.Network.Document**, **Office.FileNew**, **PowerPoint.Show.7**, **Word.Document.6**, for example. Figure 2.5 shows an open **ProgID** subkey, whose Contents Pane points to a **Document.Identifier** key.

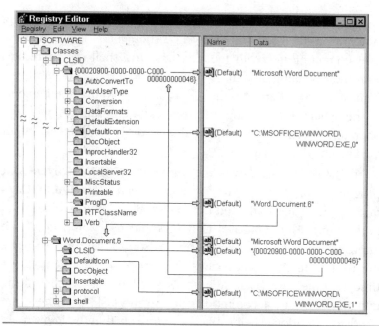

Figure 2.5 *This composite Registry Editor window shows the relationship between a* **{CLSID}** *key and a* **Document.Identifier** *key. The former's* **ProgID** *subkey specifies the* **Document.Identifier** *key, where a* **CLSID** *subkey points back to the* **{CLSID}** *key.*

Shell, Shellex, and ShellNew Key Structures

Many **Filename-Extension** and other subkeys lead to one of several subkeys that specify various shell functions, each of which is described in this section. But first, what is a shell?

The Shell Defined

As anyone who has shucked an oyster knows, a *shell* is that hard calcium-like structure that tries to protect its owner (in this case, the oyster) from the outside world (usually a hungry diner). In the jargon of the computer, the word is a general descriptor of any program that protects—or *tries* to protect—the operating system from the user, and vice versa. The general idea is that the user communicates with the shell and the shell communicates with the operating system. Acting as an interface between these parties, the shell translates the needs of one into the requirements of the other. By so doing, the user can communicate with the operating system in something that approaches human, rather than machine, language.

In DOS, the shell was the well-known **COMMAND.COM** program, which accepted a command such as **FORMAT C: /s** from the user and translated it into something the machine could understand. The Windows GUI (graphic user interface) is an improved shell (according to current wisdom) that further shields the user from the complexities of the operating system. From time to time, the basic Windows shell needs some unique enhancements to accommodate a specific task, and these are handled by various shell subkey structures within the Registry. In each case, the information contained under one of these subkeys pertains only to the item beneath which the subkey appears. Typical examples are some of these keys are given here.

Overview of Shell, Shellex, and ShellNew Keys

For future reference, this section briefly summarizes the principle functions of these keys, with further details given in the sections that follow. Although the Registry itself is inconsistent in its use of upper- and lowercase letters to label the keys, this book follows the style shown here in all text explanations. However, the illustrations show whatever style the programmer used when that key was written. Thus, you may discover **Shell** and **shell**, **ShellEx**, **Shellex**, and **shellex**. There is one exception to the rule: there are no variations on the **ShellNew** key.

Shell	Action keys such as **Edit**, **Open**, **Play**, **Print**.
Shellex	Handler routines for Context menus and Property sheets.
ShellNew	Documents listed on the cascading New menu, accessed via the **New** option on the Desktop Context menu and the Explorer File menu.

Action Keys

A subkey under the **Shell** key may sometimes be referred to as an *action key*, because the key and its own subkeys support a specific action supported by the application or file type under which the key appears. The most common Registry action keys are described in the **Shell** section that follows, but other such keys may be installed by various software applications. In most cases, the key will function in a manner similar to one of those described here.

The Shell Key

Each action key under the **Shell** key contains instructions that pertain only to the item under which the **Shell** key appears. If a **Shell** key appears under a **FileType** or a **Document.Identifier** key (both of which were described earlier), then the names of action subkeys beneath the **Shell** key appear as options on the Context menu, when a file matching that **FileType** or **Document.Identifier** is selected. The first letter (usually) of the menu option is underlined, as in, **Open** or **Print**.

If a **Shell** subkey appears under a **File Extension** key, then refer to the associated **FileType** or **Document.Identifier** key for information about that file's action subkeys and Context menu options. Refer to "Context Menu Editing" in Chapter 4 if you would like to change an option name as it appears on the Context menu and/or select a different letter to be underlined.

The action keys listed here are usually followed by a **Command** subkey, which specifies the executable file that will perform the specified operation on the file whose Context menu is open.

NOTE

The name of any action key has no special significance, other than serving as a convenient Context menu indicator of the action that will occur if that menu option is selected. In most (but not all) cases, the name of the key is the name that appears on the Context menu. However, that name may be changed as desired, without affecting the operation of the key itself. Refer to "Change Option Name and/or Underlined Letter" in Chapter 4 for information about how to edit the name of an action key on the Context menu.

*The descriptions given here pertain only to actions initiated via the Context menu They have no effect on the way an open application handles the same task. Thus, if the **Open** subkey under, say, the **txtfile** key were missing, that action would not appear on the Context menu for any text file. However, if the Notepad applet itself were opened, its own File menu's **Open** option would continue to function in the normal manner.*

CONFIG

The **config**(uration) subkey appears as a **Shell** subkey under the **scrfile** (screen saver) key. Its **Command** subkey shows only a %1 in the Contents Pane Data column, which signifies that the selected filename should be executed. In the specific case of a screen saver file—**DANGER~1.SCR**, for example—simply typing the filename on a command line is sufficient to configure the system to use that screen saver.

CPLOPEN

This key appears under the **cplfile** key's **Shell** subkey. It might as well have been labeled **open** instead of **cplopen**. If any file with a **CPL** extension is selected, its Context menu shows a default **Open with Control Panel** option at the top of the menu, because that phrase appears in the **cplopen** subkey's (Default) Data column. If selected, the Control Panel applet whose filename is highlighted will open, thereby bypassing the intermediate step of opening Control Panel itself. To open two or more such applets simultaneously, highlight the appropriate *filename*.**CPL** files and then select the **Open with Control Panel** option.

EDIT

This subkey is found under the **Shell** key in the **batfile, regfile,** and **txtfile** tree structures. In each case, its **Command** subkey specifies that the selected **BAT**, **REG**, or **TXT** file will be loaded into the Notepad applet for editing.

EXPLORE

This subkey is found under the **{CLSID}\Shell** key for the **Folder, Inbox,** and **Microsoft Network** subkeys. In each case, it opens the selected object in the two-paned Explorer view, in which the left pane shows the Desktop and the right pane is the Contents Pane for the selected folder. The **Open** subkey on the same Context menu displays the Contents Pane only.

FIND

This subkey is located under the **{CLSID}** keys for *My Computer* and *Network Neighborhood,* and it is under the **Directory** and **Drive** keys. In each case, a **Command** subkey launches **EXPLORER.EXE**. A **ddeexec** (dynamic data exchange/execute) subkey specifies a subroutine embedded within **EXPLORER.EXE** that is to be executed (which in this case is **FindFolder**). Refer to **ddeexec** in the "Miscellaneous Other Subkeys" section later in this chapter for more information about the **ddeexec** subkey.

A **Find** subkey under the {**CLSID**} key for the Microsoft Network executes a separate **MSNFIND.EXE** file.

INSTALL

This special-purpose subkey appears under the **inffile** (**INF** file) and **scrfile** (screen saver) keys. If a Context menu for either file type is opened, the **Install** option will run the executable file that installs the selected file. In either case, a **Command** subkey specifies the appropriate command line, and a %1 parameter at the end of that line indicates that the specific file selected is the one to be installed.

NEW

If this option appears when a document file's Context menu is opened, select it to create a new copy of the same document. In most cases, the appropriate executable file loads a duplicate copy of the selected document, which must now be named and saved.

Note, however, that the file type may not be the same as the original document. For example, if the **New** option is selected from the Context menu of a rich-text format document (**RTF** extension), a copy of the document will be loaded into the user's word processor, as expected. However, it will be saved in that word processor's default format unless the user selects the **Save As** option and specifies the **RTF** format.

OPEN

As its name suggests, this key leads to a **Command** subkey that specifies the executable program that will open the selected file.

OPENAS

This special-purpose key appears under the **Unknown** key's **Shell** subkey (see "HKCR\Unknown" earlier). This key structure is used when Windows 95 is not sure which executable program is appropriate to open or print the selected file, in which case the Context menu lists an **Open With...** option. If selected, the **openas** key's **Command** subkey displays an Open With dialog box, in which the user is prompted to specify the program to use to open the file.

The dialog box includes an **Always use this program to open this file** checkbox, which really means "use the selected program to open any file with the same extension as this one." If the box is checked, then the next time a file with the same extension is selected, the Context menu will display an **Open** option instead of the **Open With** option. However, other options appropriate to the same program may not appear on the menu. Refer to "Add Other Missing Options to Context Menu" in the "Context Menu" section of Chapter 4 for further details, and instructions on how to edit the Registry so that all appropriate options will appear on the Context menu.

PLAY

The **AudioCD, AVIFile,** and **CDAfile** keys contain this subkey, and in each case, a **Command** subkey specifies the executable program (**cdplayer.exe** or **mplayer.exe**) that loads and plays the selected file. In the case of an **AVI** file, a /close switch on the executable's command line closes the media player after the file has finished playing. If you would prefer to keep the media player open at the end of a playback, the switch may be deleted, as described in "Command Line Editing" in Chapter 4.

PRINT

Common to most document subkeys, the **Print** option opens the appropriate executable program, loads and prints the selected file, and then closes the executable program.

PRINTTO

If present, the **Printto** key's **Command** subkey specifies the executable file with command-line switches and/or parameters to be used if a file is dragged to a printer icon. For example, if you drag a document file to a printer icon and drop it there, the application cited in the **Command** subkey opens, prints the document, and then closes again.

If the **Shell** subkey under a **FileType** key lacks the **Printto** and **Printto\Command** subkeys, then drag-and-drop printing is handled by the **Print** subkey (described earlier). Refer to "Drag-and-Drop Print Editing" in Chapter 4 for suggestions on changing the application used to print a document file.

The Shellex Key

The **Shellex** (shell extension) key usually contains one or more **Handler** subkeys such as those whose contents are described here. In each of the following examples, the keys provide some additional feature or features not otherwise available—hence the name *shell extension*. As with the **Action** subkeys under the **Shell** key described earlier, the presence of these **Handler** subkeys under a specific **Shellex** subkey makes sure the features do not appear where they are not needed or usable.

CONTEXTMENUHANDLERS

In addition to options placed on a Context menu by the **Shell** key's **Action** subkeys (described earlier), other options may be placed there via a **ContextMenuHandlers** subkey under a **Shellex** key, as shown here:

Object	Context Menu Options
Microsoft Network	Connection Settings, Delete
My Computer	Map Network Drive, Disconnect Network Drive
Network Neighborhood	Map Network Drive, Disconnect Network Drive
Recycle Bin	Empty Recycle Bin
Drive (removable)	Copy Disk

In each case, these unique Context menu options are specified by a **ContextMenuHandlers** subkey. For example, Figure 2.6 shows the default Context menu for the Network Neighborhood. The **Connection Settings** and **Delete** options are placed on that menu by the **Shellex** key's **ContextMenuHandlers** subkey, located under the Microsoft Network's **CLSID** key, which is **{00028B00-0000-0000-C000-000000000046}**. The figure also shows how the menu would appear if the **ContextMenuHandlers** subkey were missing.

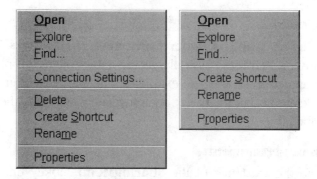

Figure 2.6 *The Network Neighborhood's Context menu is on the left, while the version on the right shows the effect if the* ***ContextMenuHandlers*** *subkey is missing.*

The **ContextMenuHandlers** key may also contain its own subkeys, such as those briefly described here.

BriefcaseMenu

Because this subkey appears as a **ContextMenuHandlers** subkey only under the **Asterisk** and **Folder** keys, it is applied to all files and folders within the Briefcase. Refer to the **Asterisk** or **Folder** keys for a description of how it functions in either location.

IconHandler

This subkey is found under the **lnkfile, piffile,** and a few other keys, where it does just about what you would expect it to do. To illustrate, use Explorer to search the **C:\Windows** folder and its subdirectories for ***.LNK** or ***.PIF** files. Open the Context menu for any such file, and its icon should appear near the top of the **General** tab, placed there by the **IconHandler,** whose Contents Pane Data column points to the {00021401... key. If the **IconHandler** subkey were missing, a generic document shortcut icon would appear there instead.

SharingMenu

This subkey appears under **ContextMenuHandlers** in the **Folder** and **Printers** keys only. As the name suggests, it places a **Sharing** option on the Context menu. There are however, a few considerations that might not be immediately apparent; these are described here.

Sharing and the Printers Subkey

Despite the existence of the **SharingMenu** subkey under the **Printers\Shellex\ContextMenuHandlers** key, the **Sharing** option does not appear on a printer icon's Context menu unless the following two conditions are met:

1.   A printer is installed on a local (not network) port.

2.   Print sharing is enabled. To do so, open Control Panel's Network applet, click the **File and Print** [*sic,* should be **Printer**] button, and place a check mark next to **I want to be able to allow others to print to my printer(s)**, which is the long way to specify "enable printer sharing."

PropertySheetHandlers

The subkey beneath any key with this name serves as a pointer to a **{CLSID}** key. Figure 2.7 shows two subkey formats that may be used; each is briefly reviewed here. In each case, the parenthetical reference is to a subkey used here to illustrate the format under discussion.

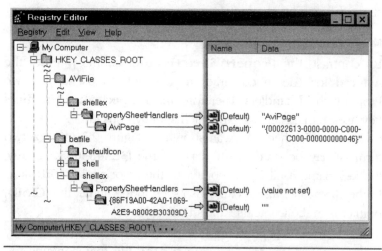

Figure 2.7 The AVIFile key's PropertySheetHandlers *subkey points to an AVIPage subkey, which in turn points to the {CLSID} key associated with AVI files. By contrast, the batfile key's PropertySheetHandlers subkey leads directly to a {CLSID} pointer.*

SINGLE PROPERTY SHEET (AVIFILE)

In some cases, the **PropertySheetHandlers** key supports a single property sheet, as in the case of the **AVIFile** key shown in Figure 2.7. Here, the Contents Pane for the **PropertySheet Handlers** key shows AviPage in its Data column, a subkey with that name appears below it, and that key's own Contents Pane points to the {00022613... **CLSID** key associated with the **AVI** file. That key's **InProcServer32** subkey's Contents Pane contains the following information:

```
(Default)     "C:\WINDOWS\SYSTEM\mmsys.cpl"
```

This indicates that the **mmsys.cpl** file contains the Property sheet information required by **AVI** files. If that file is missing, then the **Details** and **Preview** tabs on an **AVI** file's Properties sheet will also be missing.

MULTIPLE PROPERTY SHEETS (ASTERISK)

By contrast, the **PropertySheetHandlers** subkey under the **Asterisk** key (described earlier in the chapter) must support two Property sheet handlers. Therefore, the **PropertySheetHandlers** key itself remains empty, and each subkey beneath it supports its own property sheet. As was shown in Figure 2.3, one of two formats may be used. In the case of the {3EA48300... subkey, the key name itself is the pointer to the associated {CLSID} key. In the **BriefcasePage** subkey, also seen in the figure, the {CLSID} pointer is in the Contents Pane's Data column.

As in the **AVIPage** example earlier, the specified {CLSID} key contains the path and filename for the file that contains the appropriate Property sheet data.

A Property Sheet Handler for a Dialog Box

Strictly speaking, a dialog box, like the one shown in Figure 2.4, might not be thought of as a Property sheet, because it is not accessed via some Context menu's **Properties** option. Nevertheless, its various components may be modified via a subkey that resembles the just-described **PropertySheetHandlers** key. At the bottom of Figure 2.8, the Contents Pane for **FileTypesPropertySheetHook** refers to a **{CLSID}** key, which in turn contains an **InProcServer32** subkey whose own Contents Pane specifies the **URL.DLL** file that places the Contents Type (MIME): line in the **Options** dialog box.

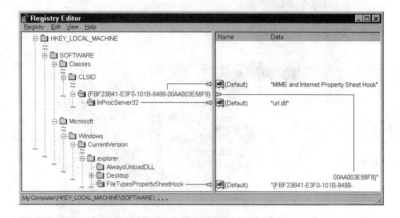

Figure 2.8 The *Microsoft* key's *FileTypesPropertySheetHook* points to the *{CLSID}* key in the *CLSID* section. To better illustrate the relationship, the *{FBF23B41-...* key is shown here under the **HKEY_LOCAL_MACHINE** key, because that's where the *Microsoft* key also resides. The former key only is also discussed in the "HKEY_CLASSES_ROOT" section in this chapter.

The ShellNew Key

If the Desktop Context menu's **New** option is selected, a cascading menu displays a list like that shown in Figure 2.9. For each menu option, a **ShellNew** key will be found under the **File Extension** subkey associated with that document type. For example, Figure 2.10 shows the **.bmp** and **.doc File Extension** subkeys, whose

Contents Panes point to a **Document.Identifier** subkey (described earlier), which in these cases are **Paint.Picture** and **Word.Document.6,** respectively. The Contents Pane for each of these keys lists the text that appears on the cascading New menu, and the **Shell\Open\Command** subkey specifies the executable file that will be launched to create the appropriate new document on the Desktop.

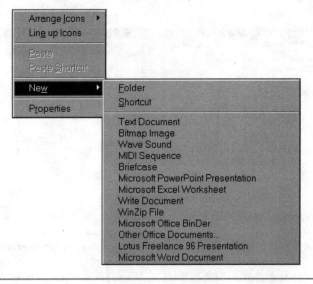

Figure 2.9 On the Desktop menu, the *New* option leads to a cascading menu of available new document types.

The role of the **ShellNew** key itself varies depending on the information in its Contents Pane. To illustrate this, open the **ShellNew** subkey under any **File Extension** key and note the word that appears on the second line in the Contents Pane, then find that word in the list that follows. In each of these examples, the contents of the Data column determine the action taken, as described here.

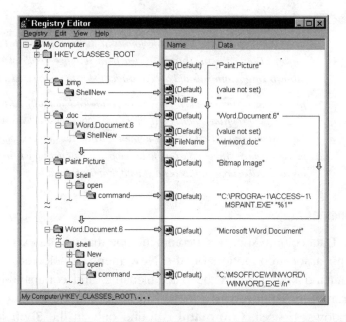

Figure 2.10 *In this composite Registry Editor window, the* ***.bmp***
key's ***ShellNew*** *subkey shows a NullFile entry in its Contents Pane.*
Therefore, if ***New Bitmap Image*** *is selected from the New menu*
shown in Figure 2.9, the MS Paint applet will open, but a template
file will not be loaded. By contrast, the ***.doc*** *key's* ***ShellNew*** *subkey*
shows a FileName entry whose Data column specifies ***winword.doc****,*
a template document found in the ***C:\Windows\ShellNew*** *folder. If*
Microsoft Word Document *is selected from the New menu, this file*
will be loaded into Microsoft Word.

NOTE

*The examples included here are representative of those seen on
several typical Windows 95 systems. However, variations have been
noted between systems, which may be due to the influence of various
third-party applications.*

Assuming the ***File Extension*** *key contains a* ***ShellNew*** *subkey (not
all of them do), then if a new file of that type is placed on the Desktop
via the Context menu's* ***New*** *option the filename will take the
following format:*

```
New <FileType>.<ext>
```

*where **FileType** is the text string found in the associated **FileType** subkey's Data column. Thus for a new bitmap image, a title of **New Bitmap Image.bmp** would appear under the icon on the Desktop.*

*In the four examples given here, only **Command** actually runs an executable program when the appropriate option is selected on the Context menu's cascading **New** menu. The other entries simply place a new document file on the Desktop, without actually running the executable program associated with that file format.*

Command

The Data column specifies a command line that will be executed if the associated option on the **New** menu is selected. The command line specifies the path, filename, and command-line parameters required to create the specified new item. In Windows 95 itself, **Command** is found only in the **ShellNew** key's Contents Pane for the following two subkeys:

Briefcase (.bfc subkey): A New Briefcase icon is placed on the Desktop the first time this option is selected. If it is selected again, a New Briefcase (2) icon appears, and so on.

Shortcut (.lnk subkey): If this option is selected, of course Windows 95 has no idea which application requires a new shortcut. Therefore, a Create Shortcut dialog box prompts the user to enter the desired command line or to browse for the desired application.

Data

If a binary data string appears in the Data column, that string is written into a new file of the appropriate format. For example, a multimedia application may write a Data entry into the Contents

Pane in the **.mid** (MIDI file) and/or **.wav** (Wave file) key's
ShellNew subkey, such as the 18-byte hexadecimal sequence
shown in Figure 2.11. This is the standard header that appears at
the beginning of any MIDI file, as also shown by the shaded area
in the Debug window in the same figure. If this sequence is
present in the Data column, then the application that wrote the
data entry supports MIDI recording, and therefore the **New MIDI
Sequence.mid** file in the **C:\Windows\Desktop** folder should
be 18 bytes long.

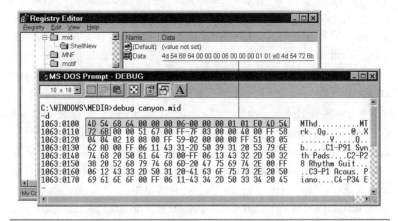

Figure 2.11 *If the **MIDI Sequence** option on the New menu
(Figure 2.9) is selected, the **.mid** file's **ShellNew** subkey opens a
new MIDI file. The 18-byte hexadecimal string seen in the
Contents Pane's Data entry is the header which appears at the
beginning of any MIDI file. In the MS-DOS Prompt—DEBUG
window, the shaded area shows that header as it appears in the
CANYON.MID (or any other) MIDI file.*

If the **.mid** subkey does not contain a **ShellNew** key, then of
course there will be no **MIDI Sequence** option on the Desktop
Context menu's cascading **New** menu. Refer to "Add Menu
Option" in the "Desktop New Menu" in Chapter 5 for information
on how to add a MIDI sequence or other option to that menu.

If a Data *line is followed by a* NullFile *line (described later), then the latter takes precedence and the* Data *line is ignored.*

NOTE

FileName

When *FileName* appears in the Name column, the Data column specifies a new document file that will be placed on the Desktop, not unlike the binary header just described. However, the binary header is written as a new file, while a new document file is actually a copy of a blank document file currently located in the **C:\Windows\ShellNew** folder. This blank file may be quite a bit larger than the 18-byte MIDI header described earlier, because it contains all the basic data required for any new file created in the same format.

If the new document file's icon is subsequently double-clicked, the executable file that loads the file is the one specified under the **FileType** subkey associated the **File Extension** key. To locate it, open the **File Extension** key itself and note the **FileType** listed in its Contents Pane. Then locate the subkey with that name and open its **Shell\Open\Command** subkey. The path and filename for the executable file are located in the (Default) row's Data column, as shown by the **Word.Document.6** example in Figure 2.10.

*The **New** subkey, which also happens to appear under the same **Shell** subkey is not part of this discussion of the Desktop Context menu's cascading New menu. It is instead one of the **Action** subkeys that were described earlier, in the "Shell Key" section.*

NOTE

NullFile

The Data column shows an empty pair of quotation marks. As with the **Filename** description, the command to open the associated file type is found under the **FileType** subkey associated with the **File Extension** key. In this case, a null file (of zero-byte length) is created on the Desktop. A Nullfile entry is found under the **.bmp** and other subkeys, because the specific format of the file you want to create is, of course, unknown, and therefore Windows 95 cannot predict the correct file header to write into the new file. Presumably, you will open the null file, add something to it, and then save it in whatever format you prefer, at which time the correct header will be written into the file.

Other HKCR Subkeys

This section covers a few important **HKCR** subkeys that may need a bit of explanation. Their descriptions were put off until now, because a passing acquaintance with the **Shell** and **Shellex** key structures (described earlier) may make it easier to wade through some of what follows here.

In a few cases, a heading appears for a subkey that one might expect to find, even though that subkey does not exist. In each such case, there is a brief explanation of how the associated item is supported in the absence of a subkey. Figure 2.12 summarizes the relationship between many of the subkeys described in this section.

AudioCD

This subkey is linked to the **Drive** and **Folder** subkeys, both of which are described later. Its purpose is to specify a File Type icon and to support the **Play** option required by audio compact discs. Refer to the **AutoRun** key for information pertaining to CD-ROM (data) discs.

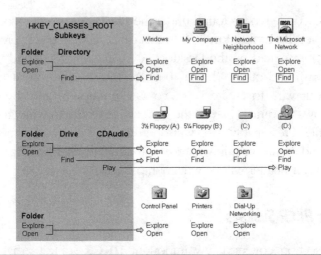

Figure 2.12 *A few Context menu options are shown here under various Desktop and Explorer icons. The horizontal lines and arrows indicate the various* **HKEY_CLASSES_ROOT** *subkeys where each option originates. The three boxed* **Find** *options are supported separately by a* **Shell\Find\Command** *subkey under the {CLSID} key associated with each object.*

DefaultIcon

The icon specified here appears only on the list of Registered File Types on the **File Type** tab, where it is identified as *AudioCD*.

Shell

Although each option listed here appears on the Context menu for any audio compact disc, only the **Play** option is directly supported by a subkey in this section.

> **Explore**: This option is placed on any audio CD's Context menu by the **Shell\explore** subkey found under the **Folder** key.
>
> **Find**: This option is placed on the Context menu by the **find** subkey under the **Drive** key.

Open: Similar to the **explore** subkey described earlier, this option appears on the Context menu through the **Shell\open** subkey under the **Folder** key.

Play: This is the only CD audio option supported by a subkey under the **CDAudio** key. Its **Command** subkey specifies that the CDPlayer applet will be used to play the audio compact disc.

*If the **Shell** key's own Contents Pane Name and Data columns show (Default) and "play" respectively, then the executable file (**cdplayer.exe**, or similar) listed in the **play** key's **Command** subkey will play an audio compact disc as soon as it is inserted in the CD-ROM drive. Refer to "AutoPlay and AutoRun" in Chapter 5 for information about customizing this feature.*

Shellex Subkey

This key is conspicuous by its absence here, so of course there are no **ContextMenuHandlers** or **PropertySheetHandlers** subkeys either. The functions usually supported by these subkeys are handled via the **Drive** key's **Shellex** subkey structure, as described in the "Drive" section later.

AutoRun

This subkey is written into the Registry if both of the following conditions are met:

1.   The **Auto insert notification** box is checked (open **Device Manager**, highlight the specific CD-ROM drive, click the **Properties** button, select the **Settings** tab).

2.   A CD-ROM containing an **AUTORUN.INF** file is inserted in the CD-ROM drive *after* Windows 95 has opened. (Refer to "Hard Drive Icon" in Chapter 5 for the reason and method of adding an **AUTORUN.INF** file to a hard drive.)

If these conditions are met, an executable program (usually **AUTORUN.EXE**) specified in the CD-ROM's **AUTORUN.INF** file is executed when the disc is inserted in the drive. If the disc is subsequently removed, its **AutoRun** subkey remains in place, but it is rewritten if another CD-ROM is inserted in the drive, provided that disc contains an **AUTORUN.INF** file in its root directory. In any case, the contents of that file are written into the **AutoRun** subkeys, as shown here and in Figure 2.13:

AUTORUN.INF File Contents	Subkey *	Contents Pane Data Column
[autorun]		
OPEN=AUTORUN\AUTORUN.EXE	command	E:\AUTORUN\AUTORUN.EXE
ICON=AUTORUN\WIN95CD.ICO	DefaultIcon	E:\AUTORUN\WIN95CD.ICO

*Full **HKEY** paths are **AutoRun\3\Shell\AutoRun\Command**, and **AutoRun\3\DefaultIcon**.

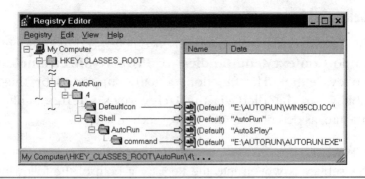

Figure 2.13 *In this typical **AutoRun** key example, the **4** subkey signifies drive 4, that is, drive **E**. Fresh Contents Pane Data, such as that shown in the illustration, is written into the Registry whenever a CD-ROM with an **AUTORUN.INF** file is inserted in the CD-ROM drive.*

The numbered subkey immediately below the **AutoRun** key indicates the drive letter (2 = C, 3 = D, 4 = E, etc.). Under default conditions, the **AutoRun** key leads to a numbered subkey for the CD-ROM drive only, which is drive **E** (*4*) in the preceding example. The entire **AutoRun** structure is erased from the Registry every time Windows 95 closes and does not appear again until the next time the conditions listed earlier are met. However, if there is a valid **AUTORUN.INF** file on any hard drive partition (as described in Chapter 5), then the **AutoRun** key and the subkey(s) referring to the hard drive remain in place, and only the CD-ROM subkey is erased.

NOTE
*The **AutoRun** key described here refers only to CD-ROM (data) discs. Refer to the **AudioCD** key for details about playing audio compact discs in a CD-ROM drive.*

DIRECTORY

Within the Registry, a *Directory* may be described as a special-case folder, that is, a folder that contains nothing but files and possibly some file subdirectories. In other words, it's just what a directory was in the days before Windows 95. Refer to the **Folder** key below for additional information on the distinction between a folder and a directory.

DefaultIcon

The icon specified here appears only on the list of Registered File Types on the **File Type** tab, where it is identified as "File Folder" (open Explorer's View menu, select **Options**, click **File Type** tab).

Shell

The **Shell** key leads to the single action key described here.

FIND

This subkey places the **Find** option on a folder's Context menu, but only if that folder meets the **Directory** conditions described earlier.

Drive

As its name suggests, this key supports the system's diskette, CD-ROM, and hard drives. A few functions unique to this key are described here. Because the **{CLSID}** keys described later do not directly identify the functions they support, a parenthetical reference in the section head has been added to reveal the purpose of the key.

DEFAULTICON

The icon listed here is the one seen next to **Drive** in the Registered File Types list on the **File Types** tab (to view the list, open Explorer's View menu, select **Options** and then the **File Types** tab). It has no effect on the various drive icons used to identify various diskette and hard drives. These icons are not directly specified in the Registry but may nevertheless be changed as described in the "Icons Not Specified by a DefaultIcon Key" section in Chapter 4.

SHELL

Although three actions appear on any drive's Context menu, only one is supported by a subkey here in the **Drive** section.

> **Find**: This is the only subkey found under the **Drive** key's **Shell** subkey. If any drive's Context menu is opened, this key supports the menu's **Find** option.

> **Explore** and **Open**: Although both options appear on any drive's Context menu, they are placed there via the **Shell\explore** and **Shell\open** subkeys found under the **Folder** key.

Shellex and ContextMenuHandlers

Although these keys were described in the **Shellex** section earlier, a few of the options that appear on a drive's Context menu are briefly reviewed here. Note that only one of these options is directly supported by a **ContextMenuHandlers** subkey under the **Drive** key.

> **{59099400-57FF-11CE-BD94-0020AF85B590}** (**Copy Disk** option): The **Copy Disk** option on the Context menu is supported by the **{59099400...** subkey here, which is simply a pointer to a subkey of the same name under the **CLSID** section. That key's **InProcServer32** subkey supports the **Copy Disk** option, which appears on the Context menu for diskette drives only.

> **Eject**: Although this option appears on the Context menu for CD-ROM and other removable-media drives (except diskette), there doesn't seem to be a subkey associated with it, even though it is supported via the **SHELL32.DLL** file. For the moment then, it appears to be hard-coded into the operating system.

> **Format**: Because the **Format** option is unique to diskette and hard drive Context menus, you might reasonably expect to find a **ContextMenuHandlers** subkey here that supports this function. However, such a key does not exist, and the **Format** function also appears to be hard-coded into the system via the **SHELL32.DLL** file.

> **Sharing**: This Context menu option is supported by a subkey under the **Folder** key's **Shellex** subkey. Refer to that key's **ContextMenuHandlers\SharingMenu** subkey for additional details.

Shellex and PropertySheetHandlers

These keys are also described in the **Shellex** section, with the following subkeys unique to the **Drive** key briefly described here.

> **{D3B1DE00-6B94-1069-8754-08002B2BD64F}** (**Tools** tab) and **Disk Tools**: On some systems, only the **{D3B1DE00 ...** subkey is present, and its Contents Pane is empty. On

others, the Contents Pane points to a **Disk Tools** subkey, and that key's Contents Pane cites the **{D3B1DE00 ...** subkey. In either case, in the **HKCR\CLSID** section, the **{D3B1DE00 ...** key's own Contents Pane describes it as *Disk Tools Extension* and its **InProcServer32** subkey cites a **C:\Windows\System\disktool.dll** file, which does not exist on most systems. On some OEM versions of Windows 95, the **{D3B1DE00 ...** key may be cited as above, yet the key itself is missing from the **CLSID** section described earlier.

When present, "Disk Tools Extension" and/or the subkey named **Disk Tools** would certainly suggest that this subkey structure has something to do with the **Tools** tab on any drive's Properties sheet. However, the absence of the **DISKTOOL.DLL** file and the missing **{D3B1DE00...** subkey indicate that this entire key structure does nothing yet, and in fact, the presence and function of the **Tools** tab is unaffected if part or all of it is deleted.

This subkey is cited here as a specific example of a structure that seems to be nothing more than a placeholder for a file that, if installed in the future, will support the indicated function. However, in the absence of that file, the function is supported internally by other means.

Compression: If MS Plus! is installed, this subkey's Contents Pane points to a **{7C7E55A0...** subkey whose **InProcServer32** subkey supports a **Compression** tab on the selected drive's Properties sheet. Some Windows 95 OEM versions also add this subkey.

Sharing: The **Sharing** tab on a drive Property sheet is supported via the **MSSharing** subkey under the **Folder\ shellex\PropertySheetHandlers** key.

Folder

There seem to be two Microspeak definitions for a *folder*: outside the Registry, the term usually defines what used to be known as a directory or subdirectory. Within the Registry, a *folder* is any object that can be opened to reveal other objects. Thus, each of the following items is classified as a folder:

Briefcase

CD-ROM drive

Control Panel

Dial-up networking

Diskette drive

Explorer folder (any)

Hard drive

Microsoft Network

My Computer

Network Neighborhood

Printers

Recycle Bin

DefaultIcon

The icon specified here appears only on the list of Registered File Types on the **File Types** tab, where it is identified as *Folder* (open Explorer's View menu, select **Options**, click **File Types** tab).

Shell

The subkeys found under this key support options that appear on every folder's Context menu. In addition to the conventional file folder formerly known as a directory, other folders include **My Computer**, **Network Neighborhood**, all drives, and the **Control Panel**, **Printers**, and **Dial-Up Networking** folders.

EXPLORE

This subkey supports the **Explore** option, in which the Explorer opens a window with two panes: Folders and Contents.

FIND

Because the **Folder\Shell** key does not lead to a subkey with this name, the **Find** option on any Context menu is supported by a **Find** subkey located elsewhere, such as under the **Directory** or **Drive** key described earlier in this section. For other objects (My Computer, Network Neighborhood, Microsoft Network, etc.), a **Shell\Find** subkey is located under the {**CLSID**} key associated with that object. Still other folders (Control Panel, Printers, Dial-Up Networking) do not require a **Find** option on their Context menu.

OPEN

Similar to the **Explore** option, this subkey supports the **Open** option on every folder Context menu, in which the Explorer opens a single-pane Contents window.

Shellex and ContextMenuHandlers

This key combination leads to the two subkeys described here:

BriefcaseMenu: If the Context menu for a **Briefcase** folder is opened, the subkey supports the appearance of the **Update** option on the Context menu. If the Context menu for the equivalent folder outside the Briefcase is selected, the **Update** option does not appear, because this option is appropriate only to objects located in the Briefcase.

SharingMenu: Although the name may imply the existence of a Sharing menu, this subkey actually supports the **Sharing** option on the Context menu.

Shellex and PropertySheetHandlers

The subkeys described here support various tabs that appear on the Properties sheet for any folder whose Context menu supports a **Properties** option. Note that this menu option is disabled for the **Control Panel**, **Printers**, and **Dial-Up Networking** folders.

> **BriefcasePage**: If the Context menu for a folder in any Briefcase is opened and its **Properties** option is selected, this subkey supports the **Update Status** and **Update Info** tabs.

> **MSSharing**: Under the conditions just described for **BriefcasePage**, this subkey supports the **Sharing** tab on a folder's Properties sheet.

Miscellaneous Other Subkeys

This final HKCR section describes a few additional subkeys that may be found under one or more of the previously-described keys.

ddeexec (Dynamic Data Exchange/execute)

If this key appears under a **Shell/Open** or **Shell/Print** key, its Data column specifies a subroutine embedded within an executable program. The name of this executable program may be found by opening the **Command** subkey, which appears above the **ddeexec** subkey, as shown by these typical examples.

Subkeys	Command subkey shows:	ddeexec subkey shows:
Drive\shell\find	Explorer.exe	FindFolder
Folder\shell\explore	Exporer.exe /e /idlist, %I, %L	ExploreFolder
Folder\shell\open	Explorer.exe /idlist, %I, %L	ViewFolder
Word.Document.6\		

(continued...)

Subkeys	Command subkey shows:	ddeexec subkey shows:
shell\New	**Winword.exe /n**	`"[FileNew("%1")]"`
shell\open	**Winword.exe /n**	`"[FileOpen("%1")]"`
shell\print	**Winword.exe /n"**	`"[REM_DDE_ Minimize]`
		`[FileOpen("%1")]`
		`[FilePrint 0]`
		`[DocClose 2]"`

In each line the first column lists a subkey structure under the **HKCR** key. If the final subkey in that column is opened, its **Command** and **ddeexec** subkeys show the executable program and its subroutine, as listed in the second and third columns.

The information in the subkeys under the **ddeexec** key may, of course, be viewed by sequentially opening each key and noting the Contents Pane's Data entry. The same information may be seen more conveniently by opening Explorer's View menu. For example, Figure 2.14 shows a Microsoft Word Document entry in the Registry and as it appears by taking the following steps:

1. Open Explorer's View menu, select **Options**, and click on the **File Types** tab.

2. Highlight **Microsoft Word Document** in the list of Registered File Types.

3. Click on the **Edit** button.

4. Highlight **Print** in the Actions box.

5. Click on the **Edit** button.

The various Registry entries in the Contents Pane Data column at the top of the figure appear on the Editing action sheet, as also shown in Figure 2.14. If the check mark in the **Use DDE** box is cleared, all entries below it will be cleared from the sheet and deleted from the Registry. For information about any listed item, click on the **?** button in the upper-right-hand corner of the Editing action sheet, and then point to any entry on the sheet.

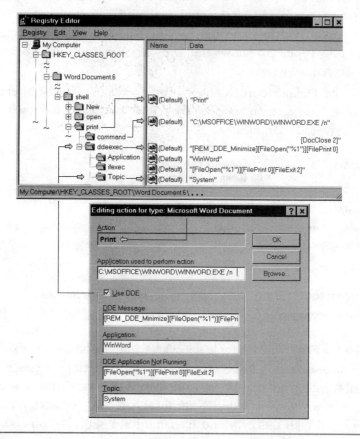

Figure 2.14 *The Registry Editor window at the top shows various Contents Pane entries for the open subkeys under the* **Word.Document.6** *key's* **Shell** *subkey. The bottom part of the figure shows how this information is presented to the user. To view this data, open the Explorer's View menu, select* **Options**, *click on the* **File Types** *tab, and highlight* **Microsoft Word Document**. *Then click on the* **Edit** *button, highlight* **Print**, *and click on the next* **Edit** *button. Similar data should be seen with any other Windows 95 word processor.*

DefaultIcon

As its name suggests, this subkey specifies the icon that appears next to any object associated with the key under which it appears. If **Options** on the Explorer's View menu is selected, the **File Types** tab shows the same icon next to the associated registered file type.

The **DefaultIcon**'s Contents Pane contains a (Default) entry whose Data column specifies the icon to be used, as shown by these typical examples:

Subkey	Contents Pane shows:	
	Name	Data
exefile	(Default)	`"%1"`
Paint.Picture	(Default)	`"C:\Progra~1\Access~1\MSPAINT.EXE,1"`
{645FF040...	(Default)	`"C:\WINDOWS\SYSTEM\shell32.dll,32"`
	empty	`"C:\WINDOWS\SYSTEM\shell32.dll,31"`
	full	`"C:\WINDOWS\SYSTEM\shell32.dll,32"`
{00020900-...	(Default)	`"C:\MSOFFICE\WINWORD\WINWORD.EXE,0"`
Word.Document.6	(Default)	`"C:\MSOFFICE\WINWORD\WINWORD.EXE,1"`

The `%1` in the first example specifies that the icon for any exefile (*filename*.**exe**) is to be taken from the executable file itself. If that file does not contain an icon, then Windows 95 displays one of its own generic icons. Note that if the `%1` parameter were replaced with the path and filename for a specific icon source (as in the **Paint.Picture** example), then *all* files with an **exe** extension would display that icon, instead of their own icon.

The **{645FF040-...** example is a special case that handles the Recycle Bin icon. If the bin is empty, the empty-wastebucket icon specified on the **empty** line is displayed. However, when any file is erased (actually, moved to the Recycle Bin), the icon changes to a full wastebasket, as specified on the **full** line. In either case, as the Recycle Bin is emptied and then refilled, the appropriate icon specification is copied to the (Default) line and displayed on the Desktop.

DEFAULTICON PRECEDENCE

The {00020900-... and **Word.Document.6** subkeys demonstrate another unique case in which a specified default icon is superseded by another default icon located elsewhere in the Registry. For example, Figure 2.5 showed the {**CLSID**} and **Document.Identifier** keys for a Microsoft Word document, and both of these keys contain a **DefaultIcon** subkey. If both subkeys were absent, Windows 95 would create a Word document file icon consisting of a dog-eared blank page with a miniature version of the **WINWORD.EXE** icon superimposed on it. If only the **DefaultIcon** subkey under the {**CLSID**} key is present, the icon specified there appears next to every Word file. However, if the **DefaultIcon** subkey under **Word.Document.6** is also present, then the icon specified there takes precedence over the one under the {**CLSID**} key. The same comments apply to any other case in which a **DefaultIcon** subkey appears under a {**CLSID**} key and under a **Document.Identifier** key—the latter key being the one specified under the {**CLSID**} key's **ProgID** subkey.

Refer to "Changing the Default Icon" in Chapter 5 if you would like to change the icon associated with an executable program or document file.

A FEW DEFAULTICON VARIATIONS

In all cases, the icon specified by a **DefaultIcon** key appears next to the associated file type on Explorer's **File Types** tab and next to all files of the same type when viewed in an Explorer window. There are, however, a few cases in which the **DefaultIcon** subkey specifies the file type icon but has no effect on a nonfile object viewed in an Explorer window. Although each of the objects listed here uses the same icon as shown on the File Types tab, its presence in an Explorer window is independent of the **DefaultIcon** subkey.

HKCR Subkey	Registered File Types
AudioCD	AudioCD
Directory	File folder
Drive	Drive
Folder	Folder
My Briefcase	Briefcase

Column 1 lists the subkey under which the **DefaultIcon** subkey appears, and column 2 specifies the name shown in the Registered File Types list, which is viewed by opening the Explorer's View menu, selecting **Options** and then clicking the **File Types** tab. Refer to "Changing the Default Icon" in Chapter 3 if you would like to change the icon associated with any of these objects.

MIME

This subkey is inserted below the **HKCR** key if MS Plus! has been installed, or it may be added by OEM versions of Windows 95.

DATABASE AND CONTENT TYPE

As the key names suggest, this is a database of MIME content types. In the Contents Pane for each subkey, an Extension entry specifies the extension associated with that content type. In effect, this is a reverse-sequence listing of MIME **File Extension** subkeys that appear near the top of the **HKCR** section. Thus, the MIME subkeys shown here are equivalent to the indicated **File Extension** subkeys:

HKCR Subkey	Name	Data
MIME\Database\Content Type\audio/wav	Extension	`".wav"`
.wav	Content type	`"audio/wav"`
MIME\Database\Content Type\text/plain	Extension	`".txt"`
.txt	Content type	`"text/plain"`

QuickView

Each subkey under this key lists a file extension recognized by the QuickView applet. If the applet has not been installed, these file-extension subkeys are still present, and each one's Contents Pane gives a description, as in these typical examples:

Key	Contents Pane Data Column
.ASC	`"ASCII File"`
.BMP	`"Windows Bitmap Graphics File"`
.DLL	`"Dynamic Link Libraries"`
.DOC	`"ANY of a number of word processing file formats"`
.INI	`"configuration files"`

If QuickView is installed (via Control Panel's Add/Remove Programs applet, Accessories component), then a subkey is added beneath every file-extension key. Each one has the same name and contents, as shown here:

Subkey Name	Contents Pane Data Column
{F0F08735-0C36-101B-B086-0020AFF07DD04F}	`"SCC Quick Viewer"`

After the final file-extension subkey, a **Shell\Open\Command** subkey specifies the executable file. As elsewhere in the Registry, the {**F0F08735...** subkey in the **CLSID** section specifies the **.dll** file that supports QuickView.

CHAPTER 3

The Windows 95 Registry Structure, Part II

This chapter continues the discussion of the Registry Editor's **HKEY** structure that began in Chapter 2. Fortunately, the five **HKEY**s described here require little more space than that devoted to the single **HKEY_CLASSES_ROOT** key in Chapter 2.

HKCU: HKEY_CURRENT_USER key [HKU*UserName* or HKU\.Default]

The information contained within the seven subkeys of **HKCU** pertains to the user who is currently logged on, hence the *Current User* designation. As with the **HKCR** key described in the previous chapter, a new **HKCU** is created as Windows opens. Its contents come from the current user's profile, which is stored under a **username** subkey under the **HKU (HKEY_USERS)** key described later, and shown in Figure 3.1. If the system is not configured for multiple users, or if the user bypasses the password prompt by pressing the **Escape** key, then **HKCU** takes its data from the **.Default** subkey (note the leading period) found under **HKU**.

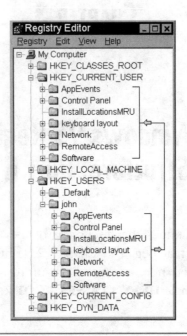

Figure 3.1 *If two subkeys appear under the **HKEY_USERS** key, one is labeled.**Default** and other is the name of the current user. As shown here, the contents of the latter key also appear under the **HKEY_CURRENT_USER** key. On a single-user system, the contents of the.**Default** key appear there instead.*

The seven **HKCU** subkeys are listed in Table 3.1, with additional details offered here.

AppEvents

Within the context of Windows 95, an *event* is just about any action whose occurrence can be celebrated in sound, if not quite in song. Such events range from the trivial to the profound, that is, from a menu popup to a general protection fault. Subkeys under the **AppEvents** key structure provide the necessary support, as described here.

Table 3.1 HKEY_USERS\.Default Subkeys

Subkey	Contents
AppEvents	**EventLabels** subkey contains labels that appear in the Sound applet's Events: box. **Schemes** subkey contains subkeys with path and filename for waveform files specified in Sound applet's Events: box.
Control Panel	See Table 3.2.
InstallLocationsMRU	The locations from which applications were recently installed (MRU = most recently used).
keyboard layout	Two or more subkeys with data about keyboard layout, language, etc.
Network	Persistent and Recent network connection subkeys.
RemoteAccess	**Address** and **Profile** subkeys for Microsoft Network or other (if installed, otherwise subkeys are empty).
RunMRU †	(Windows 95 Resource Kit erroneously reports location here.)
Software	Data on Windows 95 software.
StreamMRU †	(Windows 95 Resource Kit erroneously reports location here.)

† Actual location is **HKEY_USERS\.Default\Software\Microsoft\Windows\ CurrentVersion\Explorer**.

EventLabels

For each subkey in this section, the Contents Pane's (Default) entry lists a label for a single sound event, which may be viewed via the Control Panel Sounds applet. The Events window on that applet's Properties sheet displays a list of these event labels, each read from one of the subkeys under the **EventLabels** key.

Note that each **EventLabels** subkey is responsible for the label only; the sound itself is specified via the **Schemes** subkey, which is described later. Table 3.2 lists the **EventLabels** subkeys installed by Windows 95, and Figure 3.2 further illustrates the relationship between this subkey, the **Sounds** tab, and the **Schemes** subkey.

Table 3.2 *Control Panel Sounds Tab Events and Equivalent Eventlabels Subkey*

Sound †	Subkey Name ‡	Sound †	Subkey Name ‡
Windows			
Asterisk	**SystemAsterisk**	Minimize	**Minimize**
Close program	**Close** §	New Mail Notification	**MailBeep**
Critical stop	**SystemHand**	Open program	**Open** §
Default sound	**.Default**	Program error	**AppGPFault**
Exclamation	**SystemExclamation**	Question	**SystemQuestion**
Exit Windows	**SystemExit**	Restore Down	**RestoreDown**
Maximize	**Maximize**	Restore Up	**RestoreUp**
Menu command	**MenuCommand**	Start Windows	**SystemStart**
Menu popup	**MenuPopup**		
Windows Explorer			
Empty Recycle Bin	**EmptyRecycleBin**		
Sound Recorder		**Media Player**	
Close program	**Close** §	Close program	**Close** §
Open program	**Open** §	Open Program	**Open** §

†   Indicated event name appears on **Sounds** tab on Control Panel's Sounds Properties sheet.

‡   Full subkey path is **HKU*username*\AppEvents\EventLabels*Subkey name*.**

§   Same subkey label shared by Windows, Sound Recorder, and Media Player sections in Events list.

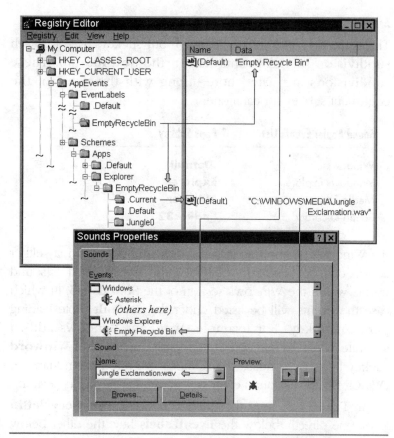

Figure 3.2 *The Control Panel Sounds applet's* **Properties** *tab derives its information from the* **HKCU** *keys shown here.*

Schemes

This key leads to two subkeys that define sounds associated with various Windows 95 applications.

APPS

The **Apps** (applets) subkey leads to four subkeys, one for each subdivision of the Events list on the **Sounds** tab. These subdivisions are listed here, along with the name of the equivalent subkey for each one:

Sound Applet Events List	Apps Subkey
Windows	**.Default**
Windows Explorer	**Explorer**
Media Player	**MPlayer**
Sound Recorder	**SndRec32**

If a Windows 95 application supports sound events, it may either add its own section and subkey to these lists or install its sound events within the Windows section of the **Sounds** tab, in which case the events will be listed under the **.Default** (note leading period) subkey. For example, Word for Windows adds a separate Winword section in the Sounds applet and a **Winword** subkey here. By contrast, the CompuServe Information Manager (WinCIM) adds its sound events to the regular Windows section.

In Figure 3.2, note that there are two **EmptyRecycleBin** keys: one directly below the **EventLabels** key, the other below the **Schemes\Apps\Explorer** key. The **.Current** (again, note leading period) subkey's Data entry specifies the specific sound that will be heard when the Recycle Bin is flushed, and the filename written there is seen in the Sounds Properties' Name box, as shown in the figure. Other subkeys specify the sounds available within each available scheme.

NOTE

*Perhaps the Microspeak Dictionary ran out of words, for as Figure 3.3 shows, the same name (.Default) has different meanings within the **AppEvents** key structure. Note that just below the **Schemes\Apps** key, a .Default subkey leads immediately to another .Default subkey. The first contains nothing more than the* word "Windows" which appears at the head of the Events list on the **Sounds** tab, as shown in Figure 3.2. The next leads to the subkeys that specify the sounds available for the event associated with the other **.Default** subkey seen earlier, under the **AppEvents \ EventLabels** key. That is, of course, the "Default sound" event; the **.Current** subkey at the bottom of the figure specifies the path and filename for the sound associated with that event.

Needless to say, there is no relationship between the use of **.Default** as a subkey name and the (Default) entry in every Contents Pane's Name column

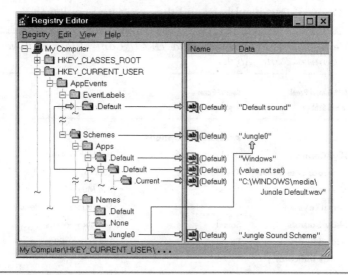

Figure 3.3 The first **.Default** key refers to the event of that name, while the third **.Default** key leads to the subkeys that list various sounds that may be applied to that event (only the **.Current** sound appears here). The other **.Default** key specifies the name ("Windows") that appears at the head of the Events list.

NAMES

There is a subkey under the **Names** key for each sound scheme listed on the drop-down list that appears in the Schemes box near the bottom of the **Sounds** tab, as shown by the partial list in Figure 3.3. Because the "Jungle Sound Scheme" is currently enabled on this system, the **Jungle0** key name appears in the **Schemes** key's Contents Pane, as also seen in the figure.

Control Panel

This subkey leads to additional subkeys that support various Desktop characteristics that can be configured via various Control Panel applets (Accessibility Options, Display, Mouse, Regional Settings). Table 3.3 is a cross-reference guide between the **Control Panel** subkeys and the associated applets.

Table 3.3 Cross-Reference Guide: HKCU\Control Panel Subkeys and Control Panel Applet

HKCU\Control Panel Key and Subkey	Control Panel Applet and Tab	Check Box, Other
Accessibility	**Accessibility Options**	
HighContrast	Display	Use high contrast
KeyboardResponse	Keyboard	Various
MouseKeys	Mouse	Use MouseKeys
SerialKeys	General	Support serial key devices
ShowSounds	Sound	Use ShowSounds
SoundSentry	Sound	Use SoundSentry
Status Indicator †		
Stickykeys	Keyboard	Use StickyKeys
TimeOut	General	Automatic reset
ToggleKeys	Keyboard	Use ToggleKeys
Appearance	**Display**	
Schemes	Appearance	Scheme box
Colors	**Appearance**	Color boxes

HKCU\Control Panel Key and Subkey	Control Panel Applet and Tab	Check Box, Other
Cursors	**Mouse**	
Schemes	Pointers	Scheme box
desktop	**Display**	
	Screen Saver	
	Background	Wallpaper
	Plus! (if installed)	Visual settings
ResourceLocale	(Not accessible via Control Panel)	
WindowMetrics	Appearance	Item and Font boxes
International	**Regional Settings**	
	Regional settings	Drop-down menu ‡
	Time	

† This (empty) subkey is written the first time Stickykeys is enabled. Contents Pane entries written when Stickykeys is disabled.

‡ Indicated region is read from KERNEL32.DLL file, not from Registry.

NOTE

*Informal tests suggest that the **Accessibility** key's **Status Indicator** subkey is not fully operational. The Contents Pane's **Docked** entry shows 0x00000001 (1) in the Data column, even on an undocked laptop computer. In fact, the key seems to be among the missing on OEM versions of Windows 95.*

InstallLocationsMRU

The Contents Pane of this subkey simply lists the last five locations from which software has been installed. A typical list might look something like this:

Name	Data
(Default)	(value not set)
a	"A:\"
b	"D:\hp2\"
c	"D:\hp3\"
d	"e:\"
e	"e:\win95\"
MRUList	"aedcb"

The MRUList (most-recently-used list) entry indicates the sequence in which the listed sources were used. Because the sequence shows the earliest sources were *c* and *b* ("D:\hp3\" and "D:\hp2"), we might reasonably infer that a "D:\hp1\" source has recently departed the list.

Keyboard Layout

The **Keyboard Layout** is written into the Registry if more than one keyboard language layout has been installed via the **Language** tab in Control Panel's Keyboard applet. If so, a **Preload** subkey leads to a series of numbered subkeys—one for each installed language. In each case, the Contents Pane lists the eight-digit number that identifies the language (00000409 = English (United States), for example), and subkey **1** specifies the default language.

Network

On a network system, if a network drive or folder is mapped to a local drive letter, a record of that connection appears under one or both of the two subkeys shown in Figure 3.4 and described here.

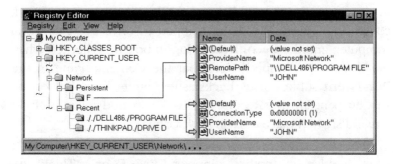

Figure 3.4 *The **Network** key's **Persistent** and **Recent** subkeys specify various network connections.*

Persistent

If a check mark is placed in the **Reconnect at logon** box when the network drive or folder is mapped to a local drive letter, then this key leads to a subkey whose label is that drive letter. The Contents Pane specifies the network provider, the path to the remote source, and the name of the local user who mapped the drive. If the **Reconnect at logon** box is subsequently cleared, the Contents Pane entries are deleted.

*Various messages may be seen as Windows 95 opens and closes, depending on the contents of the **Persistent** key and the actual system status. Refer to Chapter 8 for information about such messages.*

NOTE

Recent

The same information is also stored under this subkey, but the format is slightly different, as shown here and in Figure 3.4.

Subkey(s)	Mapped drive identified as:	Comment
Persistent	**\\DELL486\PROGRAM FILE**	Data column in Contents Pane
Recent	**././DELL486./PROGRAM FILE**	Subkey label

In this example, the **C:\Program Files** folder on a network computer (Dell486) has been mapped to drive **F** on the local computer, and the **Reconnect at logon** box was checked when the drive was mapped. Note that the Contents Pane in the **Persistent** subkey uses backslashes, while the label of the subkey beneath the **Recent** key uses a period followed by a forward slash in place of each backslash.

The **Recent** key also shows a recent connection to a network drive on another computer (drive **D** on a ThinkPad). Note also that despite its long filename capabilities, Windows 95 continues to use only the first 12 characters of the mapped device name, and these are forced into uppercase.

RemoteAccess

The subkeys found here provide remote-access information, as summarized here.

Addresses

The Contents Pane lists the current user's remote-access providers, such as the Microsoft Network, with additional details under the **Profile** subkey described later. On a system not set up for remote access, the name of the local computer is found here instead.

Profile

This key leads to one or more subkeys, each named for one of the access providers listed in the **Addresses** key cited earlier. In each case, the Contents Pane provides additional details about that provider, along with the current user's account name. Password information is not given here.

Software

This critical key contains a subkey for each manufacturer whose Windows 95 software (not hardware) has been installed on the system. Needless to say, these keys vary considerably from one system to another, depending on what software is present. The format in which data is stored also varies, because there are no standards to prescribe how such entries should be written into the Registry. Refer to "Variations in Data Format" in Chapter 4 for a few examples of such differences.

NOTE

*The subkey information found beneath this **Software** key pertains to software configuration for the current user only. Thus, if the system is set up for multiple users, the names and content of the **Company Name** subkeys found here will vary according to the current user's preferences.*

*User-independent data for the same software application is stored under the **HKLM\SOFTWARE** key (described later), and such data applies to all users. To help distinguish one key from another, note that the key name is **Software** here, and **SOFTWARE** under the **HKLM** key.*

Software Company Name

A subkey under each **Company Name** key leads to one or more additional subkeys—one for each of that manufacturer's installed applications. Each such key leads in turn to subkeys specific to that application.

The Microsoft Subkey

It probably won't come as a surprise to discover a key with this name on every Windows 95 system. As with any other **Software**

Company key, it leads to one or more (or in this case, *many* more) subkeys—one for each installed applet, application, or other Microsoft-installed component. To better illustrate the differences between the **Software** and **SOFTWARE** keys in general, and the **Microsoft** subkeys in particular, refer to the "Microsoft Software/SOFTWARE Keys" section, which appears after the "HKLM" section in this chapter.

HKLM: HKEY_LOCAL_MACHINE Key [SYSTEM.DAT]

The information contained within this key is stored in the hidden **SYSTEM.DAT** file in the **C:\Windows** folder, and two of its subkeys (**Config\000**x and **SOFTWARE\Classes**) are the sources for the **HKCR** (see Chapter 2) and **HKCC** keys (discussed later). By default, **HKLM** contains the seven subkeys described here. In addition, one or more other subkeys may be inserted by third-party Windows 95 applications. If so, the identity of the application is probably listed in the Data column of the Contents Pane's (Default) entry.

Config and 000x

The **Config** key contains one or more subkeys labeled **000**x, where x = 1, 2, 3, and so on. Each such subkey contains a hardware configuration profile available to the local machine. For example, a laptop might have a **0001** subkey for its docked configuration and a **0002** subkey for its undocked configuration. Or a desktop system might have one configuration that takes some external device into account and another that is used when that device is not physically present. Either computer might have one or more additional hardware configuration profiles, in which case that many additional subkeys would also be found here.

To view the available configurations, open Control Panel's System applet and select the **Hardware Profiles** tab. The available hardware profiles are listed alphabetically. The first profile is contained in subkey **0001**, the second in **0002**, and so on. In most cases, Windows 95 determines which configuration is required as it opens and exports the appropriate **Config** subkey into the **HKCC** key described later. Refer to "Hardware Profile Editing" in Chapter 5 for assistance in creating, editing, or removing a hardware profile.

Enum

This enumerator key contains a subkey for each hardware device type connected to the system since Windows 95 was installed. As you might suspect by now, each key leads to one or more subkeys, each of which names a single physical device. Each of these has its own subkey(s), which again will vary from one system to another, depending on the manufacturer of the installed devices. For each such subkey, the Contents Pane lists Name and Data information, such as that shown in these typical examples:

Name	Data (for an External Modem)	Data (for a Network Card)
Class	Modem	Net
DeviceDesc	DeskPorte 28.8	Intel EtherExpress PRO10 (PnP Enabled)
FriendlyName	Microcom DeskPorte FAST Plug & Play	(None, perhaps the above is friendly enough)
HardwareID	SERENUM\MNP0336	INT 1030, ISAPNP\INT 1030
Mfg	Microcom, Inc.	Intel
PnP Rev	0.99	—
HWRevision	—	1.0.00

The Contents Pane for these and other devices will also list other data, as appropriate to the device. Once Windows 95 writes a key or subkey into this section, that key will remain in place even if the cited device or device type is physically removed from the system. However, a specific device key will be removed if that device is removed via a Windows 95 uninstall procedure. If Windows itself is unable to remove the device, then its key(s) can be deleted by editing the Registry, as described in Chapter 4.

The location of a specific subkey may vary from one system to another. As a typical example, the ***PNP0100** subkey identifies the system timer, which is present on any system regardless of its type. However, the subkey may be found under the **BIOS** or **Root** key, depending on the specific system type. In the case of a hard drive, its subkey will be found under the key that describes its type (**ESDI** or **SCSI**, for example).

The following sections briefly summarize some of the subkeys that may be found under the **Enum** key, with additional details provided in Table 3.4. If necessary, a parenthetical phrase describes a key whose identity may not be immediately clear from its name. It's not a bad idea to skim each of these sections, even if it does not exist on your system; many of the subkey examples given here may exist under a different key, as, for example, in the case of a hard drive. In any case, the data found in the Contents Pane should be much the same, regardless of where the key itself is actually placed in the **Enum** key structure. Needless to say, not every subkey listed here will appear on every system. In case of doubt, refer to "Registry Search Techniques" in Chapter 4 for suggestions on how to search the **Enum** key section for a specific device.

Table 3.4 *Cross-Reference Guide: Device Manager and HKLM\Enum Subkeys* *

Device Manager Tab shows Device Type, Description †	ENUM Subkey	Additional Subkey(s)‡
CDROM		
NEC CD-ROM DRIVE 501	SCSI	NEC_\ROOT&
Disk Drives		
DEC DSP3107LS	SCSI	DEC_\ROOT&
GENERIC NEC FLOPPY DISK	FLOP	GENERIC\ROOT&
GENERIC NEC FLOPPY DISK	FLOP	GENERIC\ROOT&
Display Adapters		
ATI Graphics Ultra Pro (mach32)	PCI	VEN_\BUS_
Floppy Disk Controllers		
Standard Floppy Disk Controller	Root	*PNP0700\0000
Keyboard		
Standard 101/102-Key or Microsoft Natural Keyboard	Root	*PNP0303\0000
Modem		
DeskPorte 28.8	SERENUM	MNP0336\ROOT&
Monitor		
MAG Innovision MX17F/S	Monitor	Default_Monitor\0001
Mouse		
Standard PS/2 Port Mouse	Root	*PNP0F0E\0000
Network Adapters		
Dial-Up Adapter	Root	Net\0000
Intel EtherExpress PRO/10	ISAPNP	INT 1030\00A3478A
Other devices		
APC BACK-UPS PRO	SERENUM	APC1065\ROOT&
Ports (COM and LPT)		
Communications Port (COM1)	Root	*PNP0500\0000
Communications Port (COM2)	Root	*PNP0500\0001
Printer Port (LPT1)	Root	Ports\0000

(continued...)

Device Manager Tab shows Device Type, Description †	ENUM Subkey	Additional Subkey(s)‡
SCSI Controllers		
Adaptec AHA-174X EISA Host	Root	*ADP1740\0000
PCI NCR C810 SCSI Host	PCI	VEN_\BUS_
System Devices		
Direct Memory access controller	Root	*PNP0200\0000
Intel Mercury Pentium(r) Processor to PCI Bridge	PCI	VEN_\BUS_
Intel PCI to EISA bridge	PCI	VEN_\BUS_
I/O read data port for ISA Plug & Play Enumerator	ISAPNP	READDATAPORT\0
ISA Plug and Play bus	EISA	*PNP0A00
Numeric data processor	Root	*PNP0C04\0000
PCI bus	Root	*PNP0A03\0000
Programmable interrupt controller	Root	*PNP000\0000
System board	Root	*PNP0C01\0000
System CMOS/read time clock	Root	*PNP0B00\0000
System speaker	Root	*PNP0800\0000
System timer	Root	*PNP0100\0000
HP LaserJet 4 §	Root	printer\0000
HP DeskJet 1200C/PS §	Root	printer\0001

* Shows devices installed on typical Pentium system. Key names will vary from one system to another.

† Device description is stored in last subkey listed in table.

§ Printers do not appear on **Device Manager** tab.

‡ Some subkey names abbreviated here.

BIOS

This key appears on systems with Plug-and-Play BIOS. It contains many of the devices that would otherwise be found under the **Root** key (described later).

EISA

On an EISA system, each installed EISA device will be represented here by its own subkey. At minimum, there should be a ***PNP0A00** key, whose device description is "ISA Plug and Play bus."

ESDI

If this key is present, there is an installed ESDI device in the system—most likely a hard drive. Among other items in each drive subkey's Contents Pane, a CurrentDriveLetterAssignment entry in the Name column is accompanied by the drive letter in the Data column. If the physical drive is partitioned into logical drives, the Data column will list each letter, for example, "CDE" for a drive with three partitions.

FLOP

There is one subkey immediately below this key for each installed diskette drive. As in the hard drive subkey described earlier, in each subkey's Contents Pane, a CurrentDriveLetter Assignment in the Name column is accompanied by the drive letter in the Data column.

HTREE (Hardware Tree)

This undocumented key contains a **RESERVED** subkey, under which there is a **0** subkey. The latter key may be empty, or it may contain a binary ForcedConfig or ConfigFlags entry. Taking a hint from the key name, this structure may be reserved for future use.

ISAPNP (ISA Plug-and-Play)

This key appears on an ISA or EISA system, and its subkeys specify installed ISA devices. As a typical example, an **INT1030** subkey specifies an Intel EtherExpress PRO/10 Plug-and-Play network card. This and other data pertaining to the card's configuration will be found in subkeys beneath this key.

Even if no such devices are installed, a subkey under a **READDATAPORT** key should specify the ISA Plug and Play enumerator.

LPTENUM (LPT Enumerator)

A subkey appears under this key only if a Plug-and-Play printer is configured for a parallel port. In other words, neither a conventional (non-PnP) printer nor a PnP network printer will be specified here.

Monitor and Default_Monitor Subkeys

The **Default_Monitor** subkey contains a subkey (**0001**, **0002**, etc.) for each hardware profile. As shown in Figure 3.5, the Contents Pane for each such key identifies the monitor used for that configuration. On a Desktop system, the information in each **000x** subkey is usually identical, because the same monitor is used for each configuration. By contrast, if a laptop computer uses its own screen when undocked and an external monitor when docked, then the identity of each monitor is indicated in its own **000x** subkey.

Note, however, that although these **000x** subkeys appear beneath a key labeled **Default_Monitor,** this subsection of the **HKLM** key does not reveal which monitor is currently in use. That information is instead contained in one of the subkeys under the **HKDD\Config Manager\Enum** key. Refer to "Default Monitor Subkey" in the "HKDD" section for further details.

As shown in Figure 3.5, the text string in the DeviceDesc entry's Data column may sometimes include a reference to a screen resolution such as "Super VGA 1024x768," "Laptop Display Panel (800x600)" or something similar. However, this information does not necessarily

NOTE

*indicate the actual resolution in effect when the specified device is active.
it is instead the maximum resolution supported by the installed video
driver. To find the current resolution, open the **HKLM\Config\
000x\Display\Settings** subkey (described earlier). Refer to "Settings"
in the "HKLM" section for further details.*

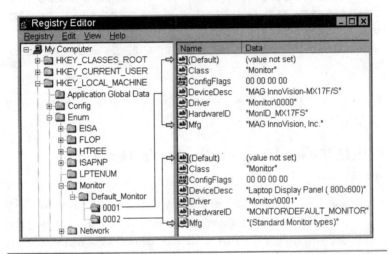

Figure 3.5 *The **Default_Monitor** key leads to subkeys defining
the characteristics of various installed monitors. In this specific
example, subkey **0001** specifies an external monitor used by a
laptop computer in its docked mode, while **0002** is the laptop's
built-in display panel.*

Network

Unlike the other subkeys under the **Enum** key, the **Network**
key's subkeys specify various network parameters, but not the
network hardware itself.

PCI

PCI-bus hardware is listed here, including PCI SCSI host
adapters, and a PCI-to-EISA bridge (if present). Each subkey
name takes the form of **VEN_*xxxx*&DEV_*yyyy***, where *xxxx* is

a vendor identification number and *yyyy* is that vendor's device number for the cited device. Typical examples are:

Subkey Name	Vendor	Device
VEN_1000&DEV_0001	NCR	PCI C810 SCSI host adapter
VEN_1002&DEV_4158	ATI Technologies	Graphics Ultra Pro (mach32)
VEN_8086&DEV_0482	Intel	PCI-to-EISA bridge
VEN_8086&DEV_04A3	Intel	Pentium processor–to–PCI bridge

The vendor and device identification are usually found in a subkey beneath the key.

PCMCIA (Personal Computer Memory Card International Association)

According to at least a few industry watchers, the acronym really meant "people can't memorize computer-industry acronyms." The more user-friendly *PC Card* term has gained recent popularity, although the acronym is still used within the Registry. Just remember that *PCMCIA* and *PC Card* may be used interchangeably, and on a system that supports PCMCIA/PC Card hardware, there should be a subkey here for every PC Card device that has been installed on the system, even if that device is not currently present.

Root

Although the Windows 95 Resource Kit states this section is for legacy devices, it may in fact contain a mixed bag of both legacy and Windows 95 devices, as described here.

LEGACY DEVICES

In most cases, there are at least a few subkeys whose name is ***PNP*xxxx*** (note leading asterisk) or **PNP*xxxx*** (no asterisk), where *xxxx* is a hexadecimal number. The asterisk denotes an item on the system board, such as a DMA or programmable interrupt controller or a numeric data processor. If the asterisk is omitted, the cited item is probably part of a plug-in adapter card.

Depending on specific system configuration, a separate **Ports** subkey may list the printer port(s), or these may be listed under a ***PNP0400** key, either in this **Root** key area or under the **BIOS** key. In addition, a **Printer** key leads to separate subkeys for each installed printer, other than those listed under the **LPTENUM** key described earlier.

WINDOWS 95 DEVICES

The Windows 95 Direct Cable Connection applet installs subkeys here for each COM and LPT port that supports this feature, and there may be additional subkeys for Net and other installed hardware, as shown by these typical examples:

Key	Subkey	Contents
MDMGEN	**COM1**	Microcom DeskPorte FAST
Net	**0000**	Dial-up adapter
PNPC031	**COM1**	Serial cable on COM1
	COM2	Serial cable on COM2
PNPC032	**LPT1**	Parallel cable on LPT1

Figure 3.6 shows a partial list of the many device subkeys found under the **Root** key. For comparison purposes, Figure 3.7 shows how some of these are listed by the Windows 95 **Device Manager** tab in Control Panel's System applet. A check mark (which does not appear in the actual screen display) indicates a device type listed under the **Root** subkey in Figure 3.6. Some of the checked items may appear instead under the **BIOS** key described earlier, if that key is present.

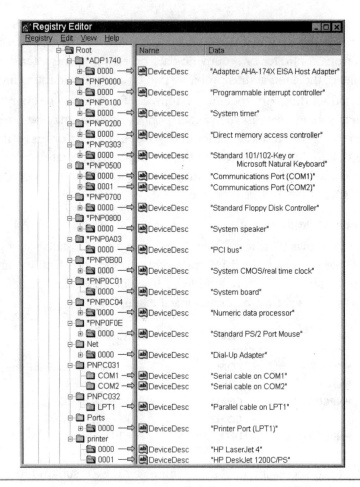

Figure 3.6 *The* **HKEY_LOCAL_MACHINE** *key's* **Enum\Root** *key may lead to a collection of subkeys like those shown here. Under each one, one or more additional subkeys specify various hardware components.*

SCSI (Small Computer System Interface)

As its name suggests, the subkeys found here define installed SCSI devices. However, a PCI SCSI host adapter will be listed under the **PCI** subkey, and not under this **SCSI** subkey.

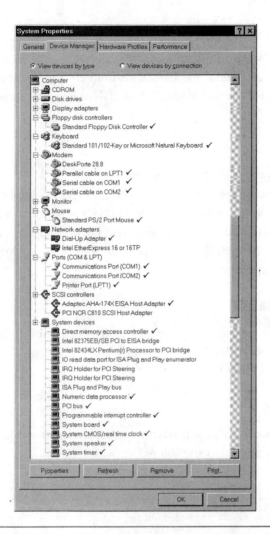

Figure 3.7 *This expanded view of a **Device Manager** tab shows many of the devices installed on the system. A check mark identifies a device specified under the **Root** subkey shown in Figure 3.6. Depending on specific system configuration, some of these devices may be specified under some other **HKLM\Enum** subkey.*

SERENUM (Serial Enumerator)

The subkeys in this section specify devices installed on a serial port, such as a serial modem or an uninterruptible power supply with serial-port notification. A serial mouse, however, is not listed here.

Hardware

The **hardware** section appears to be awaiting full implementation. According to the *Windows 95 Resource Kit,* it contains "information about serial ports and modems used with the HyperTerminal program." In fact, there are the following two subkeys in this section.

Description

Yes, but a description of what? A **System** subkey leads to a **FloatingPointProcessor** subkey, which in turn shows a **0** subkey. All three keys are empty.

Devicemap

The **devicemap** key leads to a **serialcomm** subkey, which contains nothing but the following:

Name	Data
(Default)	(value not set)
COM1	"COM1"
COM2	"COM2"

No modem information is given here, and if HyperTerminal is set to use a COM port other than COM1 or COM2, that information is also not here.

Network and Logon

This key structure is present on network systems only, where the **Logon** subkey gives the current user's username and other configuration details. The contents—but not the name—of this subkey changes on startup to specify the appropriate configuration for the current user. However, if the current user logged on by pressing the **Escape** key at the name/password prompt, then this subkey shows the name of the last person who logged on with a valid username.

Refer to the **System and CurrentControlSet** key's **control** subkey later in this chapter to get additional details about the current user.

Security

The following subkeys may be found on a system configured for remote network administration.

Access

This leads to an **Admin\Remote** subkey, which contains the name of the network administration computer.

Provider

This subkey's Contents Pane contains the following details:

Name Column	Data Column	Comment
Address_Book translator	"msab32.dll"	Network address-book
Address_Server	"(server name)"	
Container	"(server name)"	
Platform_Type	00 00 00 00	Share-level access control
	01 00 00 00	User-level access control

SOFTWARE

The subkeys under this key contain installed-software data that applies to all users, regardless of their personal configuration preferences. Thus, a Windows 95–aware software application will place a **Company Name** subkey here, as described later in this section. A subkey with the same name may also appear under the **HKCU\Software** key if the software supports individual user configurations. As already noted, this key is labeled **SOFTWARE,** while the other one is **Software.**

Classes

The subkeys under **Classes** are "buried" several levels below the Master **HKEY** in which they are actually stored. For example, the following lines show how the same subkey (**.bmp**) may be accessed here in the **HKLM** section and in the **HKCR** section:

```
My Computer\HKEY_LOCAL_MACHINE\SOFTWARE\Classes\.bmp     (level 4)
  My Computer\HKEY_CLASSES_ROOT\.bmp      (level 2)
```

The **HKCR** key structure makes access to the same information a bit more convenient, because it bypasses the intermediate **SOFTWARE\Classes** subkeys found in the **HKLM** section. Therefore, this set of subkeys was described in detail earlier, in the "HKCR" section of Chapter 2. Remember however, that if a change occurs within an **HKCR** subkey, that change simultaneously takes place here too. In fact, it is here in **HKLM** that the information is actually stored.

Description

Judging by the **Microsoft** and **Rpc** subkeys that follow, this is a description of the Microsoft RPC (remote procedure call) system. Although far beyond the scope of this book, the **uuid** (universally unique identifier) subkeys contain network address and other data needed when an application on one system needs to make a function call to a remote system.

The (*Company Name*) Subkey

No doubt there are several **SOFTWARE** subkeys that bear the name of a software manufacturer. Under each such key, there will be one subkey for each of that manufacturer's Windows 95–compatible software products that are installed on the system. Although the specific *Company Name* subkey structure will vary from one system to another, there's very little doubt that every system will have a **Microsoft** subkey under its **HKLM\SOFTWARE** key. Because there's no escaping this key and its multiple subkeys, it is explained separately at the end of the "HKLM" section. Refer to "The Microsoft Software and SOFTWARE Subkeys" for all the gory details, which should generally apply to other **Company Name** subkeys as well.

System and CurrentControlSet

As the key names suggest, the **System** and **CurrentControlSet** keys lead to data that controls how the system (that is, Windows 95) configures itself as it opens. This data is found under the two subkeys described here.

Control

On a network system, the **control** key's Contents Pane usually shows a CurrentUser entry, whose Data column lists the name of the current user, which is read from the **HKLM\Network\Logon** key (described earlier). The information in that key was written when Windows 95 opened and prompted the user to enter a name and password. However, if the name/password prompt is disabled, the current user name is the one that was entered immediately after Windows 95 was installed. If the prompt is enabled, but bypassed by pressing the **Escape** key at the name/password prompt, then there is no **CurrentUser** entry here. Nor does this entry appear on a non-networked single-user system.

Figure 3.8 illustrates the sequence on a network system when the user enters a valid user name and password. To verify this, type in a valid name in any distinctive mix of upper- and lowercase letters and note its appearance in the **Logon** and **control** subkeys, as illustrated in the figure. Then restart Windows and note that the User name prompt shows the previous user name just as it was typed at the beginning of the previous session. Now press the **Escape** key to open in the default user mode. The Registry's **Logon** key will continue to show the previous user name, while the **control** key will not. Also note there is no stylistic consistency between the opening prompt (User name), the **Logon** key entry (username), and the **control** key entry (Current User).

A few of the subkeys that appear under the **control** key are briefly described here.

COMPUTERNAME

With luck, you don't need to be told what this key contains.

IDCONFIGDB

No doubt the key name means "Database of Configuration Identification(s)," and its Contents Pane displays entries such as those shown here:

Name	Data (Laptop)	Data (Desktop)
CurrentConfig	"0002"	"0001"
FriendlyName0001	"Docked"	"Original Configuration"
FriendlyName0002	"Undocked"	(Other configuration(s), if any)

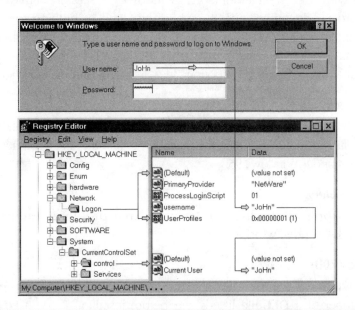

Figure 3.8 *If a user logs on with a valid password, the user name is written into the Registry's* **Logon** *and* **control** *keys. If the next user bypasses the user/password prompt by pressing the* ***Escape*** *key, the* **Logon** *key retains the previous user's name, but the* **control** *key does not.*

The CurrentConfig entry specifies which of the listed configurations is currently enabled. On some laptop systems, the CurrentConfig number may not change unless the computer is powered off and back on again as part of the docking/undocking procedure.

SessionManager

From its name, one might deduce that this key has something to do with the management of a Windows 95 session, although Microsoft documentation elsewhere has little or nothing to say about a Session Manager. Nevertheless, the subkeys found here contain much information that may be helpful to the advanced user looking for troubleshooting clues, as briefly summarized here.

APPPATCHES

Each subkey under the **AppPatches** key lists a specific application. Additional subkeys contain the patch(es) required if that application is run under Windows 95.

CHECKBADAPPS

The applications listed here may have problems running correctly under Windows 95.

CHECKVERDLLS

A Windows 95 application is supposed to check the version number of a **DLL** file listed here before installing its own **DLL**, which may be an earlier version. Some do, some don't. Refer to the "Check DLL Files" section in Chapter 7 for information about troubleshooting DLL-related files.

HACKINIFILES

This key's Contents Pane Data column cites a single line in each of three **INI** files, yet there seems to be no relationship between the line here and the equivalent line there. The key name suggests some sort of file "hack," yet a modification in the Data column has no effect on the **INI** file, and vice versa.

Known16DLLs

Windows 95 searches various folders for 16-bit **DLL** files in the Default Search Order shown here. However, if a **DLL** file is listed in the **Known16DLLs** key's Contents Pane, then the search order for that file is as shown in the Revised Search Order column.

	Default Search Order	Revised Search Order
1.	Current folder	C:\Windows\System
2.	C:\Windows	C:\Windows
3.	C:\Windows\system	Current folder
4.	Executable file folder	Executable file folder
5.	Folders specified by PATH	Folders specified by PATH

KnownDLLs

This key's Contents Pane specifies the **DLL** files that are loaded into memory when Windows 95 starts, even if no application requires them.

VMM32

Each subkey in this section is the name of a former virtual device driver file that is now part of the **VMM32.VXD** file in the **C:\Windows\System** folder.

Services

This key leads to a long series of subkeys, which may specify various drivers, provide descriptions of installed hardware, or furnish other information pertaining to system configuration.

Arbitrators

The four subkeys under the **Arbitrator** key specify the resources that Windows 95 has allocated, as shown in Figure 3.9 and described here.

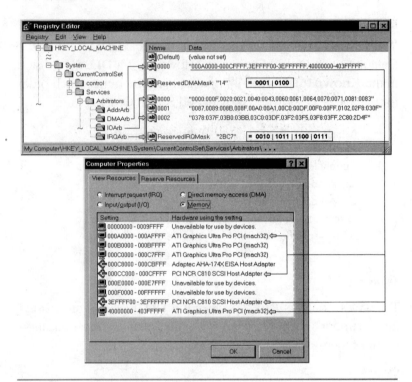

Figure 3.9 *The* **Services\Arbitrators** *key leads to subkeys for arbitration of various resources. The Computer Properties window at the bottom of the illustration shows how address resources are displayed on the Device Manager's* **View Resources** *tab.*

ADDRARB

This address arbitrator lists the memory addresses that Windows has assigned to hardware devices. Figure 3.9 shows how Device Manager's **View Resources** tab reports the same information. In this specific example, a legacy sound card occupies the 000E0000 - 000E7FFF memory range, and the system ROM BIOS is at 000F0000 - 00FFFFFF. Although the **View Resources** tab shows both blocks as "Unavailable for use by devices," neither is listed in the **AddrArb** key's Contents Pane.

DMAA<small>RB</small>

The Direct Memory Address Arbitrator uses a bit mask format to specify the reserved DMA configuration. In the example shown in Figure 3.9, the bit mask is hexadecimal 14, whose binary equivalent specifies DMA 4 and 2, as indicated by the underlined decimal numbers below the binary value.

```
Hex   ─────────binary─────────
14  =   0   0   0   1   0   1   0   0
        7   6   5   4   3   2   1   0
```

IOA<small>RB</small>

Here, each numbered entry in the Name column specifies some of the I/O (input/output) ports used by known hardware devices. There are about eight such ports listed in each row, and the list proceeds sequentially from I/O port 0000 to the highest port used by a known device. The port assignments are separated by commas, and a port range is indicated by a colon between the starting and ending port number, as shown here:

```
0087, 0089:008B, 008F, 00A0:00A1, 00C0:00DF
```

The first two entries would appear as 0087 - 0087 and 0089 - 008B in the Device Manager's input/output (I/O) list. If that list shows a port as "In use by unknown device," that port does not appear on the list in the **IOArb** key's Contents Pane.

IRQA<small>RB</small>

The Interrupt Request Arbitrator subkey follows the style of the **DMAArb** subkey described earlier. Thus, the ReservedIRQMask shown in Figure 3.9 specifies the IRQs indicated here by the underlined numbers under the binary value.

```
Hex   ───────────────── binary ─────────────────────────
2BC7 =   0    0    1    0   1   0   1   1   1   1   0   0   0   1   1   1
        15   14   13   12  11  10   9   8   7   6   5   4   3   2   1   0
```

Class

There is a subkey here for every supported class of hardware device, as illustrated here by a few of the many subkeys that may be found in this section.

DISPLAY

This key leads to one or more numbered (**0000, 0001,** etc.) subkeys—one for each configuration. Each in turn leads to a **DEFAULT** and a **MODES** subkey, as shown in Figure 3.10. The **DEFAULT** subkey specifies the display driver and its default mode, as shown here:

Name	Data	Default Color Depth	Default Resolution
Mode	"8,640,480"	$8 = 2^8 = 256$ colors	640,480 = 640 x 480

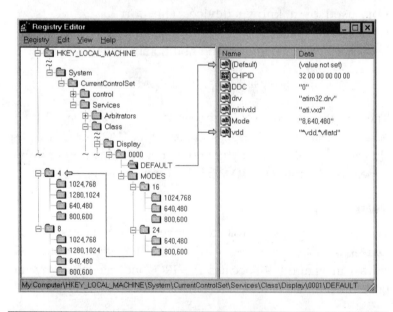

Figure 3.10 *In this illustration, the* ***DEFAULT*** *key's Contents Pane specifies the current video drivers, while the* ***MODES*** *subkeys list the various color depths and resolutions supported by the installed driver.*

The mode specified here is not necessarily the currently enabled color mode, which is specified beneath yet another **Display** key, as described in the "HKCC\Display\Settings" section later in the chapter (see also Figure 3.17). The subkeys under the **MODES** key list each available color depth (16, 24, 4, 8 in this example), and another level of subkeys specifies the screen resolutions available at each color depth. The Contents Pane of each of these keys is empty.

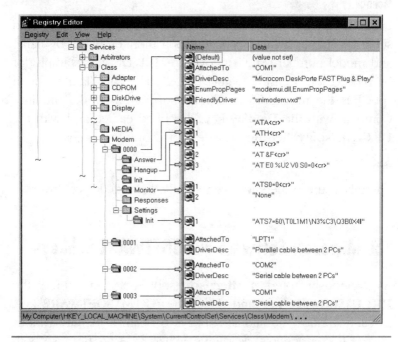

Figure 3.11 *The* **Modem** *key leads to one or more numbered subkeys, one for each communications device. In this example, the modem itself is specified by the* **0000** *key, whose subkeys list various AT commands. The other three subkeys (* **0001–0003** *) specify DCC (Direct Cable Connection) devices. For each device, the Contents Pane seen here shows a partial list of its actual parameters.*

MODEM

The Contents Pane of each numbered subkey lists details about a modem or other installed communications device, as shown in

Figure 3.11. Beneath each such key, additional subkeys specify commands appropriate to that device, such as the modem AT commands shown in the figure. If the Windows 95 Direct Cable Connection has been installed and enabled, a separate subkey appears here for each available cable connection, even if a DCC cable is not physically attached.

MONITOR

Each DriverDesc entry in the Contents Pane of the numbered subkey(s) beneath this key identifies a monitor, either by name and model number (MAG Innovision MX17F/S, for example) or by type (Laptop Display Panel 800 x 600). The MaxResolution specifies the maximum resolution supported by the monitor. Compare with the **Display** key, described earlier, and with the **HKCC\Display\Settings** key described later in this chapter.

VxD

There is a subkey here for every installed virtual device driver.

The Microsoft Software and SOFTWARE Subkeys

As previously noted, a **Microsoft** subkey appears under the **HKCU\Software** key and under the **HKLM\SOFTWARE** key. In each location, additional subkeys beneath it identify various Microsoft components, as shown in Figure 3.12. Because both these key structures are found on every Windows 95 system, a comparison is offered here, to give a better idea of the differences between subkeys with the same name. Although these details apply only to the specific subkeys described here, similar comparisons can be made between most other **Company Name** subkey systems that appear under the **HKCU\software** and **HKLM\SOFTWARE** keys.

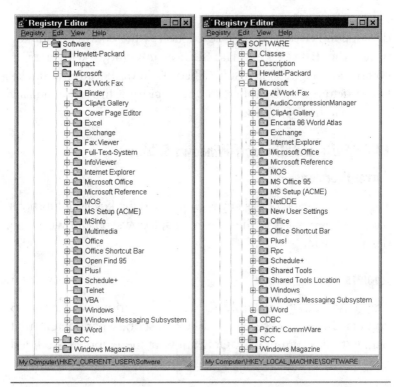

Figure 3.12 *A comparison of the subkeys found under the* **Microsoft** *key in the two Registry locations indicated in the Status Bars at the bottom of each window. Note that not all subkey names appear in both locations.*

In the comparisons that follow, remember that subkeys under **HKCU\Software** pertain to the current user only and will therefore change if a different user logs onto the system. By contrast, those under **HKLM\SOFTWARE** pertain to the basic software installation on the local machine, without regard to a specific user's personal configuration. If a **Company Name** subkey appears under **HKLM\SOFTWARE** only, then it may be inferred that the cited software is not separately configurable for multiple users.

In the following descriptions, each **HKCU** subkey description is followed by a description of the equivalent subkey under the **HKLM** key. The section concludes with a brief comparison of the Microsoft Office 95 keys, because a similar key structure may be found in any Registry if this (or a similar) office suite has been installed.

HKCU\Software\Microsoft\Windows Subkey
CurrentVersion

The Contents Pane of this key is empty, and the key itself functions solely as a repository of the subkeys that follow, some of which are described here.

Applets

This key leads to multiple subkeys for various Windows 95 applets. In each case, the subkey describes parameters that pertain to the current user. Only a few of these applets are listed here.

CDPLAYER

The **Settings** subkey's Contents Pane lists the various settings that determine the appearance and playing characteristics of the CDPlayer applet. These settings are refreshed when the applet closes and then used to set up the applet the next time it opens.

FREECELL

The Contents Pane lists games won and lost and other critical information that should not fall into enemy hands.

REGEDIT

The FindFlags entry stores the current Find parameters of the Registry Editor in DWORD format, as shown by this default entry:

Name	Data
FindFlags	0x00000003 (3)

The legal values are set by the first four bits of the DWORD, as shown here:

0	0	0	0		0	0	0	0		0	0	0	0		1	1	1	1
15	14	13	12		11	10	9	8		7	6	5	4		3	2	1	0

Bit	Decimal Value	Signifies
0	1	Match whole string only
1	2	Keys
2	4	Values
3	8	Data

Thus, if bits 0 and 1 are set, then a decimal value of 3 (2 + 1) in the Data column indicates the **Keys** and **Match whole string** boxes are checked. A decimal value of 15 (8 + 4 + 2 + 1) signifies all boxes are checked, and so on.

Explorer

The subkeys found here define various details pertaining to the current user's Explorer configuration.

ExpView

The Contents Pane of the Explorer View key has a single Settings entry, in which the binary number sequence in the Data column specifies the current size and position of the Explorer window, as well as the state of the Toolbar and Status Bar options.

RecentDocs

The Contents Pane of this key lists the most recently used (that is, opened) documents; this is the list seen on-screen if the Start menu's **Documents** option is selected. Figure 3.13 shows that the

list is stored in the Registry in binary format, and the Edit Binary
Value window inset shows the contents of one of these strings.
Note that the filename seen in the window (**README.TXT**) is
followed by a shortcut filename (**Readme.txt.lnk**), and this
shortcut file is stored in the **C:\Windows\Recent** folder.

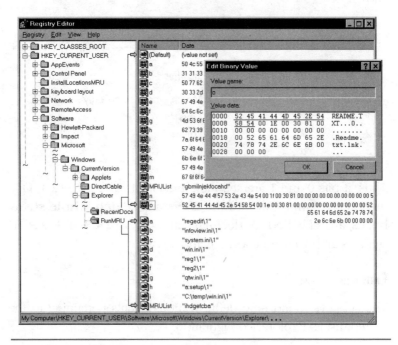

Figure 3.13 *The contents of the Start menu's cascading*
Documents *option are written into the* ***RecentDocs*** *key in*
binary format. By contrast, the contents of the ***Run*** *option's drop-*
down menu are stored in the ***RunMRU*** *key in text string format.*

The MRUList (most recently used) entry in the Contents Pane
indicates the sequence in which these documents were opened.

RunMRU

This key's Contents Pane lists the most recently used (that is,
run) items that were accessed via the Start menu's **Run** option.

The list may be viewed by clicking on the **down arrow** in the Run dialog box. As with the **RecentDocs** key described earlier, an MRUList specifies the order in which these items were run. But unlike the **RecentDocs** key, here the Contents Pane lists each item in string (ASCII text) format, as shown in Figure 3.13.

Shell Folders

Here, the Contents Pane lists the paths to various Windows 95 folders.

Policies

If the System Policy Editor has been used to impose certain restrictions on the current user, these restrictions will be listed here. Refer to "System Policy Editor" in Chapter 5 for details about using this utility.

Explorer

The Contents Pane lists various restrictions that are in place, as shown here by a few typical examples:

Name	Data	Comments
NoFind	0x00000001 (1)	Disables **Find** option
NoRun	0x00000001 (1)	Disables **Run** option
NoSetFolders	0x00000001 (1)	Disables **Folders on Settings** option

Network

In similar fashion, the Contents Pane describes restrictions imposed on network operations.

Keep in mind that any restrictions found under either of these subkeys can be easily disabled by the knowledgeable user, either by editing the appropriate line to change the DWORD from 1 to 0 or by simply erasing the line.

NOTE

HKLM\SOFTWARE\Microsoft\Windows Subkey

CurrentVersion

By contrast with its empty **HKCU\Software** counterpart, the Contents Pane of this **CurrentVersion** key contains much information about the Windows 95 installation, including product ID number and name and the identity of the registered user (owner) and organization (company name).

Applets

Again in contrast with the **HKLM\Software\...** subkey described earlier, this **Applets** key has comparatively few subkeys beneath it.

BACKUP

This subkey is written into the Registry the first time the Windows 95 Backup utility is used. Its Contents Pane describes the various backup configurations that are available, and a TapeDriveDetected entry indicates the presence (1) or absence (0) of a tape drive.

CHECK DRIVE

The Contents Panes in this key's **LastCheck** and **LastSurface Check** subkeys contain an entry for each drive letter that has been tested by the ScanDisk utility.

Setup

The Contents Pane of this key, which has no **HKCU** equivalent, contains a list of paths to various Windows 95 components.

OPTIONALCOMPONENTS

Here, the Contents Pane lists most (but not all) of the subkeys found beneath this key. Each such subkey identifies a specific

Windows 95 component (Accessibility, CD Player, Character Map, and so on), and the following information appears in the Contents Pane:

Name	Data	Comments
INF	`"filename.inf"`	The **INF** file that installs this component
Installed	`"0"` or `"1"`	1 = installed, 0 = not installed
Section	`"section name"`	The section of the **INF** file cited above

WINBOOTDIR

One of the few unmysterious Registry keys, this one contains just what you would expect from its name.

Explorer

The subkeys found here define various details pertaining to the configuration of the local machine, regardless of which user is currently logged on.

DESKTOP, MYCOMPUTER, AND THE NAMESPACE SUBKEYS

The Contents Panes of the **Desktop** and **MyComputer** keys are both empty, but both keys lead to a **NameSpace** subkey, which brings up the question: what's a *NameSpace?* It appears to be nothing more than the space on the Desktop itself or within an open My Computer window. In both areas, a certain number of object icons are seen, and of those, a few are specified under these two **NameSpace** subkeys, as listed here:

Desktop\NameSpace Subkeys	Contents Pane Data Column
`{00020D75-0000-0000-C000-000000000046}`	Inbox
`{00028B00-0000-0000-C000-000000000046}`	The Microsoft Network
`{645FF040-5081-101B-9F08-00AA002F954E}`	Recycle Bin
`{FBF23B42-E3F0-101B-8488-00AA003E56F8}`	The Internet

My Computer\NameSpace Subkey	Contents Pane Data Column
{992CFFA0-F557-101A-88EC-00DD010CCC48}	Dial-Up Networking

In each case, the subkey name serves as a pointer to the {CLSID} subkey beneath the **HKCR** key described in Chapter 2, and the Contents Pane reveals that key's identity. If one of the subkeys listed earlier is not present under the **NameSpace** key, then that object does not appear in the indicated NameSpace.

LastBackup, LastCheck, LastOptimize

If one or more of these keys are present, its Contents Pane Name column shows a listing for each drive letter, and the Data column specifies the number of days that have elapsed since the indicated function was last performed. The information contained here may be viewed via the **Tools** tab on the ·Properties sheet for any drive, as indicated here:

Subkey Name	Tools Tab
LastBackup	Backup status
LastCheck	Error-checking status
LastOptimize	Defragmentation status

Shell Icons

This subkey appears under the **Explorer** key if MS Plus! is installed, and its Contents Pane specifies icons in the new **COOL.DLL** file and in other MS Plus! files. These icons supersede various default icons formerly taken from the **SHELL32.DLL** file, and if MS Plus! is not installed, the user may still add a **Shell Icons** subkey to accomplish the same effect. For details on how to add or edit this subkey, refer to "Icon Not Specified in a DefaultIcon Subkey" in Chapter 5.

HKCU\Software\Microsoft Office\95 Subkey

The open **IntelliSearch** subkey in Figure 3.14 indicates that the current user has used the **Answer Wizard** option that appears on the Help menu in Microsoft Office applications, as well as on the Office 95 Shortcut bar. Note that there is no clue in the Registry itself to reveal that **IntelliSearch** has anything to do with the Answer Wizard feature. However, if any item in the Contents Pane's Name column is double-clicked, the Edit Binary Value window (also seen in the figure) opens, and a question may be seen on the right-hand side of that window. The next time the user opens PowerPoint's Answer Wizard, this inquiry will reappear in the Wizard window. If some other user logs on later and uses PowerPoint's Answer Wizard, this inquiry will not be seen.

In a similar manner, other subkeys found under the **Microsoft** or any other **Company Name** key in this **SOFTWARE** section will apply only to the current user.

HKLM\SOFTWARE\Microsoft\Microsoft Office\95 Subkey

By contrast, each subkey in this section specifies parameters that apply to anyone who uses the version of Microsoft Office 95 installed on this system, regardless of user name. For example, in the open **Wrapper\Filters** subkey at the bottom of Figure 3.14, the Contents Pane shows text data that appears if any user clicks the **Open a Document** button on the Office Shortcut bar. The data in the figure is shown on seven lines, just as it will appear in the *MS Office* application's Open dialog box. In the Registry itself, the data actually appears as a lengthy one-line text string.

It may be worth pointing out that Figure 3.14 offers another example of the Registry's inconsistent use of data storage formats.

While the just-described text appears as conventional ASCII characters, the four Data lines at the top of the Contents Pane in the same figure show regular text in hexadecimal format. For more on this subject, refer back to "Data Format Comparisons" in Chapter 1.

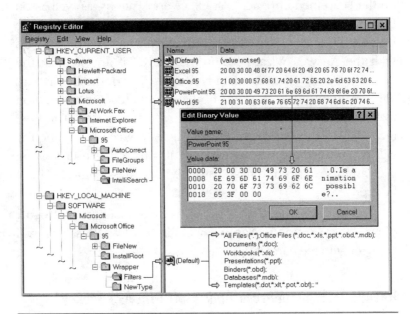

Figure 3.14 The **IntelliSearch** key reveals questions the current user has asked the Microsoft Office 95 Answer Wizard. At the bottom of the illustrations, the **Filters** key lists the options that will appear if any user clicks the **Open a Document** button on the Office Shortcut bar.

HKU: HKEY_USERS [USER.DAT]

According to Microsoft documentation, this key contains "the .Default subkey plus all previously loaded user profiles for users who have logged on." But, in fact, it does not. There is indeed a

.Default subkey, which, as its name implies, specifies the default user configuration for anyone who logs on without a user profile. Thus, if no password prompt appears as Windows 95 opens or if it does appear but the user simply presses the **Escape** key instead of entering a user name and password, then data contained within the **.Default** key is used to configure the session, and no other subkey is seen beneath the **HKEY_USERS** key.

When a new user logs on for the first time, a custom **USER.DAT** file is created for that user in a new **C:\WINDOWS\ Profiles*username*** folder. Initially, the file contains two versions of the **C:\Windows\USER.DAT** file, the first of which is an exact replica. This is followed by a revised version, in which all references to *.Default* are changed to *username*, along with other changes appropriate to the new *username* configuration. As this user tailors the configuration to suit personal preference, these changes are made only within the *username* section of this custom **USER.DAT** file. The .Default section remains an untouched "carbon copy" of the original **C:\Windows\USER.DAT** file.

When the Registry Editor is subsequently opened, the **HKEY_USERS** key shows two subkeys, one named **.Default** and the other labeled with the ***username*** under which the user logged on. Figure 3.15 shows such a key, with its **.Default** and ***username*** (**john**, in this example) keys expanded to show their subkeys. In this case, the **.Default** set is ignored, and the ***username*** set is replicated under the **HKEY_CURRENT_USER** key, as also shown in the figure. Note that the **.Default** key's **Software** subkey shows only four manufacturer's subkeys, while the same subkey under the ***username*** key shows six, and these are of course also seen under the **HKCU** key. This indicates that when the current user logged on for the first time, only four software applications had been installed, and the present user subsequently installed two more applications.

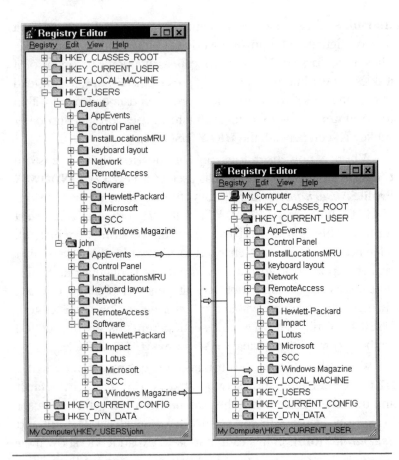

Figure 3.15 *At the left of the illustration, the current user's Software list includes a few items not available to a .Default user. As in Figure 3.1, this list is part of the current user's configuration that is written into the* **HKEY_CURRENT_USER** *key shown at the right.*

If nothing else, the simple expedient of showing only a **.Default** and a current **_username_** subkey prevents one user with busy fingers from "fixing" some other user's configuration.

To summarize, if HKU shows a **.Default** key only, then that key is replicated under **HKCU**, but if a second (**_username_**) key is present, then that key is replicated instead. In either case, the subkeys themselves were described in the **HKCU** section earlier in the chapter.

HKCC: HKEY_CURRENT_CONFIG key [HKLM\Config\000*x*]

As shown in Figure 3.16, the data seen here is derived from the **HKLM\Config\000*x* subkey**, where 000*x* is the subkey for the current hardware configuration. If there is only one such configuration (as on most desktop systems), then the information is taken from **HKLM\Config\0001**, which is the only subkey under the **Config** key.

Assuming there are two or more 000*x* subkeys under **HKLM\Config** (as on many laptops that support both docked and undocked configurations), then each one contains the three subkeys described in this section. However, only the specific subkey set found here in **HKCC** is currently enabled.

Note that **HKCC** does not reveal the identity of the specific **HKLM\Config\000*x*** key from which it is derived.

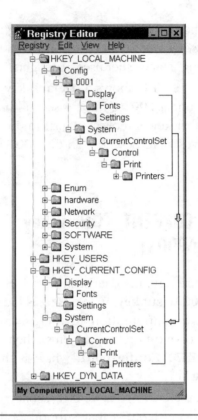

Figure 3.16 *Hardware configuration information in the* ***HKEY_LOCAL_MACHINE****'s **Config\0001** key is written into the* ***HKEY_CURRENT_CONFIG*** *key, as seen here. On a laptop computer there would be two numbered* ***Config*** *subkeys, one each for docked and undocked modes. In either case, the appropriate one is written into the* ***HKCC*** *key when the system is powered on.*

Display

This key leads in turn to the **Fonts** and **Settings** subkeys. In Figure 3.17, the composite Contents Pane illustrates typical entries within both subkeys.

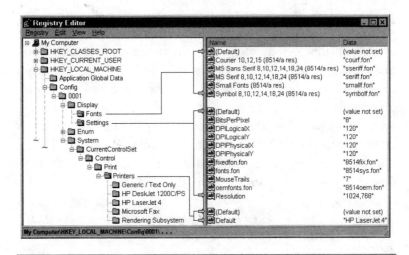

Figure 3.17 *The **Fonts** key specifies screen fonts formerly listed in the* [fonts] *section of **WIN.INI**, while the **Settings** key specifies system fonts from the* [boot] *section of **SYSTEM.INI**, where the same font listings are still retained. The **Printers** key simply lists the current default printer, while other installed printers are identified by empty subkeys below it.*

Fonts

This subkey specifies the screen fonts that were formerly listed in the [fonts] section of **WIN.INI**.

Settings

This subkey defines color depth (BitsPerPixel) and other screen characteristics and specifies the system fonts that were formerly loaded via the [boot] section of **SYSTEM.INI**. These fonts are still listed there, however, for the benefit of applications that don't recognize the Windows 95 Registry.

The Resolution entry specifies the current horizontal and vertical resolution, in pixels (1024,768, for example).

Enum

If present, this key may contain various subkeys (**BIOS**, **Root**, **SCSI**, etc.), which in turn specify Plug-and-Play BIOS or other elements. Note, however, that an element found here represents a formerly available device that has been removed from the system configuration. Because the structure of this key varies as edits are made from within the Device Manager, refer to "HKCC: The Enum Subkey" in Chapter 4 for more details about the keys that appear in, and disappear from, this area.

*There is another **Enum** subkey that appears directly under **HKLM**, as described earlier in the chapter.*

N O T E

System

This key leads to a series of empty (value not set) subkeys and finally to the **Printers** subkey, which specifies the current default printer, as shown in Figure 3.17. If more than one printer is installed, there are additional subkeys beneath the **Printers** key for each one. These subkey labels serve as a simple list of available printers, but the keys contain no further information.

HKDD: HKEY_DYN_DATA key [system RAM]

The dynamic data displayed under this **HKEY** is created fresh every time Windows 95 opens. The data is written into RAM and continuously updated in **HKDD**, as required. The data is displayed here under the following two subkeys.

Configuration Manager

This key is also known as the *hardware tree*, because its contents define the current hardware configuration of the system. The root of this hardware tree is the **Enum** subkey, described next.

Enum Subkey

This hardware enumerator key leads in turn to an extensive series of subkey branches, each labeled with an eight-character hexadecimal number (**C111326C, C113CBB4**, for example). In the Contents Pane for each of these subkeys, a HardwareKey data entry serves as a pointer to a subkey series, which may be found within the **HKLM\Enum** key section described earlier.

Table 3.5 lists Contents Pane entries taken from some of the many **C ...** subkeys found under the **Enum** subkey on a typical personal computer. In each case, the actual **C...** key name is not given, because it will vary from one configuration to another. The first column lists a subkey sequence found under the **HKLM\Enum** key described earlier. The final column shows the information displayed in the DeviceDesc row, which would be seen if the final subkey in the indicated area is opened.

Table 3.5 *Contents of Typical HKEY_DYN_DATA Key's Enum Subkey* *

In Contents Pane, HardWareKey entry points to this HKLM\Enum subkey:	DeviceDesc(ription), taken from the indicated HKLM\Enum subkey
EISA*PNP0A00\0	ISA Plug and Play bus
FLOP\GENERIC_NEC_FLOPPY_DISK_	GENERIC NEC FLOPPY DISK (A)
FLOP\GENERIC_NEC_FLOPPY_DISK_	GENERIC NEC FLOPPY DISK (B)
HTREE\RESERVED\0	(empty)
HTREE\ROOT\0	(a non-existent key)

In Contents Pane, HardWareKey entry points to this HKLM\Enum subkey:	DeviceDesc(ription), taken from the indicated HKLM\Enum subkey
ISAPNP\INT1030\00A3478A	Intel EtherExpress PRO/10 (PnP Enabled)
ISAPNP\READDATAPORT\0	IO read data port for ISA PnP enumerator
MONITOR\DEFAULT_MONITOR\0001	MAG Innovision MX17F/S
NETWORK\JADM\0000	HP JetAdmin
NETWORK\JADM\0002	HP JetAdmin
NETWORK\MSTCP\0000	TCP/IP
NETWORK\NETBEUI\0000	NetBEUI
NETWORK\NETBEUI\0002	NetBEUI
NETWORK\NWLINK\0000	IPX/SPX-compatible Protocol
NETWORK\NWLINK\0002	IPX/SPX-compatible Protocol
NETWORK\VREDIR\0000	Client for Microsoft Networks
NETWORK\VREDIR\0001	Client for Microsoft Networks
NETWORK\VREDIR\0004	Client for Microsoft Networks
NETWORK\VREDIR\0005	Client for Microsoft Networks
NETWORK\VSERVER\0000	File and printer sharing for Microsoft Networks
NETWORK\VSERVER\0001	File and printer sharing for Microsoft Networks
NETWORK\VSERVER\0002	File and printer sharing for Microsoft Networks
NETWORK\VSERVER\0003	File and printer sharing for Microsoft Networks
NETWORK\VSERVER\0008	File and printer sharing for Microsoft Networks
NETWORK\VSERVER\0009	File and printer sharing for Microsoft Networks
NETWORK\VSERVER\0010	File and printer sharing for Microsoft Networks
NETWORK\VSERVER\0011	File and printer sharing for Microsoft Networks
PCI\VEN_1000&DEV_0001\...	PCI NCR C810 SCSI Host Adapter
PCI\VEN_1002&DEV_4158\...	ATI Graphics Ultra Pro (mach32)
PCI\VEN_8086&DEV_0482\...	Intel PCI to EISA bridge
PCI\VEN_8086&DEV_04A3\...	Intel Mercury Pentium Processor to PCI bridge
ROOT*ADP1740\0000	Adaptec AHA-17X EISA Host Adapter

In Contents Pane, HardWareKey entry points to this HKLM\Enum subkey: †	DeviceDesc(ription), taken from the indicated HKLM\Enum subkey
ROOT*PNP0000\0000	Programmable interrupt controller
ROOT*PNP0100\0000	System timer
ROOT*PNP0200\0000	Direct memory access controller
ROOT*PNP0303\0000	Standard 101/102-Key or MS Natural Keyboard
ROOT*PNP0500\0000	Communications Port (COM1)
ROOT*PNP0500\0001	Communications Port (COM2)
ROOT*PNP0700\0000	Standard floppy Disk Controller
ROOT*PNP0800\0000	System speaker
ROOT*PNP0A03\0000	PCI bus
ROOT*PNP0B00\0000	System CMOS/realtime clock
ROOT*PNP0C01\0000	System board
ROOT*PNP0C04\0000	Numeric data processor
ROOT*PNP0F0E\0000	Standard PS/2 Port Mouse
ROOT\NET\0000	Dial-Up Adapter
ROOT\PNPC031\COM1	Serial cable on COM1
ROOT\PNPC031\COM2	Serial cable on COM2
ROOT\PNPC032\LPT1	Parallel cable on LPT1
ROOT\PORTS\0000	Printer Port (LPT1)
ROOT\PRINTER\0000	HP LaserJet4
ROOT\PRINTER\0001	Generic / text only
ROOT\PRINTER\0002	HP DeskJet 1200C/PS
SCSI\DEC_____DSP3107LS_____4	DEC DSP3107LS (hard disk)
SCSI\NEC_____CD-ROM_DRIVE:5012	NEC CD-ROM DRIVE:501
SERENUM\APC1065\...	APC BACK-UP UPS PRO S/N: xxxx
SERENUM\MNP0336\...	DeskPorte 28.8 (modem)

*__Enum key__ leads to multiple subkeys, each labeled with an eight-character hexadecimal number (not shown here). Hex subkey labels vary from one configuration to another.

Although the previously described __HKLM\Enum__ subkey lists every device ever installed on the computer, only those devices currently in use will appear under the __Enum__ subkey here in the __HKDD\ConfigManager__ section. The information shown in these keys is continuously updated and is therefore valid whenever it is displayed.

Default Monitor Subkey

Figure 3.18 shows a typical example of the relationship between a subkey here in the **HKDD\ConfigManager\Enum** section and the associated subkey in the **HKLM\Enum** section. In this specific example, the **C1151CF0** subkey's Contents Pane shows the following information:

Name	Data
HardWareKey	"MONITOR\DEFAULT_MONITOR\0001"

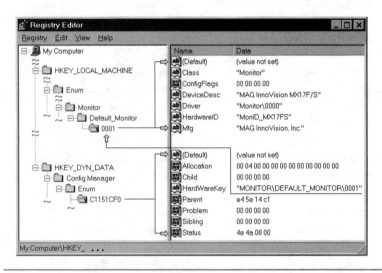

Figure 3.18 *In the open **C1151CF0** key in this **HKEY_DYN_DATA** section, the Contents Pane's **HardWareKey** listing specifies a subkey in the **HKEY_LOCAL_MACHINE** section where the default monitor is identified. In a similar manner, each such subkey has a **HardWareKey** listing that points to some other hardware component.*

The Data column specifies the subkey in which the monitor is actually identified. To locate that key, add **HKEY_LOCAL_ MACHINE\ Enum** to this entry and ignore the all-uppercase style shown here. The complete key name, therefore, is:

```
HKEY_LOCAL_MACHINE\Enum\Monitor\Default_Monitor\0001
```

In Figure 3.18, the DeviceDesc entry in that key's Contents Pane identifies the current monitor as a MAG Innovision MX17F/S.

NOTE *If a laptop computer is configured for an external default monitor when attached to a docking station, it is usually possible to toggle between that monitor, the laptop's own screen, or both—typically, by holding down the **Fn** key and pressing **F7** (or similar). This action, however, has no effect on the information displayed in the subkeys just described.*

PerfStats (Performance Statistics)

This section provides the dynamic links to performance statistics that may be monitored on-screen via the System Monitor applet. Its size is enormous, as may be demonstrated by highlighting the key and exporting it to a **PERFSTAT.REG** file, whose file size will be 4,827,877 bytes. This is an ASCII translation of RAM-resident PerfStats data and would not otherwise be found in a file, because neither **SYSTEM.DAT** nor **USER.DAT** maintains a record of this subkey. Nevertheless, the file size and content may help to better understand the amount of data contained here.

If you do export this subkey, make sure you erase the file after examining it; it wastes a lot of space and can't be re-imported anyway. Refer to Chapter 4 for more information about Registry import/export operations.

In Figure 3.19, the **StatData** subkey under the **PerfStats** key is opened, and its Contents Pane shows the items currently available to the System Monitor. The various Name entries seen here are derived from other subkeys found under the **PerfStats** key in the **HKLM** section, as illustrated by the **KERNEL** and **VFAT** key examples shown in the figure, where information in the Data column (not shown in the figure) is derived and constantly refreshed, as necessary, from system RAM.

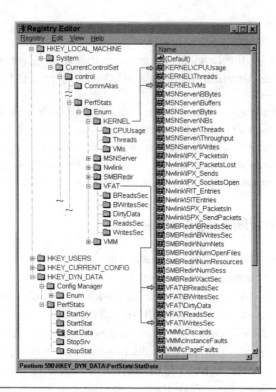

Figure 3.19 *In this **HKEY_DYN_DATA** key sample, the Contents
Pane shows a partial list of items in the **StatData** subkey's
Contents Pane. Each item in the Name column is read in from
the indicated section of the **HKEY_LOCAL_MACHINE**'s
PerfStats key. The Data column entries (not shown here) are
dynamically read into the key and continuously refreshed
during the course of any Windows 95 session.*

To illustrate how all this works, open the System Monitor's Edit
menu, select the **Add Item** option, and then select **Memory
Manager**. Next, scroll down the Item list and select **Swapfile
size** and **Swapfile in use**. The System Monitor window should
now look like the one shown at the top of Figure 3.20. Highlight
either graph, and the Status Bar at the bottom of the window
displays the graph name, followed by the last—that is, the
current—value and the peak value, both expressed in decimal

notation. The figure shows how the Status Bar reports changes, depending on which graph is selected.

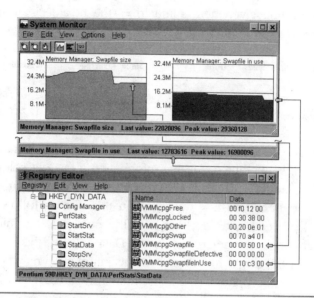

Figure 3.20 *Data shown in the* **StatData** *key's Contents Pane can be read via the System Monitor applet. Four-byte binary data in the Contents Pane is converted to a decimal value displayed in the System Monitors Status Bar and displayed by the graph. As the binary data changes in the* **HKEY_DYN_DATA** *key, so does the graph.*

Now open the Registry Editor's **HKEY_DYN_DATA\Config Manager\PerfStats\StatData** subkey and scroll to the bottom of the Contents Pane. The Swapfile and SwapfileInUse entries show the current values for these two items, and the hexadecimal data should agree with the decimal value reported as Last value in the System Monitor's Status Bar. To convert from one format to the other, remember that the Data column shows the hexadecimal value in reverse sequence. Reverse the order of the hexadecimal characters and then convert to decimal format. If the resulting value does not agree with that reported by the

System Monitor's Status Bar, open the Registry Editor's View menu, select the **Refresh** option, and try again.

The listing given here summarizes the hexadecimal and decimal values shown in Figure 3.20 for Swapfile and SwapfileInUse:

Name in Contents Pane	Data	Same, Inverted	Decimal Value
VMM\cpgSwapfile	00 00 50 01	01 50 00 00	22,020,096
VMM\cpgSwapfileinUse	00 10 c3 00	00 c3 10 00	12,783,616

In the previous discussion of the HKDD Config Manager's **Enum** subkey, it was pointed out that information in a Data column pointed to a key under HKLM's own **Enum** subkey, as illustrated in Figure 3.18. The **PerfStats** key described in this section follows the same general procedure, except that here the pointer is the information in the Name column rather than in the Data column; this was shown in Figure 3.19. Figure 3.20 shows how this information may be viewed by the user. At the bottom of the illustration, the **HKDD** key leads to the **PerfStats\StatData** subkey, whose partial contents are shown at the bottom of the Contents Pane. Here, the Name column shows a list of subkeys, each of which points to a subkey that resides under the following **HKLM** key:

```
HKLM\System\CurrentControlSet\control\PerfStats\Enum\VMM
```

This key is further illustrated in Figure 3.21, where dynamic data is again shown within the **HKDD** section, and an accompanying pointer indicates the associated **HKLM** location. In this specific example, HKLM's **cpgSwapfile** subkey offers the following information in its Contents Pane:

Name Column	Data Column	To Display Data:
Description	"Size of swap file in bytes."	Open System Monitor, highlight **Swapfile size**, click **Explain** button.
Name	"Swapfile size"	Same. Also appears in Item box.
Differentiate	"FALSE"	(Not part of data display)

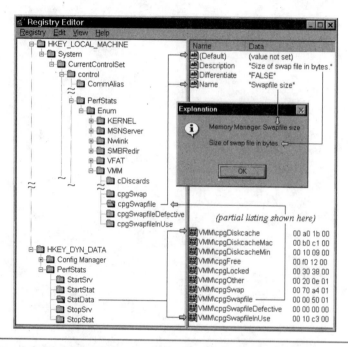

Figure 3.21 *In the.Contents Pane list at the bottom of the illustration, the **VMM\cpgSwapfile** entry in the Name column is derived from the **HKLM** subkey of that name (**cpgSwapfile**). That key pane contains the information shown by the Contents Pane at the top of the illustration, and this information is displayed to the user via the Explanation window shown in the inset.*

The Explanation box inset in Figure 3.21 shows how the Data column entries are displayed to the user. In much the same manner, dynamic data for any System Monitor item is found here under the **PerfStats** subkey, and the Contents Pane's Name column points the way to static data stored in another subkey under **HKLM**, as shown in the preceding example.

If you search the Registry for DiskCacheMac, you'll find it appears several times. It should, of course, be DiskCacheMax, but no harm is done, because the item is simply a pointer from one location to another, perhaps programmed by someone with Mac Envy.

NOTE

CHAPTER 4

The Registry Editor

In previous chapters, the Registry Editor applet was used simply as a passive device with which to view the structure of the Registry. This chapter re-introduces the Registry Editor, this time in its primary role as an editing utility.

An HKEY Review

In Chapter 2, Figure 2.1 illustrated the relationships between five of the six **HKEY**s in the Registry Editor's Key Pane. As shown in that figure, the sources of three **HKEY**s are subkeys within two of the other **HKEY**s, which for identification purposes were described as the Master **HKEY**s. For reference purposes, the six **HKEY**s are listed here, along with the source for each of them. The files that are the source of the two Master **HKEY**s are then described in some detail in the "Registry Files" section, which follows. Again, for future reference, the name of the **HKEY** contained within each file is given in parentheses.

HKEY Name	Source HKEY (or Filename)	Source HKEY's Subkey
HKEY_CLASSES_ROOT	HKEY_LOCAL_MACHINE	SOFTWARE\Classes
HKEY_CURRENT_USER	HKEY_USERS	Default (or UserName)
HKEY_CURRENT_CONFIG	HKEY_LOCAL_MACHINE	Config\000x
HKEY_LOCAL_MACHINE	SYSTEM.DAT	
HKEY_USERS	USER.DAT	
HKEY_DYN_DATA	(dynamically derived from system RAM)	

The Registry Files

The files described in this section are known collectively as *The Registry*, and their attributes are system, hidden, and read-only. Except as noted, the files are written into the **C:\Windows** folder, not the **C:\Windows\system** folder as stated in some Microsoft documentation. Table 4.1 lists the files described here and other files associated with the Registry.

Table 4.1 The Registry Editor Files

Filename	Location	Purpose
REGEDIT.EXE	C:\WINDOWS	the executable Registry Editor file
REGEDIT.HLP	C:\WINDOWS\HELP	help file
REGEDIT.CNT	C:\WINDOWS\HELP	help topics listed on Contents tab
REGEDIT.lnk	(as specified by user)	shortcut to REGEDIT.EXE (optional)
SYSTEM.DAT †	C:\WINDOWS	system-specific data
SYSTEM.DA0 †	C:\WINDOWS	backup copy
USER.DAT †	C:\WINDOWS	user-specific data for default user
USER.DA0 †	C:\WINDOWS	same, backup copy
USER.DAT †	C:\WINDOWS\ Profiles\UserName	same, for specified user (UserName) only
USER.DAO†	C:\WINDOWS\ Profiles\UserName	same, backup copy for specified user
filename.REG	(as specified by user)	ASCII text file(s) created by user, via Export option on File menu (optional)

Filename	Location	Purpose
CFGBACK.EXE ‡	Windows 95 CD-ROM	to backup Registry
CFGBACK.HLP ‡	Windows 95 CD-ROM	help file
HKLMBACK ‡	on backup set	to restore SYSTEM.DAT file
HKUBACK ‡	on backup set	to restore USER.DAT file
REGBACK.INI ‡	C:\WINDOWS	CFGBACK.EXE initialization file

† File attributes are system, hidden, read-only.

‡ Refer to Chapter 6 for details (also +s +h +r attributes).

SYSTEM.DAT (HKEY_LOCAL_MACHINE)

As explained in Chapter 3, the **HKLM** key contains the basic hardware and software configuration data that applies to the computer, without regard to the current user. Its **Config** subkey leads to one or more numbered subkeys, one for each available hardware configuration (**0001** = docked, **0002** = undocked, and so on). All of this data is written into a single hidden **SYSTEM.DAT** file in the **C:\Windows** folder.

SYSTEM.DA0

If Windows 95 opens successfully, a copy of **SYSTEM.DAT** is written into a hidden **SYSTEM.DA0** file, which is also in the **C:\Windows** folder. By definition, this file is known to be valid, because a new version is only created if Windows 95 opens successfully. Consequently, it can be used as a recovery device if Windows 95 fails to open on a subsequent session. In that case, the **SYSTEM.DA0** file is copied to **SYSTEM.DAT**, and Windows 95 should open in its last valid configuration.

SYSTEM.1ST

This hidden file is written into the root directory immediately after the Windows 95 setup procedure concludes successfully. Although described in some Microsoft documentation as a "copy of the Registry," it is in fact a copy only of the initial **HKLM** key configuration. Because Windows 95 does not upgrade this file, it soon becomes out-of-date as Windows 95 itself is configured and reconfigured. Nevertheless, it may be better than nothing if all other attempts to recover the Registry fail. Refer to "SYSTEM.1ST" in Chapter 7 for additional troubleshooting details.

USER.DAT (HKEY_USERS)

The **HKU** key contains one or two subkeys, the first of which is always labeled **.Default.** This key contains configuration data that pertains to the default user; that is, to any user who logs on and bypasses the password prompt by pressing the **Escape** key. If the system is set for single-user operation, then only the **.Default** subkey is found under the **HKU** key, and its contents are read from and written to the **USER.DAT** file in the **C:\Windows** folder.

Custom Profiles

If the following conditions are met, a **C:\Windows\Profiles** folder is created, and that folder contains one or more **UserName** folders, as shown in Figure 4.1:

1. The system is configured for a UserName and password prompt.

2. On the Passwords Properties sheet's **User Profiles** tab, the following radio button is enabled: **Users can customize their preferences and desktop settings. Windows switches to your personal settings whenever you log on.**

If these conditions are met, then a new **UserName** folder is created
in the **C:\Windows\Profiles** folder when a new user logs on for
the first time. The **UserName** folder holds the user's own **USER.DAT**
file, which initially contains two copies of the **C:\Windows**
USER.DAT file. One is an exact duplicate, while in the other all
.Default keys are rewritten as **UserName,** as shown here:

Duplicate version of C:\Windows\USER.DAT
```
[HKEY_USERS\.Default]
[HKEY_USERS\.Default\Control Panel]
[HKEY_USERS\.Default\Control Panel\Appearance]
(and so on...)
```
Revised version to specify UserName
```
[HKEY_USERS\john]
[HKEY_USERS\john\Control Panel]
[HKEY_USERS\john\Control Panel\Appearance]
```
(and so on...)

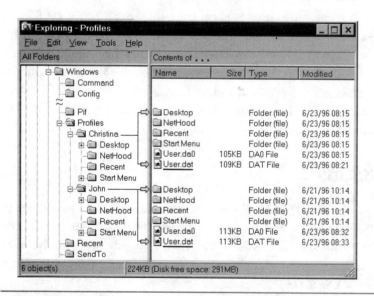

Figure 4.1 *If Windows 95 is configured for multiple users, a*
C:\Windows\Profile folder holds a separate folder for each user.
*Each such **UserName** folder contains the user's own **USER.DAT***
*file and a **USER.DA0** backup copy. Subfolders (**Desktop** and*
others) hold the user's customized configuration information.

The Registry Editor now shows two subkeys under the **HKU** key, one labeled **.Default**, the other **UserName.** In this case, the latter subkey is written into the **HKCU** key, as was illustrated in Figure 2.1. As the user makes configuration changes, these are written into the **UserName** section of the **USER.DAT** file in that user's folder, while the **.Default** section remains unchanged.

As Windows 95 opens, it reads the **C:\Windows\USER.DAT** file, on the assumption that no user name will be specified. However, if the user logs on as **John** (or whatever), then the **C:\Windows\Profiles\John\USER.DAT** file is read, and its settings supersede those of **C:\Windows\USER.DAT**. You can note this by observing the opening wallpaper, which is specified in **C:\Windows\USER.DAT**. After the logon prompt, this changes to the wallpaper specified in the user's personal **USER.DAT** file, located in the place just described.

If some other user logs on later, that user's **USER.DAT** file is read, and again the **HKU** key shows a **.Default** and a **UserName** subkey—the latter now labeled for the current user. Some Microsoft documentation states that the **HKU** key contains a subkey for *every* user, but in fact it only shows two subkeys, regardless of how many users may have logged on to the computer in the past.

USER.DA0

Like the **SYSTEM.DAT** file described earlier, a backup copy of **USER.DAT** is written into a hidden **USER.DA0** file in the **C:\Windows** folder when Windows 95 opens successfully. Also, if the user enters a valid user name and password, a copy of that user's **USER.DAT** file is likewise copied as **USER.DA0**, both of which are in the **C:\Windows\Profiles\UserName** folder.

Once Windows 95 has opened, no **USER.DA0** file will be updated if a new user logs on via the Start menu **Shut Down** option's **Close all programs and log on as a different user** radio button.

USER.1ST

Unlike the **SYSTEM.1ST** file cited earlier, there is no equivalent **USER.1ST** file.

Registry Editor Menu Details

Chapter 1 presented a brief overview of all Registry Editor menus (see Figure 1.4). Additional details are given here for those menu options frequently used during an editing session. In the following descriptions, these options are listed alphabetically under each menu.

Registry Menu

As noted in Chapter 1, the Registry menu, shown here in Figure 4.2, is equivalent to the File menu found on most other Menu Bars.

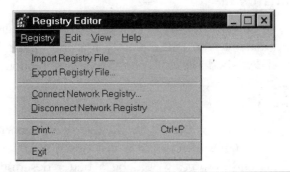

Figure 4.2 *The Registry Editor's Registry menu.*

Connect Network Registry .

In theory, this option allows the user to connect to a Registry on a network computer. The fact that the option is enabled suggests this might indeed be possible, if only one could penetrate the Microsoft documentation to learn the means to do so. However, a careful reading between the lines reveals the following disconnected facts:

1. Remote Registry Service will not work with share-level security; in other words, it requires user-level security.

2. User-level security requires a user database.

3. Windows 95 does not support a user database.

Therefore, Windows 95 alone does not support the Remote Registry Service, which is required to use this option. Apparently, a Windows NT or NetWare server is required to enable this feature.

Disconnect Network Registry

Given the explanation of the **Connect** option, it should come as no surprise that this option is disabled.

Export Registry File

Use this option to export all or part of the current Registry to a script file that may be subsequently imported back into the Registry, as described in the "Export Operations" section later.

Import Registry File

Assuming a previous version of the Registry has been saved to a script file via the **Export** option just described, this option imports (actually, *merges* would be a better description) the contents of that file back into the Registry. Refer to the "Import Operations" section later for additional details.

Print

To print all or part of the Registry, highlight the desired key or subkey and select this option. A Print dialog box like the one shown in Figure 4.3 appears, with the **Selected branch** radio button in the Print range area enabled. To print the entire Registry, either highlight **My Computer** in the Registry Editor window or click on the **All** radio button. But before doing so, refer to "Registry Print Jobs" for additional details about printing the Registry.

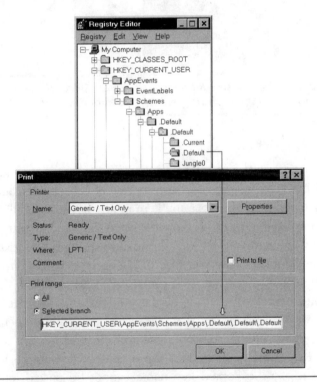

Figure 4.3 *In this Registry Editor Print dialog box, the enabled radio button next to **Selected branch** indicates the specified key will be printed. Put a check in the **Print to file** box to print an ASCII text copy of the selected key to a file instead of to the printer.*

Edit Menu

The options on the Registry Editor's Edit menu are shown in Figure 4.4 and summarized here.

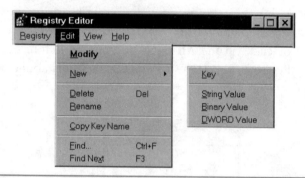

Figure 4.4 *The Registry Editor's Edit menu. Select the **New** option to open the cascading menu also shown in the figure.*

Copy Key Name

This option is not part of the original retail version of Windows 95 but has been added to some recent OEM versions. If available, simply highlight any key or any item in any key's Contents Pane, and then use the option to copy the open key's full Registry path to the Clipboard, where the information is stored in text and OEM text formats only. Because the Registry Editor's Edit menu does not offer a **Paste** option, press **Ctrl+V** to paste the copied key name into any other Registry location, into the Find window's Find what box (described later) or into any document whose **Paste** option supports text and OEM text formats. The **Copy Key Name** option does not save a picture image to the Clipboard, so the copied key name cannot be pasted into the Paint applet or another application that requires this format.

Delete

Simply highlight the desired key or Contents Pane entry and use this option to delete it. Because the deleted item cannot be undeleted, you may want to export the key in which it appears, in case you decide later that the item should not have been deleted.

If one of the six **HKEY**s is highlighted, the **Delete** option is disabled. If any Contents Pane's (Default) entry is highlighted, the option is not disabled, even though that item cannot be deleted. If you attempt to do so anyway, an "Unable to delete all specified values" message appears, and the delete action is ignored.

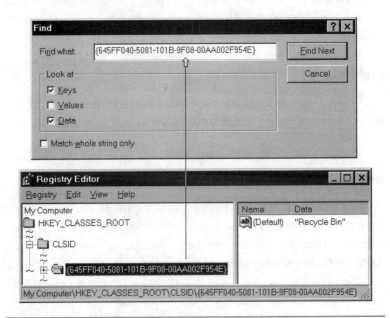

Figure 4.5 *Use the Edit menu's **Copy Key Name** option (if available) to copy a lengthy {**CLSID**} key name to the Clipboard, then paste the key name into the Find dialog box's Find what area. This is more reliable than entering such data at the keyboard.*

To delete multiple entries, hold down the Control key while highlighting the entries to be deleted. Or hold down the Shift key and select the first and last entries to be deleted. Then use the Delete option (or press the Delete key) to delete all selected entries. Either technique functions in the Contents pane, but not the Key pane.

Find

Select this option (or press **Ctrl+F**) to open the Find dialog box shown in Figure 4.5. Type the text you wish to find into the Find what box, check one or more of the boxes below it, and press the **Find Next** button to begin the search. Refer to "Registry Search Techniques" later in this chapter for suggestions on searching the Registry.

Find Next

This menu option finds the next occurrence of the selected text string, but it's much faster to simply press **F3** to perform this operation.

New

To add a new entry to the Registry, first highlight the appropriate existing key in the Key Pane and then select this option to open the cascading New menu whose options are described here. Note that if **My Computer** is highlighted, all New menu options will be disabled, because it is not possible to add a new **HKEY** nor to add an entry to the My Computer Contents Pane.

Key

If this option is selected, a new subkey is added directly beneath the currently opened **HKEY** or subkey. As shown in Figure 4.6, an open key appears with a boxed New Key #1 legend. If you do not rename the key, and select the **Key** option again, a New Key #2 key will be added.

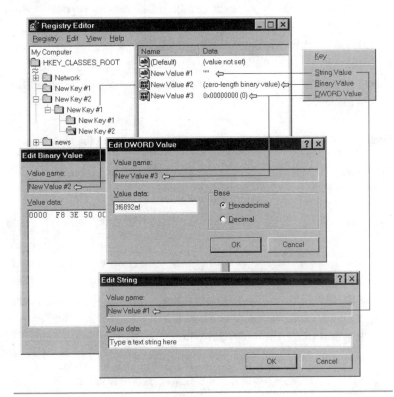

Figure 4.6 *If a small icon next to a Name entry in the Contents Pane is double-clicked, an Edit Value dialog box opens in whatever format is appropriate for the data on that line.*

To add a subkey beneath either key, highlight the new key and again select the **Key** option. Repeat as desired to create the required key structure. Rename each new key either as it is created or later, as desired.

String, Binary, or DWORD Value

To add an entry to the Contents Pane of any key, highlight that key and then select the appropriate format from the cascading **New** menu. In each case, a boxed `New Value #x` entry will appear in the Name column of the Contents Pane, and the Data column will show an empty value in the appropriate format. For example, if a new entry is created in sequence in each of the three available formats, the Contents Pane would show the following entries:

Name	Data	format (on *New* menu)
New Value #1	`""`	String value
New Value #2	(zero-length binary value)	binary value
New Value #3	0x00000000 (0)	DWORD value

Double-click on any entry in the Name column to open one of the Edit dialog boxes shown in Figure 4.6. Then type the desired data into the Value data box in the format appropriate for that data. In the figure, the Contents Pane shows the initial null entries, and each dialog box shows a typical Value data entry, which will replace the null data when the **OK** button is clicked.

NOTE

The Registry Editor automatically encloses every Data column text string in quotes. Therefore, do not type quotes in the Value data box when editing a string, unless an additional set is required for other purposes.

Rename

Highlight any key or Contents Pane icon (or Name entry) and then select this option to rename the selected item. If the **Rename** option is disabled, it is not possible to rename that item.

View and Help Menus

All options on these menus were described in the "View Menu" and "Help Menu" sections of Chapter 1.

Context Menus in the Registry Editor

Figure 4.7 shows the Context menu for any key in the Registry Editor's Key Pane. The **Delete** and **Rename** options are disabled if an **HKEY**'s Context menu is opened. The figure also shows the Context menus for entries in the Contents Pane Name and Data columns.

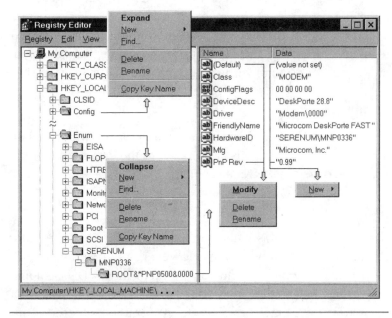

Figure 4.7 *If a key's Context menu is opened, the first option is either **Expand** or **Collapse,** depending on the status of the selected key. In the Contents Pane, Context menu options vary according to whether an item in the Name or the Data column is selected.*

With the exception of the options described here, all other options on these menus (**Find, New,** etc.) are the same as those already described.

Collapse

A minus sign to the left of any key indicates that subkeys beneath it are displayed, in which case the **Collapse** option appears at the top of the menu. If selected, the subkey structure collapses (disappears) and a plus sign appears next to the key.

Expand

If a plus sign appears to the left of any key, the **Expand** option appears at the top of the menu; if selected, the key structure expands to show the subkeys beneath it. If no sign appears next to a key, then the **Expand** option is visible but disabled, indicating that no further action is possible at this subkey level.

Modify

Selecting this Contents Pane option simply opens whatever Edit window (see Figure 4.6) is appropriate to the data format of the highlighted item in the Name column.

New

As already noted, this is the same as any other Registry Editor Context menu's **New** option. However, its appearance as a single-option Context menu for any item in the Data column may at first be puzzling, especially because the option does not appear if an item in the Name column is selected. But, notwithstanding its position here in the Contents Pane's Data column, it continues to function as described earlier and illustrated in Figure 4.4.

Registry Editing Techniques

Before even *thinking* about editing the Registry, make sure you've made a complete backup copy of the hidden **SYSTEM.DAT** and **USER.DAT** files. The files themselves are described later in this chapter, and Chapter 6 reviews various backup procedures that may be used. In most cases, Windows 95 is clever enough to protect itself against Registry mishaps, but it never hurts to buy a little extra insurance—at least until you're comfortable enough with the Registry to patch it up if it gets hurt by accident.

Backup a Contents Pane Entry

Keep in mind that the Registry Editor does not support an **Undo** option, which means that all edits are final. Also, if you edit any key that appears at two locations, the edit occurs simultaneously at both those locations (**HKCR\.bat** and **HKLM\SOFTWARE\Classes\.bat,** for example). Therefore, in addition to the overall backups described in Chapter 6 and the Registry export procedures described later in this chapter, it's not a bad idea to make a copy of a Contents Pane entry prior to editing it, especially if the original data is lengthy and/or complex, as shown in this example:

```
C:\Windows\rundll.exe setupx.dll,InstallHinfSection
DefaultInstall 132 %1
```

If you edit a line like this and then decide to restore the original, you may have trouble doing so unless your memory is excellent—or you have a backup line available.

Use the following procedure to make a single-line backup of any Contents Pane entry:

1. Double-click on the Name entry icon to be copied.

2. Press **Ctrl+C** to copy the highlighted Value data line, then click on the **OK** button.

3. Create a new entry called *<whatever>***bak**.

4. Double-click on its Name entry icon.

5. Press **Ctrl+V** to paste the copied data into the Value data box.

Now you can edit the original entry as desired, and if it doesn't work, reverse the procedure to restore the original data. This technique may prove convenient if you edit several Contents Pane entries and then want to selectively restore some, but not all, to their original state. Refer to "Registry Tracker Applet" in Chapter 6 for an alternative method of recording line changes.

Illegal Edits

In most cases, a *disabled* (grayed) option on the Edit menu indicates it is not possible to use that option on the highlighted Registry key. For example, if **My Computer** is highlighted, the **Delete**, **Rename**, and **Copy Key Name** options are disabled. Or if an **HKEY** is highlighted, **Delete** and **Rename** are disabled.

In other cases, an Edit menu option may appear to be available, even if it is not. To illustrate, highlight the **(Default)** item in any Contents Pane and then select the **Delete** option. After the "Are you sure?" message appears, an "Unable to delete all specified devices" message appears, indicating that this item cannot be removed.

Although the Registry Editor protects its contents from certain disastrous accidents, it nevertheless permits the user to make many potentially life-threatening operations without comment. Therefore, reread everything you can find about backup procedures before making any serious moves.

Registry Navigation Keys

Table 4.2 lists various keystroke combinations that may be useful during a Registry editing session.

Table 4.2 *Registry Editor Navigation Keys**

Keyboard Key	Primary Action	Secondary Action †
Down Arrow	Open next-lowest key on same level	
Up Arrow	Open next-highest key on same level	
Right Arrow	Expand open key	Open next-lowest key
Left Arrow	Open next-highest key	Collapse its subkeys
Alt Home	Open **My Computer** icon	
Alt Home Left Arrow	Same, and collapse **HKEY**s	
Tab	Toggle between Key and Contents Panes	
F1	Help	
F2	Rename open key	
F3	**Find, Find Next**	
Alt F4	Exit Registry Editor	
F5	Refresh	
F6	Toggle between Key and Contents Panes	
F10	Highlight Registry menu	
Shift F10	Open Context menu	Close Context menu

*   List does not include **Alt** keys for menus or menu options. Refer to underlined letters on Menu Bar and in menu options.

†   If listed, action occurs on alternate key presses.

INI Files and the Registry

As noted in Chapter 1, there is a certain amount of interaction between the Registry and various **INI** files. While some **INI** data is transplanted to the Registry, Windows 95 may also add or revise **INI**-file data every time Windows 95 starts, so that it contains information appropriate to the current user. So, if you see something in an **INI** file immediately after installing a new application, and whatever it is has disappeared the next time you look, it's probably been relocated to a Registry subkey. Likewise, if remaining **INI**-file content changes from one session to another, it's a sure sign that the Registry is at work in the background.

As one more example of what can happen, if you change wallpaper from within Windows 95, **WIN.INI** retains the old wallpaper specifications for the moment, even though the new wallpaper appears on-screen. But the next time Windows 95 opens, it checks the Registry and rewrites **WIN.INI** as required to bring it into conformity with the Registry.

As a result of these file interactions, you may want to keep an eye on your **INI** files—especially **WIN.INI**—until you become familiar with the Registry's mode of operation.

Search Techniques

In order to edit a Registry Key or Contents Pane entry, first you need to find it. If you know the location you need, the fastest way to access it is usually to successively click on the plus signs next to the appropriate **HKEY** and its subkeys until the desired key is found and opened. However, if you're not sure where the Key or Contents Pane entry is located, use the Edit menu's **Find** option to search for it.

It's usually possible to hasten the search action by checking only one box in the "Look at" area of the Find dialog box. To verify this, time a search for **StopStat** (an **HKDD** subkey) with all three boxes checked and again with only the **Keys** box checked. The latter search may take about half the time of the former.

Obviously, every Registry key exists in the Key Pane, so there's no point wasting time searching the other two areas. However, a reference to the *name* of a key may be found in either column in the Contents Pane, as was shown in Figures 3.18 through 3.21 of the previous chapter. Most filename citations are found in the Data column, although there are a few filename lists in the Name column of the **InstalledFiles** and **VMM32Files** subkeys under the **HKLM\System\CurrentControlSet\control** key.

Given a bit of experience, it should be possible to predict the location of an item with some degree of certainty, and by checking only the appropriate box, to find it in much less time than it would take to search the whole works.

Registry Search Indicators

The customary "busy" mouse pointer does not appear during a Registry search. Instead, the Find box shown in Figure 4.8 remains on-screen until the search has concluded. If the search is successful, then the found item is highlighted. If the search is unsuccessful, the Registry Editor does not display a "not found" message. However, a "Finished searching" message does appear, as also shown in the figure. If **F3** is pressed repeatedly to find all occurrences of the search item, the same message appears if **F3** is pressed after the final successful search.

Binary and DWORD Searches

The **Find** option is unable to find binary or DWORD data stored in the Contents Pane's Data column. If you need to find specific data in either format and you know the general area where it should be, export only the appropriate key structure and then use your word processor's **Find** option, as shown in these examples:

Format	Data Column shows	Search for
binary	45 3a 8d ac d4	45,3a,8d,ac,d4
DWORD	0x00087439 (554041)	dword:00087439

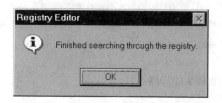

Figure 4.8 *The Find box is displayed during a Registry search operation, but the usual "busy" mouse pointer does not appear. When no more search items are found, a Registry Editor box shows a "Finished Searching" message.*

Binary and DWORD data are written into a Registry script file as shown in the Search for column above and in Figure 4.9. Therefore, search for binary data by entering the hexadecimal byte characters separated by commas. In a DWORD search, the leading "0x" and the parenthetical decimal equivalent are not written into the script file, but the "dword:" prefix is. Depending on context, it may be helpful to begin the search with that prefix, to avoid finding {**CLSID**} entries that contain the same character string.

Copy/Paste Search Techniques

For most find operations, it's sufficient to type the desired data into the *Find what* box and then to search for it. However, if you've encountered a complex key name or Data column entry and you want to find other occurrences of that item, you may prefer to copy the highlighted data to the Clipboard and then paste it into the Find what box. Although the Registry Editor's Edit menu does not support a **Copy** option, and the familiar **Ctrl+C** combination does not always work, one of the following techniques will still permit you to copy any item in the Registry Editor window.

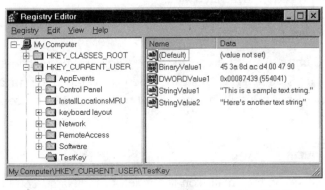

TestKey saved via the Export option   *TestKey* saved to a PRN file

REGEDIT4

[HKEY_CURRENT_USER\TestKey]   [HKEY_CURRENT_USER\TestKey]
"StringValue1"="This is a sample text string."   StringValue1=This is a sample text string.
"BinaryValue1"=hex:45,3a,8d,ac,d4,00,47,90   BinaryValue1=45,3a,8d,ac,d4,00,47,90
"DWORDValue1"=dword:00087439   DWORDValue1=39,74,08,00
"StringValue2"="Here's another text string"   StringValue2=Here's another text string

---

Figure 4.9 *This "do nothing" key's Contents Pane shows examples of binary, DWORD, and string data. For comparison purposes, the text examples below the window show how this data is exported into a Registry script file (left) and printed to a file (right). Note the differences in the use of quotes, format of DWORD data, etc.*

Key Name

If your version of Window 95 supports the Edit menu's **Copy Key Name** option (described earlier), use that option to copy a lengthy key name, such as the **{CLSID}** number shown at the bottom of Figure 4.5. Paste that string into the Find what box, cut the **HKEY_CLASSES_ROOT\CLSID** at the head of the string, and then search for other occurrences of that unique string.

If the **Copy Key Name** option is not available, use the data column procedure described later.

Name Column

A Name entry cannot be copied to the Clipboard by highlighting it and pressing **Ctrl+C**. Instead, open its Context menu and select the **Rename** option. The boxed name can now be copied via **Ctrl+C**.

Data Column

Double-click on the small icon to the left of the Name entry and then press **Ctrl+C** to copy the highlighted Value data box.

Device Searches

Sometimes the identity of a device may be obvious from the name that appears to the left of its key. For example, if a key name is **NEC___CD-ROM_DRIVE:5012** (see Figure 5.6 in the next chapter), it should be reasonably clear that the key refers to a CD-ROM drive manufactured by NEC. Others keys are not quite so obvious though, as shown by the **SERENUM** (Serial Enumerator) and **MNP0336** subkeys in Figure 4.10. If either subkey is highlighted, the Contents Pane simply shows (Default) and (value not set), neither of which is very informative. To track down the necessary information in this specific example, open the **HKLM\Enum** key that appears immediately below the last **000x** key and look for a **SERENUM** subkey. Note that this **Enum** key is at a different level than the subkeys of the same name that may appear under one or more of the **000x** keys just above it. Its own subkeys specify various serial devices, one of which is **MNP0336**. Open the **ROOT...** subkey immediately below it to display a list of its contents, which includes sufficient information to identify the device hiding behind the **MNP0336** key. Use the same general technique to find information about other devices listed under any **000x** key's **Enum** subkey. Or in any other location where an ambiguous key name is discovered, search the Registry for other occurrences of that name, one of which may lead to a clue (or another subkey) that will identify the device.

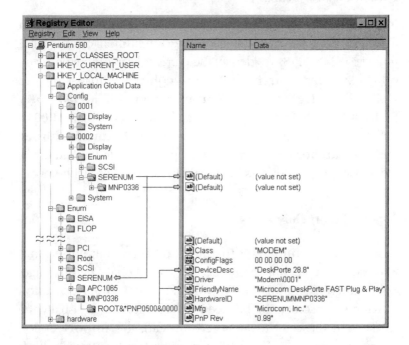

Figure 4.10 _If a key name or its Contents Pane data is ambiguous, a search for another key of the same name often leads to data sufficient to identify the device._

General Hardware Search

As another hardware device–search technique, highlight the **HKLM\Enum** key and search the Data column for a likely device description (system timer, HP DeskJet, SyQuest EZ135, etc.). To find all system drives (diskette, CD-ROM, hard drive), search the Name column for **CurrentDriveLetterAssignment** to find drive **A**. Then press **F3** repeatedly to find each successive drive letter. Once the desired item is found, note the key and subkey in which that device is specified.

Default Monitor Search

In Figure 3.18 in the previous chapter, the DeviceDesc entry in that key's Contents Pane identified the current monitor as a MAG Innovision MX17F/S. To identify the current default monitor in any other system, search the Data column entries in the **HKDD\ConfigManager\Enum** section for **MONITOR\ DEFAULT_MONITOR**, note the actual **000x** key (usually, **0001**), and then find that key under the **HKLM\Enum\Monitor\ Default_Monitor** key. As in the example shown in the figure, the DeviceDesc entry indicates the monitor name and model number.

Import/Export Operations

In becoming familiar with these actions, remember that Microspeak definitions rarely follow conventional English usage. For example, neither the **Import** nor the **Export** operation actually *move* something between two locations, as is usually the case when these terms are used. Instead, the **Import** option *merges* a copy of a saved (that is, *exported*) Registry file back into the Registry, while **Export** *saves* a copy of the selected key(s), while leaving the original in place.

Import Operations

To import a saved Registry file back into the current Registry, select **Import Registry File** on the Registry menu, highlight the desired file, and click on the **Open** button. Notwithstanding its ambiguous name, the button actually merges the selected file into the Registry. At the conclusion of the import action, the following message is displayed:

```
Information in path\filename.REG has been successfully
entered into the registry.
```

Remember to keep in mind the following unique characteristics of the import action:

1. An imported Contents Pane entry will overwrite a current Registry entry of the same name.

2. An imported Contents Pane entry will be added to the current Registry if that entry does not already exist there.

3. An existing entry in the current Registry will be left undisturbed if the imported file does not contain a replacement for it.

These characteristics apply to every key, subkey and Contents Pane entry in the current Registry. For example, Column 1 in the following table shows a hypothetical **AnyName** key and its three subkeys in the Registry. Column 2 shows the contents of a previously created **AnyName.Reg** file about to be imported into the Registry, and Column 3 shows the contents of the revised Registry after the file has been imported.

Original Registry Contents	Imported File Contents	Revised Registry Contents
AnyName	AnyName	AnyName
Subkey **A**	Subkey **A**	Subkey **A**
Contents Pane entry **w**	Revised entry **w**	Revised entry **w**
Subkey **B**	——	(Subkey **B** and its contents unchanged)
Contents Pane entry **x**	——	
Subkey **C**	Subkey **C**	Subkey **C**
Contents Pane entry **y**	Identical entry **y**	Rewritten entry **y**
	New entry **z**	New entry **z**
	Subkey **D** (*new*)	Subkey **D** (*new*)

Note that the imported **AnyName.Reg** file has not completely replaced the previous version of the **AnyName** key. Instead, it updated the Contents Pane entry **w** under subkey **A,** left subkey **B** untouched, revised subkey **C,** and added a new subkey **D.** If subkey **B** is no longer wanted, it will have to be deleted as a separate operation.

If it is important that an existing key/subkey structure be completely replaced by a new version, use the following procedure:

1. Export the existing key, as **AnyName.BAK** (just in case—you can always erase it later).

2. Delete the **AnyName** key in the current Registry.

3. Import the new **AnyName.Reg** file into the Registry.

Or, refer to "The INF File" later for an alternative method of handling a Registry import, which may be convenient if the same information must be imported into several Registries.

Export Operations

To save all or part of the Registry, highlight any branch (that is, any key or subkey), and then select the **Export** option to open the Export Registry File dialog box shown in Figure 4.11. The Selected Branch box near the bottom of the dialog box verifies the name of the key that is about to be exported. Both that key and all subkeys beneath it will be saved to a file, whose name must be entered in the File name box.

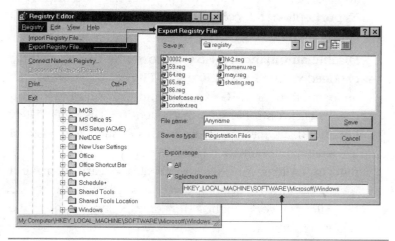

Figure 4.11 *When the **Export Registry File** option is selected, the name of the open Registry key appears on the Selected branch line in the Export Registry File dialog box. Click on the **All** radio button if you would rather export the contents of the entire Registry.*

EXPORT STATUS MESSAGE

There is none. The mouse pointer may change to the busy mode hourglass (or similar) icon while data is being exported, but no message appears at the conclusion of the operation, other than the mouse pointer returning to its normal appearance.

Import/Export Tips

If you plan to use the Registry Editor's **Import** and **Export** options frequently, you might want to consider the following suggestions:

Set up a Registry folder. Create a dedicated **C:\Registry** (or similar) folder for Registry files and then a **Registry** shortcut icon. Open that icon's Context menu, select **Properties**, and click on the **Shortcut** tab. Type **C:\Registry** in the Start in box, click on the **Apply** button, and then click **OK**. The next time you select the **Import** or **Export** option, the contents of the **C:\Registry** folder will appear in the dialog box.

Disable automatic Registry imports. By default, any file exported via the **Export Registry File** option is saved with an extension of **REG**, and—again, by default—if you double-click on a file with that extension it is immediately imported back into the Registry. This is quite convenient if it's what you want to do, but if you make a practice of regularly editing the Registry, it's all too easy to make a mess of things by accidentally double-clicking the wrong file. After you've done this a few times, consider one of the following alternatives:

Revise the Registration association. Open Explorer's View menu, select **Options**, and click on the **File Types** tab. In the list of Registered file types, select **Registration Entries** and click on the **Edit** button to open the Edit File Type dialog box, whose Actions box shows Edit, **Merge** (in boldface type), and Print. Highlight the **Edit** action and click on the **Set Default** button to make **Edit**, rather than **Merge**, the default (boldface) action. The next time you double-click (accidentally or on purpose) a file with the **REG** extension, the file will open in Notepad for editing, which may be preferable to an accidental Registry merge. When you really *do* want to merge a file into the Registry, do so via its Context menu.

The action described here does not affect a double-click action from within the Import Registry File dialog box, but if you've gone to the trouble to open that box, then presumably you really do want to merge something into the Registry.

Use some other extension. As an alternative to the preceding suggestion, use an extension other than **REG** for potentially hazardous Registry files. Assuming you've created a dedicated **C:\Registry** folder, the presence of say, a few **.re_** files in addition to the usual **.reg** files should be no cause for confusion. If you double-click on a *filename*.**re_** file, Windows 95 will have no idea what to do with it, so it won't get imported into the Registry by accident. When you are ready to import it, use the Registry Editor's **Import** option. Or refer to "Add Merge Option" in the "Context Menu Modifications" section of Chapter 5 for additional suggestions about setting up a permanent **.re_** (or similar) key in the Registry.

Creating a Registry Script File for Importing

Some sources warn against editing the Registry directly and recommend instead that a Registry script file be created and then imported into the Registry. In most cases, however, this may be more trouble than it's worth. Although the file is in straight ASCII text format, the proliferation of slashes, double-slashes, and commas turn file creation into a tedious procedure at best, and it may be even easier to mis-edit the file than to mis-edit. the Registry itself.

Even if duplicate information must be entered into several Registries, it's usually easier and faster to edit one Registry

directly and then export the appropriate section(s) to a script file
that can be subsequently imported into other Registries.
Nevertheless, here are a few guidelines for creating a Registry
script file for those occasions when you feel the urge to do so.

The REGEDIT4 File Header. Whenever the **Export** option
(described earlier) is used, a 12-byte header is written into
the file, consisting of the word **REGEDIT4,** followed by
two sets of line-feed/carriage-return bytes, as shown by the
underlined portions of the following Debug script excerpt:

```
D:\registry>debug network.reg
-d
146B:0100  52 45 47 45 44 49 54 34-0D 0A 0D 0A 5B 48 4B 45   REGEDIT4....[HKE
146B:0110  59 5F 43 55 52 52 45 4E-54 5F 55 53 45 52 5C 4E   Y_CURRENT_USER\N
146B:0120  65 74 77 6F 72 6B 5D 0D-0A 22 52 65 73 74 6F 72   etwork]..\"Restor
. . .
146B:01A0  45 5D 0D 0A 22 52 65 6D-6F 74 65 50 61 74 68 22   E]..\"RemotePath"
146B:01B0  3D 22 5C 5C 5C 5C 44 45-4C 4C 34 38 36 5C 5C 43   ="\\\\DELL486\\C
146B:01C0  22 0D 0A 22 55 73 65 72-4E 61 6D 65 22 3D 22 4A   "..\"UserName"="J
-
```

If this header is slightly altered (**REGEDIT** or **REGEDIT3**,
for example), no error message will be seen when the
Import option is selected, even though the file will not be
imported into the Registry.

Use of Backslash and Quotes in Registry Script File.
Figure 4.12 shows a Registry Editor window in which the
Contents Pane displays some network-related data. Note in
particular the RemotePath entry's underlined Data column,
and compare that entry against the way the same data
appears in the Registry script file, where it is also
underlined. The comparison shows that each backslash in
the Contents Pane is written as a double backslash in the
script file. In addition, the script file uses single backslashes

within the Key\subkey structure, but of course these separators do not appear in the Registry Editor's Contents Pane. As a final comparison, note the use of quotes in the script file and compare each line with its equivalent in the Registry Editor's Contents Pane.

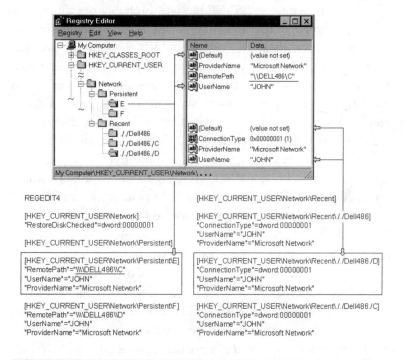

Figure 4.12 *This Registry Editor window displays the contents of a few network-related keys, while the boxed portions of the Registry script file excerpt beneath it show how that information is exported into the file. Compare the underlined RemotePath entry in both locations.*

The point of these tedious comparisons is to draw attention to the distinctive style that must be followed when editing a Registry script file. After making a few minor editing errors, you may agree that it's usually far simpler to just edit the Registry directly, and never mind the safety-first aspects of script file editing.

The INF File

Although the Windows 95 **INF** file was probably not thought of as a stand-in for the Registry script file, it does offer an alternative way to edit the Registry, which some prefer over the method just described. According to the Windows 95 Resource Kit, these "Device information (INF) files provide information used by Windows 95 to install software that supports a given hardware device." While the statement is not false, it describes only one function of an **INF** file, which can support both hardware *and* software devices. In fact, the **INF** file is actually a setup information file, and it is correctly identified as such in the list of Registered file types. With a little practice, it can be used as an alternate Registry-editing device, as described here.

If an **INF** file's Context menu is opened and its **Install** option selected, the file contents are read and significant changes may be made to the Registry, as prescribed by sections of that file, which superficially resemble the familiar **INI** file format. A few of these sections are reviewed here, to show how they affect the Registry and how they can be used to edit it, even if a new hardware or software device is not being installed.

Not all **INF** file sections, nor all lines within a section, are described here. In most cases, information to the left of the equal sign should be entered as written here, while that to the right may vary as desired. However, a subsequent section name must agree with whatever was specified in a previous section. Spaces added here for clarity may or may not be found in actual **INF** files.

Although a complete description of the **INF** file structure is beyond the scope of this chapter, a nodding acquaintance with the few details offered here may help in troubleshooting some Registry problems. For additional details, refer to Appendix C ("Windows 95 INF Files") in the Windows 95 Resource Kit. But read with care, for there are many errors in its pages, a few of which are pointed out here. In general, the CD-ROM version is more accurate than the printed version.

Windows 95 Version

This is the standard opening section for all **INF** files, as shown here.

```
[Version]                       Comments
Signature    = "$Chicago$"      Identifies a Windows 95 INF file by its beta name
Class        = Adapter          Specifies the device class.
```

The `Signature` line must be written as `$Chicago$` and not `$Windows 95$` as indicated in the print version of the Resource Kit.

Install

This section specifies additional sections of the **INF** file in which various Registry edit sections may be specified, as shown by the examples given here:

```
[DefaultInstall]                Comments
AddReg    = AddRegEntry         Name of the INF file section in which new
                                Registry entries are specified.

DelReg    = DeleteRegEntry      Name of section in which Registry
                                entries to be deleted are specified.
```

Although the **Resource Kit** cites an `[Install]` section only, the section head must be revised as shown here to enable an **INF** file to correctly edit the Registry when its Context menu's **Install** option is selected. To verify this, search the **INF** files in the **C:\Windows\Inf** folder for those that contain this section header (**cabview.inf**, **explore.inf**, **shell.inf**, for example).

Edit Registry Entries

These sections are cited on the AddReg and DelReg lines in the just-described [DefaultInstall] section. Although programmers delight in giving obscure names to sections such as these, there seems to be no performance advantage in doing so. Consequently, each section described here is given a simple name that describes what it does. *Real* programmers can, of course, change these names to help ensure minimum comprehension. Each italicized line illustrates the format in which a line should be entered, and this is followed by a few sample lines to illustrate actual Registry modifications:

```
[AddRegEntry]
HKEY, Subkey(s), Name,      Flag,    Data
HKCR, .abc,      TestLineA,  ,     "Line Enclosed In Quotes"
HKCR, .abc,      TestLineB, 0,     Line Not Enclosed In Quotes
HKCR, .abc,      TestLineC, 1,     FF, 38, 95, D3, 5F
```

The entries in this section are added to the Registry, and each item on the first line is briefly described here:

> **HKEY**—This is of course the **HKEY** under which the entry is to appear. For reasons best left unexplained, the Resource Kit refers to this **HKEY** entry as *reg-root-string*.
>
> **Subkey(s)**—This is the complete subkey structure that appears under the specified **HKEY**.
>
> **Name**—The entry written here appears in the Contents Pane's Name column.

Flag—A number here specifies the format of the data, as follows:

Flag	Data Format	Comments
0 (or none)	ASCII string	To preserve spaces in text, enclose the line in quotes.
1	Binary data	Enter hexadecimal numbers separated by commas.

Data—This entry appears in the Contents Pane's Data column. Make sure to follow the format specified by the **Flag** entry. If that entry is omitted, data will be considered as an ASCII string.

```
[DelRegEntry]
HKEY,    Subkey(s)
HKEY,    Subkey(s), Name
HKCR,    .abc
HKCU,    TestKey, StringValue1
```

As you might expect, this section specifies a subkey structure that is to be removed. The permissible entries are as described in the [AddRegEntry] section, except that there is no **Flag** entry.

If the **Name** entry is omitted, then the entire specified subkey structure is deleted. Otherwise, only the cited **Name** entry and its associated Data column entry are removed. Thus, the last two lines of code will remove the entire **HKCR\.abc** subkey structure, but only the StringValue1 entry in the **HKCU\Testkey.** Other **TestKey** entries and subkeys will be left undisturbed.

INF and REG File Comparison

As noted in the "Import Operations" section earlier in this chapter, a script file imported into the Registry may revise existing entries and add new ones, but it does not provide a means to delete a subkey or a line that is no longer needed. By comparison, the **INF** file's **DelReg** function can be used to explicitly delete either. Therefore, the relatively simple expedient of writing an **INF** to install a nonexistent device can be used as a means to place new or revised data into the Registry and to remove data that is no longer needed.

The same general procedure can also be used to delete the Recent Document and/or Run command lists, the contents of a folder, and so on. Refer to "The INF file as a Registry Editor" in Chapter 5 for a typical example of how to use the **INF** file to customize your system.

Registry Print Jobs

The following section describes various ways to handle a Registry print job. Before printing anything, however, remember that a full printout can run 500 or more pages, and that only includes the **HKEY_LOCAL_MACHINE** and **HKEY_USERS** sections. As described in Chapters 2 and 3, three of the other keys are derived from these two as Windows 95 opens, and therefore they are neither printed nor saved unless specifically selected, as described later. The dynamically created **HKEY_DYN_DATA** section is also not printed, which is probably a good thing because it would add about 1000 pages to the print job.

Print (Registry Menu Option)

Use this option only to send a small subsection of the Registry to the printer. Otherwise, consider the **Print to File** option or the **Export/Print** procedure.

Print to File

Most Print dialog boxes support a **Print to File** option, such as that shown in Figure 4.3 earlier in the chapter. By default, this action usually saves a file in a format that can be sent directly to the printer later. While this can be helpful if the printer is located elsewhere, it may be more convenient to reconfigure the option to save a straight ASCII text version of the desired Registry section to a file and then print that file. Follow the procedure described here to do so. But first, review the "Export/Print" section; it offers an alternative way to print that may be more convenient than the one described here.

1. Open the Start menu, highlight the **Settings** option, and select the **Printers** folder. Or select it via the My Computer window.

2. Double-click on the **Add Computer** icon in the Printers window.

3. When the Add Printer Wizard window appears, click on the **Next** button.

4. Select **Local printer** and click the **Next** button.

5. Scroll down the Manufacturers list, highlight **Generic** and click **Next**.

6. In the Available ports list, highlight **LPT1:** and click **Next** (or select some other port, as desired).

7. Click the **No** radio button underneath "Do you want your Windows-based programs to use this printer as the default printer?"

8. Click the **No** button underneath "Would you like to print a test page?" and click on the **Finish** button.

9.   If prompted to do so, insert the Windows 95 CD-ROM in the drive so that the necessary drivers can be installed.

At the conclusion of this operation, there should be a **Generic/Text Only** icon in the Printers window, as shown in Figure 4.13.

Figure 4.13 *If a generic printer is installed and configured to print to a file, its printer icon in the Printers window displays a diskette overlay.*

Now select the **Print** option and when the Print dialog box appears, use the **down arrow** in the Name box to select the **Generic/Text Only** printer. Click on the **Print to File** check box, give the file a suitable name, and click the **OK** button to create it. The file can be subsequently viewed in any word processor or ASCII text editor, where it can be edited before printing. Or, if the file is very short, simply send it to the printer instead of to a file.

Export/Print Procedure

Remember that the Registry menu's **Export** option saves an ASCII textfile version of the selected Registry key or keys, which can be conveniently reviewed by any word processor and then printed in whole or in part. This is by far the easiest way to handle any print job, because the exported section can be reviewed before committing the whole thing to the printer. It's also a convenient means to export and print those sections of the Registry that are not included in a full print job. For example, to print just the **HKEY_CLASSES_ROOT** section, select that key, export it, review it in a word processor, and then print it. Note the page count though, for even this "small" section of the Registry can be a paper-eater.

Print versus Export/Print

For reference purposes, Table 4.3 lists the page count and file size for typical **HKEY**s exported to a Registry **REG** file and saved to a **PRN** file. Note that in the exported file versions, the size of the full copy is 12 bytes less than the sum of the **HKEY_LOCAL_MACHINE** and **HKEY_USERS** keys, thus reconfirming that these are the only two keys saved in a full Registry export.

Table 4.3 *File Size of Typical Exported HKEYs*

HKey Name	Saved to .PRN file		Exported to .REG file	
	Page Count	File Size	Page Count	File Size
HKEY_CLASSES_ROOT	274	477,254	219	414,403
HKEY_CURRENT_USER	76	196,461	59	173,427
HKEY_LOCAL_MACHINE	546	1,101,548	472	976,050
HKEY_USERS	77	198,158	59	176,914
HKEY_CURRENT_CONFIG	2	1,651	1	1,481
HKEY_DYN_DATA	1286	5,306,623	1,018	4,848,997
Full copy †	621	1,299,706	530	1,152,952

† Exported full copy is sum of **HKLM** and **HKU** keys, less 12 bytes.

The reason for the size discrepancy is that each exported Registry file contains the following header:

```
REGEDIT4¶
     ¶
```

Each *EOL* (end of line) character (¶) signifies two bytes, which therefore adds four bytes to the 8-byte text string and accounts for the header total of 12 bytes. Because a full registry export has only one such header, its file size should agree with the sum of the two **HKEY**s cited earlier, less one 12-byte header.

Note that for each key, the **PRN** file page count and file size are considerably larger than the exported file. The reason for this may be demonstrated by exporting any convenient single key, such as the sample **Testkey** shown in Figure 4.9. Next, print the same key to a file, and then review both files in a word processor, as shown on the following page.

Note that each line in the **TESTKEY.PRN** file is slightly longer than the same line in the **TESTKEY.REG** file, which accounts for why its **PRN** file is larger than the equivalent **REG** file. The file comparison also reveals the following points about each file type:

Exported key (TESTKEY.REG)·

Name entries and Data column strings enclosed in quotes

Binary data prefaced by `hex:` or `dword:`

Binary data written in same sequence as shown in Contents Pane

Key saved to file (*TESTKEY.PRN*)

Each line padded with seven leading spaces

No entries enclosed in quotes

DWORD entry written in reverse sequence, numbers separated by commas

Exported as TESTKEY.REG

	Characters	EOL	
REGEDIT4	8	2	
	0	2	
[HKEY_CURRENT_USER\TestKey]	27	2	
"StringValue1"="This is a sample text string"	46	2	
"BinaryValue1"=hex:45,3a,8d,ac,d4,00,47,90	42	2	
"DWORDValue1"=dword:00087439	28	2	
"StringValue2"="Here's another text string"	43	2	
	0	2	
	194	16	= 210 bytes

Printed to file as TESTKEY.PRN

	Characters	EOL	
	0	2	
	0	2	
[HKEY_CURRENT_USER\TestKey]	34	2	
StringValue1=This is a sample text string	49	2	
BinaryValue1=45,3a,8d,ac,d4,00,47,90	43	2	
DWORDValue1=39,74,08,00	30	2	
StringValue2=Here's another text string	46	2	
	202	14	= 216 bytes

In both files, entries are written in the order in which they were entered or edited in the Registry, which is not necessarily the order in which they currently appear in the Contents Pane, where they are sorted alphabetically.

Variations in the Registry Structure

In any examination of the Registry, it's important to keep in mind that there is no "standard" way to store data here. For example, a DWORD was described in Chapter 1 as a four-byte sequence. It might therefore seem that the DWORD format would be used whenever data is stored within four bytes. But, search the Registry for **EditFlags** (check the **Values** box only) and you'll find many four-byte sequences are expressed as binary values rather than as DWORDs. There doesn't seem to be any consistent pattern to the choice between these formats, other than perhaps the personal preference of the programmer.

A Format Variation Example

To show how similar information may be written in more than one format, the Registry example in Figure 4.14 shows how the same information is stored by various Windows 95 applications. To create the illustration, the following three Windows 95 application windows were opened:

Manufacturer	Application	Subkey with Size, Position Data
Hewlett-Packard	JetAdmin	Position
Windows Magazine	Wintune95	Settings
Microsoft	Registry Editor	Regedit

Each application window was adjusted so its dimensions and on-screen position were the same as the others. With the Registry Editor window placed on top, each application's size-and-position subkey was opened so that its Contents Pane could be examined. Because only one Registry key can be opened at a time, the figure is a cut-and-paste composite view, edited to show all three subkeys in a single Contents Pane. Also, the illustration shows only those items pertaining to the size and position of each application window.

Note that Hewlett-Packard's **Position** subkey reports the height and width of the window, followed by the x, y coordinates of its upper-left-hand corner. In this example, the window's height and width are 544 and 803 pixels, and the upper-left-hand corner is at $x = 158$, $y = 92$ pixels, measured from the left side and the top of the screen.

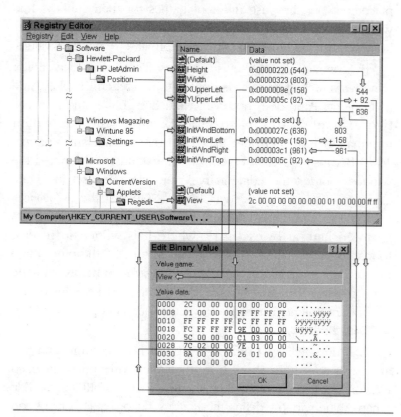

Figure 4.14 *This composite view of a Registry Editor window shows how different software applications present the same basic information in their Contents Panes. The addition examples on the right side of the Contents Pane show how to "do the math," to verify that each data set creates a window of the same size and position.*

The specified window height and top (544 + 92) mean that the bottom is at pixel 636. Therefore, the window width and left side (803 + 158) would place its right side at pixel 961. And that's just the way the *Windows Magazine* Wintune 95 utility reports the same information in its **Settings** subkey. Note that both utilities require four data entries to report the windows size and placement but they use different names for their subkeys and within the Contents Pane's Name column. The applications do, however, use the same DWORD data format to report their values.

By contrast, the subkey for Microsoft's own Registry Editor window is tucked five levels down, in the **Regedit** subkey, and its Contents Pane does not even vaguely resemble the previous two examples. In this specific example, the equivalent information is written into a 60-byte binary data entry named *View*. Because the Data column entry extends well beyond the window border, the Edit Binary Value window inset in Figure 4.14 shows the complete data string. Note that the 0x0000009e DWORD for the upper-left-hand corner in the other two applets is stored here at bytes 1C–1F, where it is written in reverse format as 9E 00 00 00. It is followed in turn by the other three DWORDs found in the *Windows Magazine* **Settings** subkey. Note also that the same hexadecimal letters appear as lowercase a–f in the Contents Pane's Data column, but as uppercase A–F in the Edit window.

A series of lines from one applet's Data column entry to another's may help show how that data will appear in each location. For general information, the final four DWORDs in the Edit Binary Value window define the Registry Editor's Split bar position (7E 01 00 00), the width of the Name (8A 00 00 00) and Data (26 01 00 00) columns, and finally, the condition of the Status Bar at the bottom of the Registry Editor window (01 00 00 00 = enabled).

Some other Microsoft applets and applications specify their window size as just described, while others don't. For example, Word version 7.0's **Data** subkey has a single entry named

Settings, whose Data column contains a 2- to 3-K binary sequence which includes the window specifications and much more, including a list of recently opened document files. By contrast, the Internet Explorer's **Document Windows** subkey defines its own window by specifying its height, width, and x and y data, but they're not DWORDs. Instead, the Explorer writes the data as binary values: that is, as separate 4-byte entries, each written in the reverse hexadecimal format found within the Registry Editor's **View** entry.

The point of this little review is to illustrate how different formats may be used to record the same information. The point to remember is: if you've seen one subkey, you definitely haven't seen them all.

The Norton Registry Editor

Version 2.0 of the Norton Utilities for Windows 95 includes a Registry Editor applet with several features not found in Windows 95's own utility. Although the same six HKEYs are displayed in its Key pane, the keys are listed in alphabetical order, as shown in Figure 4.15. In addition, the entire Registry key structure is reproduced within the *Norton Registry Advisor* key, which is also shown in the same figure. For each key and subkey found here, the Contents pane contains a pointer (not shown in the figure) to a location in an ADVISOR.HTM file, where that key's contents are described. For example, if the HKEY_LOCAL_MACHINE key is selected, the Advisor tab at the bottom of the Editor window displays a brief summary of the key, as shown in Figure 4.16.

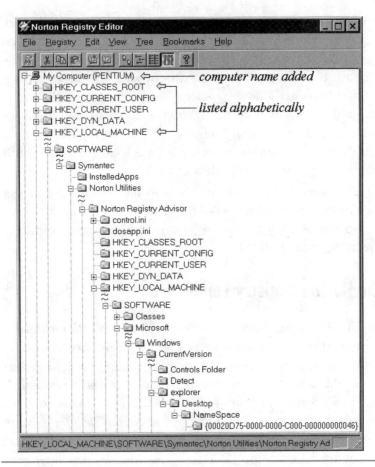

Figure 4.15 *The Norton Registry Editor lists the Registry's six HKEYs in alphabetical order and repeats the entire key structure under the Norton Registry Advisor key. In this section, the Contents pane (not shown) for each such key contains a pointer to information about that key.*

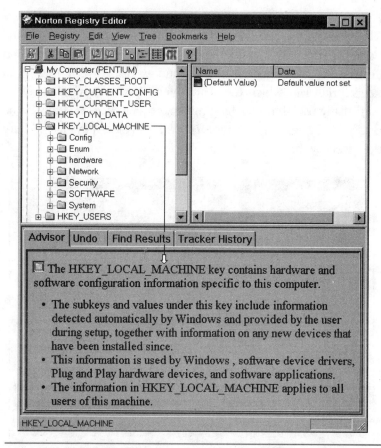

Figure 4.16 *If a Registry key or subkey is selected, the Advisor tab displays a brief summary of the key's purpose. If a summary is not available, the Advisor described the next highest key in the Registry key structure.*

Figure 4.17 displays the results of a search for the ShellFolder key (described in the *Attributes Flags* section of Chapter 5). While the Contents pane displays the first occurrence of that key, the Find Results tab at the bottom of the window displays a listing of all Registry keys in which the search item is found, which may be particularly useful in searching multiple occurrences of a key name or data entry, such as the nine *HKCR* ShellFolder keys found here (followed by the nine *HKLM* duplicates).

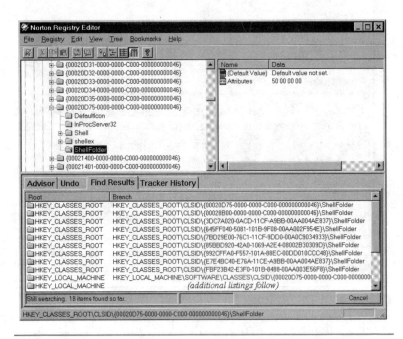

Figure 4.17 *While the Key and Contents panes display the results of the first search hit, the Find Results tab at the bottom of the Norton Registry Editor window lists all occurrences of the searched item.*

The Find Results tab may also be useful in tracing the occurrences of an item which may occur as both a key and as a Data entry.

For example, a search for the {85BBD920... number associated
with the Briefcase object turns up the following Registry citations:

Key Name	Data column shows:
HKEY_CLASSES_ROOT*\Shellex\...	
ContextMenuHandlers\BriefcaseMenu	{85BBD920...
PropertySheetHandlers\BriefcasePage	{85BBD920...
Briefcase\CLSID	{85BBD920...
CLSID\{85BBD920-42A0-1069-A2E4-08002B30309D}	"Briefcase"
Folder\Shellex\ContextMenuHandlers\BriefcaseMenu	{85BBD920...
Folder\Shellex\PropertySheetHandlers\BriefcasePage	{85BBD920...
HKEY_LOCAL_MACHINE\SOFTWARE\Classes	
(The six keys above are repeated here)	

Note that the searched number turns up once as a key name (in
the left colum, above) and five times as a Data column entry
within the Contents panes of other keys.

CHAPTER 5

Customizing the Windows 95 Registry

This chapter continues the discussion of Registry editing, with an emphasis on how to customize the Registry to configure Windows 95 according to your personal preferences. The chapter begins with a look at a few custom editing techniques, then describes various menu and icon editing procedures, and concludes with a look at a handful of editing techniques to customize a specific aspect of the Windows 95 Desktop.

Custom Registry Editing Techniques

As described in Chapter 4, the Registry may be edited by simply executing the **REGEDIT.EXE** utility and having at it. But in addition to the basic editing techniques described in that chapter, there are various other methods of editing the Registry that may prove helpful from time to time. Like just about everything else associated with the Registry, the procedures described here are for the most part undocumented. Until you are quite sure that a specific procedure works well on your system, make sure you back up the Registry before experimenting. When you are certain that a procedure will not harm the Registry, make a backup anyway.

The System Policy Editor

The System Policy Editor applet can be used to write data into the Registry to restrict access to a variety of Windows 95 features. By default, the applet (**POLEDIT.EXE**) is not installed as part of the Windows 95 setup procedure, but it is available in the **Admin\Apptools\Poledit** folder on the Windows 95 CD-ROM disc. You may prefer to leave it uninstalled and just access it from the disc as needed. If the disc is not readily available to others, this may help keep busy little fingers from "fixing" policies when no one's around to maintain order.

An Open Template File dialog box opens the first time the applet is run, and an **Admin.adm** file should be listed in the window. Highlight it and click **OK** to open a blank System Policy Editor window. Open its File menu and select **Open Registry** to display **Local User** and **Local Computer** icons, as seen in Figure 5.1. Double-click on the **Local User** icon to open the Local User Properties window and the **Policies** tab seen in the same figure. Next, click on one of the book icons shown opened in the figure to access various restriction check boxes; put a check mark in any box, and that feature will be disabled. If the **Control Panel** book is selected, five additional books are displayed, as shown in Figure 5.2. Put a check in the box under any book to display a Settings list at the bottom of the window. Then check one or more of those boxes as required.

As a result of the specific checked boxes shown in Figure 5.1, DWORD entries were written into the Contents Pane for the subkeys shown in Figure 5.3. (The NoDriveTypeAutoRun entry at the top of the Contents Pane is handled separately, as described in the "Drive Media Icons" section later in the chapter.) For future reference, Table 5.1 lists the restrictions shown in Figures 5.1 and 5.2 and identifies each subkey entry written into the Registry.

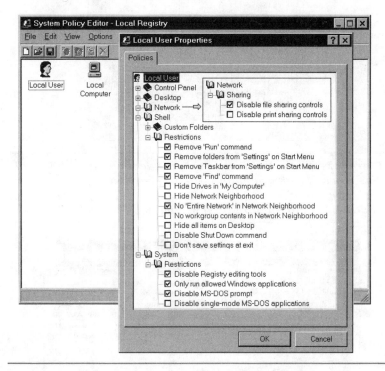

Figure 5.1 *If the System Policy Editor's **Local User** icon is selected, various restrictions can be imposed by the check boxes shown here.*

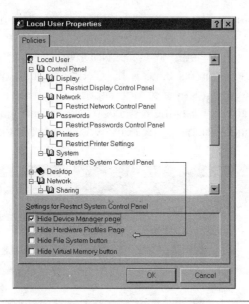

Figure 5.2 *The Control Panel book icon leads to five additional books, each of which contains a single check box. If any checked box is highlighted, the Settings area at the bottom of the window lists additional restrictions that may be imposed.*

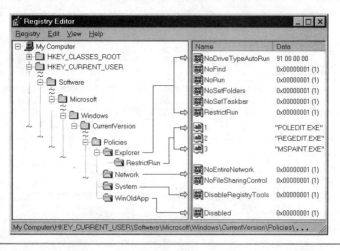

Figure 5.3 *The boxes checked in Figure 5.1 write the following entries into the **Policies** subkeys shown here. Refer to Table 5.1 for a list of these and other restrictions.*

Table 5.1a *Cross-Reference Guide: Local User Policies and Registry Subkeys* *

Policies Control Panel Book, Check Box, Settings	Registry Subkey and Entry
Display, Restrict Display Control Panel	**System**
Disable Display Control Panel	NoDispCPL
Hide Background page	NoDispBackgroundPage
Hide Screen Saver page	NoDispScrSavPage
Hide Appearance page	NoDispAppearancePage
Hide Settings page	NoDispSettingsPage
Network, Restrict Network Control Panel	**Network**
Disable Network Control Panel	NoNetSetup
Hide Identification Page	NoNetSetupIDPage
Hide Access Control Page	NoNetSetupSecurityPage
Passwords, Restrict Passwords l Control Pane	**System**
Disable Passwords Control Panel	NoSecCPL
Hide Change Passwords page	NoPwdPage
Hide Remote Administration page	NoAdminPage
Hide User Profiles page	NoProfilePage
Printers, Restrict Printer Settings	**Explorer**
Hide General and Details page	NoPrinterTabs
Disable Deletion of Printers	NoDeletePrinter
Disable Addition of Printers	NoAddPrinter
System, Restrict System Control Panel	**System**
Hide Device Manager page	NoDevMgrPage
Hide Hardware Profiles page	NoConfigPage
Hide File System button	NoFileSysPage
Hide Virtual Memory button	NoVirtMemPage

* Settings (indented in table) appear at bottom of Policies tab if box under indicated book is checked (see Figure 5.2).

Table 5.1b *Cross-Reference Guide: Local User Policies and Registry Subkeys (continued)*

Policies Book and Check Box	Registry Subkey and Entry
Network, Sharing	**Network**
Disable file sharing controls	NoFileSharingControl
Disable print sharing controls	NoPrintSharingControl
Shell, Restrictions	**Explorer** *
Remove Run command	NoRun[1]
Remove folders from Settings on Start Menu	NoSetFolders[2]
Remove Taskbar from Settings on Start Menu	NoSetTaskbar[2]
Remove Find command	NoFind[1]
Hide Drives in My Computer	NoDrives[3]
Hide Network Neighborhood	NoNetHood
No Entire Network in Net Neighborhood	NoEntireNetwork[4]
No workgroup contents in Net Neighborhood	NoNetworkGroupContents[4]
Hide all items on Desktop	NoDesktop
Disable Shut Down command	NoClose[1]
Don't save settings at exit	NoSaveSettings
System, Restrictions	**Explorer** *
Disable Registry editing tools	DisableRegistryTools[5]
Only run allowed Windows applications	RestrictRun
Disable MS-DOS prompt	Disabled[6]
Disable single-mode MS-DOS applications	NoRealMode[6]

*Unless otherwise noted, entries are in **Explorer** subkey's Contents Pane.

[1]Removes option from Start menu (after reboot).

2 Removes option from Start menu only if *both* NoSet restrictions are set

[3]Previously shared drives still viewable in Network Neighborhood.

[4]In **Network** subkey.

[5]In **System** subkey.

[6]In **WinOldApp** subkey.

*After setting the desired restrictions, if you open the File menu and select **Save**, the new policies take effect immediately. Before experimenting, review the notes given here, because some restrictions may lead to problems. Or refer to the "Restriction Recovery Procedure" in Chapter 7 if you discover such problems the hard way.*

Disable Registry Editing tools. This disables the Registry Editor while leaving other Windows applications enabled. A subsequent attempt to open the Editor will display an error message.

Disable Shut Down command. If some other policy has disabled the Registry Editor and the System Policy Editor is also unavailable, think twice before enabling this restriction. Otherwise, there will be no way to exit Windows 95 other than via the **Reset** button or power switch. While both remain effective, neither is highly recommended.

Hide all items on Desktop. This option takes effect the next time Windows 95 opens; it does what you think, with one important exception: items in the **StartUp** folder are executed. Therefore, a completely customized Desktop can be set up by selecting this restriction and then creating one or more shortcuts in the **StartUp** folder to display only those Desktop items that you want to see. Refer to "Customizing the Desktop" for additional details.

Hide Drives in My Computer. If any drive is currently shared, the contents of that drive can still be accessed via Network Neighborhood.

Only run allowed Windows applications. If this box is checked, a **Show** button appears and leads to a list of allowed applications (not shown in Figure 5.1). Enter the applications that should *not* be restricted, and those applications will be listed in the **RestrictRun** subkey seen in Figure 5.3. Note that this subkey does the opposite of what its name implies: access to applications listed in its Contents Pane will *not* be restricted, while all other applications will no longer run. Therefore, you might want to make sure the list begins with **POLEDIT.EXE** and/or **REGEDIT.EXE**. If these applications are not specified here, they too will not run, and that makes it difficult to further revise the list or to ever use the Registry Editor again.

Restricting the Default User

The System Policy Editor can offer at least some protection against the casual or unauthorized user. If the computer is configured for a user name and password prompt as Windows 95 opens, bypass the prompt by pressing the **Escape** key to log on as a default user. Then use the System Policy Editor to set restrictions that will be enabled for all users who subsequently bypass the user name and password prompt. These policies will not be enabled if an authorized user enters a valid name and password. (Refer to "HKU: HKEY_USERS" in Chapter 3 and "USER.DAT" in Chapter 4 for more information about the default user.)

If such protection against system meddlers is necessary, you may want to save the **REGEDIT.EXE** utility to diskette and then erase it from the **C:\Windows** folder. Put the diskette and the Windows 95 CD-ROM disc with **POLEDIT.EXE** on it, in a busybody-free location. Note, however, that this is *not* the ultimate security system; it can be defeated by the knowledgeable user with relatively little effort. If security problems persist, other measures will be required (corporate downsizing comes to mind).

The INF File as a Registry Editor

As mentioned in "The INF File" section in Chapter 4, the Setup Information file is primarily intended for use during a hardware or software installation procedure, when it automatically adds, modifies, or deletes various Registry entries as required by the item being installed. However, a custom **INF** file may also be written to perform various Registry housecleaning chores. When the file is subsequently "installed," it modifies the Registry as desired, even though no hardware or software device is actually being installed.

As a typical example of what can be accomplished, this section shows how to remove the various recent-history lists viewed via the Start menu's **Documents**, **Find**, and **Run** options. These lists are maintained in the Registry in the subkeys listed here and are shown in Figure 5.4.

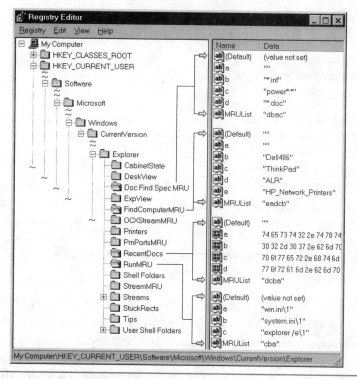

Figure 5.4 *In this composite view, the four open subkeys contain the history lists that appear if various Start menu options are selected.*

HKEY_CURRENT_USER\SOFTWARE\MICROSOFT\WINDOWS\CURRENTVERSION\EXPLORER\ ...

Subkey	Start Menu Option	Find Menu Option
Doc Find Spec MRU	Find (cascading menu)	Files or Folders ...
FindComputerMRU	Find (cascading menu)	Computer...
RecentDocs	Documents	
RunMRU	Run	

To remove one or more of the Start menu lists specified in columns 2 and 3, create a **KillList.INF** (or similar) file as shown here, but without the parenthetical comments.

```
[version]
signature=$Chicago$


[DefaultInstall]
AddReg=AddRegKey (optional)
DelReg=DelRegKey


[AddRegKey]  (this key and its contents are optional)
HKCU, Software\Microsoft\Windows\CurrentVersion\Explorer\Doc Find Spec MRU
HKCU, Software\Microsoft\Windows\CurrentVersion\Explorer\FindComputerMRU
HKCU, Software\Microsoft\Windows\CurrentVersion\Explorer\RecentDocs
HKCU, Software\Microsoft\Windows\CurrentVersion\Explorer\RunMRUDocs

[DelRegKey]  (note comma at end of each line)
HKCU, Software\Microsoft\Windows\CurrentVersion\Explorer\Doc Find Spec MRU,
HKCU, Software\Microsoft\Windows\CurrentVersion\Explorer\FindComputerMRU,
HKCU, Software\Microsoft\Windows\CurrentVersion\Explorer\RecentDocs,
HKCU, Software\Microsoft\Windows\CurrentVersion\Explorer\RunMRUDocs,
```

Each line in the `[DelRegKey]` section deletes the contents of the subkey cited at the end of the line, after which each line in the `[AddRegKey]` section writes a new (empty) replacement key to take its place. Include one or more of these lines in each section, depending on which lists you want to delete. To verify that **KillList.INF** deletes the desired lists, open its Context menu, select the **Install** option, and check the specified Registry subkey(s), which should now be empty. With the exception of the Documents list, the associated Start menu list should also be empty. An additional step is required to delete this list, as described in the next section.

Automated List Removal

Because a conventional **INF** file is usually run only once, the Context menu's **Install** option offers the appropriate means to do that. But when a custom INF file is used as a Registry-editing tool, it may be more convenient to execute it from a batch file. You could change the **INF** file's default action from **Open** to **Install,** but this would mean that if anyone double-clicked *any* **INF** file, it would be installed without so much as an "Are you sure?" warning. To obviate such potential problems, create a batch file that duplicates the install procedure, as described here:

1. Open the **HKCR\inffile\shell\install\command** subkey.

2. Double-click on the small **ab** icon at the head of the (Default) line.

3. Press **Ctrl+C** to copy the highlighted Value data entry to the Clipboard (which is easier than typing it in at the keyboard).

4. Click **OK** or **Cancel** and exit the Registry Editor.

5. Open NotePad and press **Ctrl+V** to paste the line into it.

6. Replace the %1 at the end of the line with the path and name of the **INF** file you created. The line should now look like this:

```
C:\Windows\rundll.exesetupx.dll,InstallHinfSection
DefaultInstall 132 C:\<path>\KillList.INF
```

This must be a single continuous line.

7. If your **INF** file contains a line in the `[DelRegKey]` to delete the Documents list, add the following line to this batch file:

```
erase C:\Windows\Recent\*.INF
```

8. Save the file as **KillList.BAT** (or similar).

The erase line specified in step 7 erases the shortcut files in the indicated folder, and this in turn deletes the Documents list whenever the batch file is run. If you prefer to delete all lists specified in **KillList.INF** every time Windows 95 starts, simply move the batch file into the **C:\Windows\Start Menu\Programs\StartUp** folder. Or put the batch file in some other convenient location and drag a shortcut icon onto the Desktop so that the lists can be deleted whenever it's necessary (or politically correct) to do so.

The INF File as an Import Function Supplement

As already noted in Chapter 4, the Registry menu's **Import** option can write new data into the Registry and revise existing entries by overwriting the data contained in them. However, it will not delete an existing Registry entry in the absence of a replacement line, and therefore it is not always a reliable medium for executing a complete replacement of a Registry key.

By contrast, the **INF** file structure supports two methods of deleting all or part of any subkey. In addition to the `DelReg=DelRegKey` and the `[DelRegKey]` section described earlier, an undocumented flag in the section specified by the `AddReg=` section can be used to delete a single Name and Data entry, as shown here:

```
[DefaultInstall]
AddReg=AddRegKey
```

```
[AddRegKey]
HKCR, .abc, TestEntry1, 4,
```

Assuming there is an entry in the **HKCR\.abc** key whose name is **TestEntry1**, the "4" flag shown here will remove that entry from the Contents Pane, regardless of its Data format and its apparently contradictory appearance within a section that is supposed to add data to the Registry.

The INF File as a Troubleshooting Tool

Refer to the "Restriction Recovery Procedure" section of Chapter 7 for suggestions on using the **INF** file during a Registry troubleshooting session.

INF File Warning

Because the **INF** file is a very efficient Registry-editing tool, its potential for harm should never be underestimated. Before installing any software received from a dubious source, you might want to read the contents of its **INF** file to see what it will do to your Registry, *before* letting it do it. If you discover any Registry-wrecking content, erase the entire file set and think about getting your software from other sources. If the **INF** file appears to be in order but you're not entirely sure, heed all the warnings about backing up the Registry before proceeding.

EditFlags

In many **HKCR** subkeys, the Contents Pane shows an EditFlags entry in the Name column, with a four-byte binary value in the Data column. Each of its 32 bits is an edit flag whose value (0 or 1) specifies the status of a specific aspect of the object in whose subkey the entry appears. The effect of these flags may be seen by selecting **Options** on the Explorer's View menu and then selecting the **File Types** tab. As each item in the Registered file types list is highlighted, various buttons and Edit options are disabled, according to the status of the associated bit in the EditFlags entry, three of which are shown here with their hex-to-binary conversions.

Name	Data	Registered File Type	In Subkey
EditFlags	d8 07 00 00	Application	*exefile*
EditFlags	d0 04 00 00	MS-DOS Batch File	*batfile*
EditFlags	00 00 01 00	MIDI Sequence	*midfile*

hex Data		–––––––––– binary edit flags * ––––––––––				
D8 07 00 00	1 1 0 1	1 0 0 0	0 0 0 0	0 1 1 1	0 0 0 0	0 0 0 0
D0 04 00 00	1 1 0 1	0 0 0 0	0 0 0 0	0 1 0 0	0 0 0 0	0 0 0 0
00 00 01 00	0 0 0 0	0 0 0 0	0 0 0 0	0 0 0 0	0 0 0 0	0 0 0 1
	31 30 29 28	27 26 25 24	23 22 21 20	19 18 17 16	15 14 13 12	11 10 9 8

*Final byte (bits 7-0) not shown

Currently, one or more bits in the 31-16 range may be set, and in a few cases bit 8 may also be set. Because the final byte is not used (yet), the zeros in bits 7-0 are not shown in the binary conversions.

High-Bit (31-16) Flags

Table 5.2 lists the effect of each bit that is set to "1." Thus, if **Application** is selected in the Registered file types list, the **Remove** (bit 28) and **Edit** (bit 27) buttons to the right of the list are disabled. The disabled **Edit** button prevents the status of other features from being verified, but if EditFlags is rewritten as D0 07 00 00 (to re-enable the **Edit** button), it will be found that the following options on the Edit File Type sheet are also disabled due to the indicated set bits: **Edit** (30), **Remove** (31), **Set Default** (18), **Change Icon** (17) buttons and the Description of type line (16) immediately below the **Change Icon** button.

Table 5.2 *Effect of EditFlags settings*

Bit	Data *	To View Effect: **	Effect:
in *FileType* key's Contents Pane			
31	80 00 00	Click **Edit** button	**Remove** button disabled †
30	40 00 00	Click **Edit** button	**Edit** button disabled †
29	20 00 00	Click **Edit** button	**New** button disabled
28	10 00 00	View **File Types** tab	**Remove** button disabled
27	08 00 00	View **File Types** tab	**Edit** button disabled
26	04 00 00	Reserved	—
25	02 00 00	Click **Edit** button	Item included in list ‡
24	01 00 00	View file types list	Item excluded from list
23	00 80 00	Click **Edit** button	**Content Type (MIME)** disabled
22	00 40 00	Reserved	—
21	00 20 00	Click two **Edit** buttons	**Use DDE** check box removed
20	00 10 00	Click two **Edit** buttons	Application line disabled
19	00 08 00	Reserved	—
18	00 04 00	Click **Edit** button	**Set Default** button disabled
17	00 02 00	Click **Edit** button	**Change Icon** button disabled
16	00 01 00	Click **Edit** button	Description of type line disabled
8	00 00 01	Click **Edit** button	**Confirm Open** check box cleared
in *Shell\action* (edit, open, print) key's Contents Pane			
8	01 00 00	Ignore bits 14-15 for this **Shell** subkey action only.	

*First three bytes in Data column, if only this bit is set.

Open Explorer View menu, select **Options, **File Types** tab, take action specified here.

†Note **Shell\action** key at bottom of table.

‡Required if not extension associated with file type.

Confirm Open after Download (8) Flag

As previously noted in "MIME Contents Pane Modifications" in Chapter 2, the **File Types** tab may show a MIME (Multipurpose Internet Mail Extension) content type if MS Plus! or some OEM version of Windows 95 is installed (see Figure 2.4). In this case, the Edit File Type sheet shows three check boxes, and the new **Confirm Open After Download** box is supported via the **URL.DLL** file. If the box is cleared, the EditFlags setting described earlier changes to *xx xx* 01 00, where *xx xx* indicates that the first two EditFlags bytes remain as is. Thus, D8 07 00 00 becomes D8 07 01 00, and so on. The box is generally checked for all file types with the exception of those listed here, so a confirm-open message is *not* seen after downloading.

Registered File Type	HKCR Subkey	EditFlags Data
Internet Communication Settings	x-internet-signup	00 00 01 00
Internet Shortcut	InternetShortcut	02 00 01 00
Media Clip	mplayer	00 00 01 00
MIDI Instrument Definition	idfile	00 00 01 00
MIDI Sequence	midfile	00 00 01 00
Movie Clip (AVI)	AVIFile	00 00 01 00
RealAudio	ramfile	00 00 01 00
Sound Clip (Basic)	Aufile	00 00 01 00
Sound Clip (WAVE)	SoundRec	00 00 01 00

EditFlags Override

In cases where the Edit File Type sheet shows several actions, an additional EditFlags entry in an action subkey can override the disabled **Edit** and/or **Remove** flag. For example, Figure 5.5 shows the **HKCR\batfile** key structure. In the **batfile** Contents

Pane, the set bits (31, 30) have disabled the **Remove** and **Edit** buttons on the Edit File Type sheet, as was also shown. Therefore, if **MS-DOS Batch File** is selected, these buttons are disabled regardless of which action (**Edit**, **Open**, **Print**) Is selected. As a practical result, it is not possible to change the default editor (**NOTEPAD.EXE**) to some other text editor.

To remove this restriction, add a new binary EditFlags entry to the **batfile** key's **Edit** subkey, as also shown in the figure, where the unique 01 00 00 00 flag serves as an override to the Remove and Edit flags prescribed in the **batfile** key by bits 31 and 30. Because the status of these bits is now ignored, the **Edit** button is enabled if the **Edit** action is highlighted, making it possible to specify some other application to use as a batch-file editor. The **Open** subkey's own EditFlags entry remains at 00 00 00 00, so the **batfile** key's restrictions remain in effect if this action is selected. The **Print** subkey lacks an EditFlag entry, which is equivalent to a 00 00 00 00 setting.

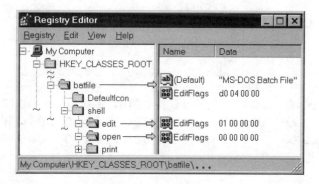

Figure 5.5 *The **batfile** key's EditFlags entry disables various buttons if **MS-DOS Batch File** is selected in the list of Registered file types. The **edit** subkey's 01 00 00 00 entry acts as an override that takes effect only if the **Edit** action is selected in the Edit File Type dialog box.*

Attributes Flags

Under the HKCR key, the {CLSID} keys associated with several Desktop objects lead to a ShellFolder subkey. That key's Contents pane contains an Attributes entry in the Name column, followed by a four-byte Data entry which functions in a similar manner to the EditFlags entry described above. Despite the *Attributes* name, the entry has nothing to do with file attributes. Instead, the 32 bits represented by the hexadecimal string in the Data column enable or disable various options on each object's Context menu, as shown by the examples below. To verify these values, open the HKCR\CLSID key and search the Data column for one of the object names given here. Open the associated {CLSID} key and find its ShellFolder subkey. The Attributes entry in the Contents pane should show the data listed here.

Object Name	Attributes	Object Name	Attributes
Briefcase	36 01 00 40	Internet	70 00 00 00
Dial-Up Networking	04 00 00 20	Microsoft Network	50 00 00 00
Inbox	50 00 00 00	Recycle Bin	40 01 00 20

hex Data	――――――――― binary edit flags * ――――――――					
36 01 00 40	0011	0110	0000	0001	0100	0000
04 00 00 20	0000	0100	0000	0000	0010	0000
70 00 00˙ 00	0111	0000	0000	0000	0000	0001
	31 30 29 28	27 26 25 24	23 22 21 20	19 18 17 16 8 7 6 5		3 2 1 0

* Third byte (bits 15-8) not shown

At present, several bits in the first byte (30-28, 26-25) may be set, and in a few cases bits 16, 6 and 5 have also been observed to be set. No bits in the third byte (15-8) appear to be used. Table 5.3 lists the effect of each bit that is set to 1. Thus, if the Internet object's Context menu is opened, it displays Properties, Delete, and Rename options because the associated bits (30-28) are set. By contrast, the Dial-Up Networking folder's Context menu displays none of these options, because the same bits are not set.

Table 5.3 Effect of Attributes settings on Context Menu Options

Bit	Data *	Enables this Context menu option: **
30	40 00 00 00	Properties
29	20 00 00 00	Delete[1]
28	10 00 00 00	Rename
25	02 00 00 00	Cut
24	01 00 00 00	Copy
16	00 01 00 00	Paste
06	00 00 00 40	unknown
05	00 00 00 20	Open and Explore [2]

*   All four bytes in Data column, if only this bit is set.

**   Attributes flags have no apparent effect on Briefcase.

[1]   Has no effect on Microsoft Network Delete option.

[2]   Recycle Bin only.

Some care should be exercised if these flags are edited. You may want to disable an existing option (Delete or Rename, for example), in which case the associated bit can be changed from 1 to 0 to do so. However, if an inappropriate Context menu option is enabled, either an error message will appear if that option is selected, or the selected option will simply do nothing.

Hardware Profile Editing

This section describes how hardware profile data is written into the Registry as various hardware devices are added or removed.

Although there should be little need to directly edit the keys described here, a quick review of this information may help to better understand the significance of some of these keys.

Consider a desktop system with only one hardware profile, typically identified as *Original Configuration*. The Device Manager shows that the system components include a SCSI CD-ROM drive. The only two subkeys under the **Config** key's **0001** key are **Display** and **System** (both described in Chapter 4). In other words, this section of the Registry contains no information about the CD-ROM drive, nor is any required here for this single-profile system. The tree is shown in Figure 5.6 in the section labeled *A*.

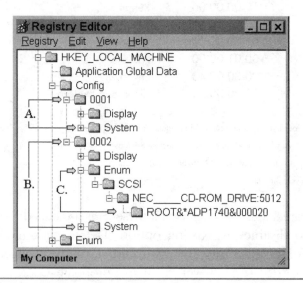

Figure 5.6 *The **Enum** subkey shown here appears if certain hardware components are removed from a hardware configuration.*

If this hardware configuration is copied as, say, Secondary Configuration, a new **0002** key appears under the **Config** key, and for the moment its contents match those of the **Config\0001** key. Again, there is no CD-ROM information in this key. But now, the CD-ROM drive is removed from this configuration only by highlighting the **CD-ROM drive**, clicking the **Remove** button, and then selecting **Secondary Configuration** in the Confirm Device Removal dialog box shown in Figure 5.7.

In Figure 5.6, the secondary configuration (**0002**) key is labeled "B." and the subsection labeled "C." shows a new **Enum** (Enumerator) subkey, which in turn contains a **SCSI** subkey. Beneath that, a subkey gives the name of the removed CD-ROM drive, followed by yet another subkey (**ROOT&...**), which specifies the SCSI adapter to which the CD-ROM drive was attached.

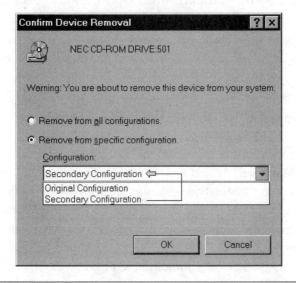

Figure 5.7 *On a multiple configuration system, a hardware device can be removed from one configuration only by selecting the second radio button and the configuration to be edited.*

If the CD-ROM is now removed from the Original Configuration too, the contents of the **SCSI** key under the **Config\0002** key will be flushed, and the CD-ROM configuration will be lost to the entire system. But assuming the drive is in fact still physically attached to the system, Windows will detect its presence the next time the system is started, and the drive will be reinstalled to the Original Configuration (assuming that's the one specified when the system restarts). However, the drive will *not* be restored to the Secondary Configuration profile until the system is restarted in that configuration. Nor will its absence be noted in the still-empty **SCSI** subkey under the **Config\0002** key.

Once the CD-ROM drive is restored to both configurations, the **0002** key will still show the empty **SCSI** subkey. But if the drive is again removed from **Config\0002**, then again the **Enum** subkey will contain the information about the missing drive. In much the same manner, information about other devices removed from this secondary configuration will be written here.

Restore hardware previously deleted from a hardware profile. The most reliable way to add hardware to any profile is to simply start the system in that configuration and leave it to Windows 95 to detect or redetect its presence. Or, double-click on Control Panel's **Add New Hardware** applet and use the Add New Hardware Wizard.

As another alternative, open the System applet, select the **Device Manager** tab, and look for the desired device. If it is listed, that means it is currently installed in at least one hardware profile. That being so, highlight the device, click on the **Properties** button, and examine the **General** tab. If there is a Device Usage section near the bottom of the window, put a check mark in the box next to the configuration that currently lacks this device.

However, if the device is connected to a SCSI or other controller, then there is no System Usage section on the device's **General** tab, and the equivalent tab on the controller's **General** tab may already be enabled, especially if other devices remain in place. In this case, you can restore the disabled device by deleting its subkey under the **Enum** key, located under the appropriate **000x** key. For example, the section labeled "C." in Figure 5.6 showed the **0002** key's **Enum** subkey. Highlight the key name of the desired device (**NEC___CD-ROM_DRIVE:5012**, in this example) and delete it. Because the

Enum key does not list any other devices, the entire **Enum** key could be deleted instead. Do *not* do this, however, if a BIOS and/or other unrelated subkeys appear here. In that case, make sure you delete *only* the device you want re-enabled.

Copy/Paste Operations

If it is ever necessary to create a new key based on the contents of an existing key, the latter key can be exported, revised as necessary, and then imported back into the Registry, as shown by this excerpt from an exported **exefile** key:

```
REGEDIT4

[HKEY_CLASSES_ROOT\exefile]
@="Application"
"EditFlags"=hex:d8,07,00,00

[HKEY_CLASSES_ROOT\exefile\shell\open]
@=""
"EditFlags"=hex:00,00,00,00

[HKEY_CLASSES_ROOT\exefile\shell\open\command]
@="\"%1\" %*"

[HKEY_CLASSES_ROOT\exefile\shellex]

[HKEY_CLASSES_ROOT\exefile\shellex\PropertySheetHandlers\PifProps]
@="{86F19A00-42A0-1069-A2E9-08002B30309D}"

[HKEY_CLASSES_ROOT\exefile\shellex\PropertySheetHandlers\{86F19A00-
42A0-1069-A2E9-08002B30309D}]
@=""

[HKEY_CLASSES_ROOT\exefile\DefaultIcon]
@="%1"
```

To write a new **abcfile** key in the same section of the Registry, open the exported file in an ASCII text editor and change every occurrence of **exefile** (shown underlined here) to **abcfile,** save the edited file, and import it into the Registry. A new **abcfile** key should now be seen, and its subkey structure and contents duplicate the **exefile** key. The key may now be edited to customize it as required.

Command Line Edits

In some cases it's possible to change the performance characteristics of a Windows 95 application or applet by editing the Data entry in the appropriate **command** subkey. As a typical example, the Media Player (**HKCR\mplayer**) applet's **play\command** subkey shows the following Contents Pane entry:

Name	Data
(Default)	"C:\WINDOWS\mplayer.exe /play /close %1"

As a result of the command-line switches shown here, if any **AVI**, **MID**, **WAV**, or other file recognized by Media Player is double-clicked, the applet loads the file, plays it, and then exits. If you would prefer to have Media Player remain open after playing the selected file, simply delete the **/close** switch.

If you know the valid command-line switches for some other application's executable file, revise the appropriate Data column entry as desired to customize the way in which that application functions.

The CLSID Generator Utility

As noted in Chapter 2, each 16-byte class identifier subkey found under the **HKEY_CLASSES_ROOT\CLSID** key is a unique (one hopes!) character string that won't be duplicated by some other object. For programmers who need to create a new CLSID number, the Windows 95 Software Development Kit CD-ROM contains a CLSID generator utility (**UUIDGEN.EXE**) in the **C:\WIN32SDK\MSTOOLS\BIN\i386** folder. The utility should be executed from a command prompt, as shown here:

```
E:\WIN32SDK\MSTOOLS\BIN\i386>uuidgen
elfd71e0-978d-11cf-aaee-444553540000
```

In this example, the utility generated the random CLSID shown on the second line. For informational purposes, the six underlined bytes are the NetworkAddress data taken from the following subkey on the machine running the **UUIDGEN.EXE** utility: **HKEY_LOCAL_MACHINE\SOFTWARE\Description\Microsoft \Rpc\UuidTemporaryData.**

If the system is not configured for network operation, the last six bytes are randomly generated, and a warning message appears. See the "Unable to determine your network address" message in Chapter 8 for further details.

Customizing the Desktop

By default, the My Computer, Network Neighborhood (if installed), Recycle Bin, and a few other objects are displayed on the Desktop every time Windows 95 starts. Some of these may be removed or relocated as described in the "Desktop Icons" section later in the chapter.

If you would prefer to simply remove all default Desktop items and set up your own custom Desktop, try the following procedure:

1.   Open the System Policy Editor and put a check in the **Hide all items on Desktop** box, as was described in the "System Policy Restriction Notes" section.

2.   Create one or more shortcut items in the **C:\Windows\ Start Menu\Programs\StartUp** folder.

The next time Windows 95 starts, the customary Desktop icons will not be displayed, but anything specified in the **StartUp** folder will be seen. For example, to display an open **Custom** folder on the Desktop, first use Explorer to create the folder as described in the "Custom Folder" section. Then write the following shortcut in the **StartUp** folder:

```
C:\EXPLORER.EXE /root, C:\Custom
```

Rewrite the shortcut's target line as required to open your own custom folder, and repeat the procedure as required to open additional folders. Shortcuts to specific applications can also be placed in the **StartUp** folder, and they too will appear on the Desktop in the usual manner.

Custom Folder

Assuming the objects described in this section are on the Desktop (or in the **My Computer** folder) for a good reason— because you use them from time to time, you probably don't want to permanently remove them. However, to reduce Desktop clutter you can move them off the Desktop and into a custom folder. To do so, create and open a **C:\Custom** (or similar) folder, then use that folder's File menu to create one or more of the following new folders within the **Custom** folder:

```
Inbox.{00020D75...
The Microsoft Network.{00028B00-0000-0000-C000-000000000046}
Recycle Bin.{645Ff040...
The Internet.{FBF23B42...
Dial-Up Networking.{992CFFA0...
```

Note that in each case, the folder name format is *name*.**CLSID,** and the CLSID number should be typed in its entirety, as in the Microsoft Network example. After typing the closing brace and pressing **Enter**, the CLSID disappears and the appropriate icon will appear under the **Custom** folder, as shown in Figure 5.8. Drag a shortcut to the Desktop and double-click on it to display the open Custom window, also shown in the figure. After doing all this, the related **{CLSID}** subkey under one of the **NameSpace** keys can be deleted. Refer to Figure 5.19 (later in the chapter) for the complete {CLSID} number for each object described here.

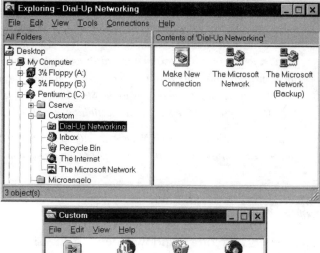

Figure 5.8 *This* **C:\Custom** *folder leads to subfolders usually found on the Desktop; each is identified by its distinctive icon rather than by the customary folder icon. The contents of the* **Dial-Up Networking** *folder appear in the Contents Pane. The* **Custom** *folder itself shows the distinctive subfolder icons and additional icons for any other object dragged into this folder. Note also that the diskette and hard drive icons have been customized, as described in the text.*

As an alternative, follow steps 1 and 2 given earlier to clear the Desktop of its usual icons and display only the custom folder(s) and/or shortcuts that are in the **StartUp** folder.

NOTE

1. As a potentially-confusing side-effect of relocating some default Desktop objects to a Custom folder, these objects are now regarded as conventional folders, and therefore will display some duplicate Context menu options and erroneous Property sheet tabs. Do not drag such an object back to the Desktop from the Custom folder, or its Context menu and Property sheet will retain these invalid options. To avoid such confusion, it would probably be better to relocate these objects to the Start menu instead. (See Add Menu Option in the Start Menu section later in the chapter.)

2. Make sure you export each NameSpace subkey before deleting it, just in case you decide to restore the object to the Desktop at a later date.

The Explorer Window

By default, every Explorer window opens in the single-pane Open mode, and every folder's Context menu shows **Open** as the default (boldface type) option. Follow the directions given under the following headings to change this mode.

Explorer Windows (all)

If you would prefer to have all folder windows open in the double-pane Explore mode, open the **HKCR\Folder\shell** key and change the (Default) entry's Data column from the empty string ("") shown in Figure 5.9 to "explore" as also shown in the figure. This changes the Context menu default option from **Open** to **Explore** and affects all folders, including **My Computer**, **Network Neighborhood**, and **Recycle Bin**.

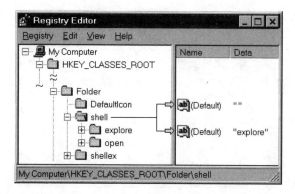

Figure 5.9 *By default, a Desktop Explorer window opens in the single-pane Open mode, because the Shell key's (Default) Data-column entry is empty. To open these windows in the two-pane Explorer mode, change the (Default) entry to "explore" as shown here.*

My Computer Window

Unless the default mode has been changed from Open to Explore mode, as just described, a double-click of the Desktop's **My Computer** icon (or any other folder icon) displays a single-pane Contents window like that shown in Figure 5.10. Because the root of this window is My Computer, it does not display the icons for **Network Neighborhood**, **Recycle Bin**, and **My Briefcase**.

To open My Computer in a two-pane Explorer view instead, open the **HKCR\CLSID\{20D04FE0...** key and add the subkeys shown within the shaded box in Figure 5.11. In the specific example shown in the figure, the new **Open\command** subkey command line (`"explorer.exe /e,,/select,C:\"`) opens the My Computer window as shown in the figure. Note that a Folders Pane now shows the complete Desktop tree, while the Contents Pane duplicates that seen in the default mode shown in Figure 5.10, except that drive **C** is highlighted. Revise the command line as desired to create some other opening format, which will affect the appearance of the My Computer window only.

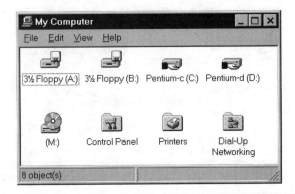

Figure 5.10 *The default single-pane Open mode for the My Computer window shows the available drives and the **Control Panel**, **Printers**, and **Dial-Up Networking** folders.*

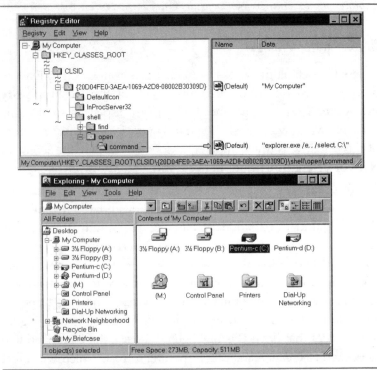

Figure 5.11 *To open the My Computer window in the two-pane mode shown here, add the **open** and **command** keys indicated by the shaded area in the Registry Editor's Key Pane.*

For information about Explorer's other command-line switches, search the Windows 95 Resource Kit index for "Windows Explorer," select **command-line switches**, and click on the **Display** button (or see page 1118 in the printed version).

Menu Editing

This section describes ways to customize the appearance of various Windows 95 menus by editing the Registry.

The Context Menu

To give you a basic idea of how a Context menu might be edited, Figure 5.12 shows the default Context menu for the Recycle Bin. The menu's **Empty Recycle Bin** option is placed there by the special **ContextMenuHandlers** subkey found under the Recycle Bin's **CLSID\{645FF040-5081-101B-9F08-00AA002F954E}\shellex** key. In this particular example, the **ContextMenuHandlers** subkey leads to yet another subkey, whose name is simply the **{645FF040...** key cited earlier. This "circular reference" may seem odd, because all it does is point back to the original **CLSID** subkey. However, you might want to take advantage of this convention to prevent the casual user from emptying the Recycle Bin. By deleting the **{645FF040...**subkey under the **ContextMenuHandlers** key, the **Empty Recycle Bin** option is removed from the Recycle Bin's Context menu, as also shown in the figure.

The **Empty Recycle Bin** option might be placed on some other Context menu, as described here and illustrated in Figure 5.12, which also shows the default Context menu for a bitmap file. To add the **Empty Recycle Bin** option to this menu, add the following subkey structure beneath the **Paint.Picture** key:

```
Key Names
Paint.Picture
   shellex
```

```
ContextMenuHandlers
    {645FF040-5081-101B-9F08-00AA002F954E}
```

Figure 5.12 *The Recycle Bin's default Context menu appears in the upper left-hand corner, while the menu to its right shows the effect of deleting the* **Empty Recycle Bin** *option. The lower left-hand corner shows the default Context menu for a bitmap file. The menu to its right shows the effect of adding the* **Empty Recycle Bin** *option.*

No entry is required in the Contents Pane of each new subkey; Figure 5.12 shows the effect on the Context menu, which now displays the new option.

Although this little exercise is of no practical value, it does show how the Context menu can be modified by deleting or adding various Registry subkeys.

STYLE OF CONTEXT MENU OPTION NAMES

The first few options on any Context menu are usually derived from the names of subkeys that appear directly under the selected object's **shell** subkey. To revise the wording of any of these options, edit the appropriate Contents Pane as desired. For example, Figure 5.13 shows the Context menu for a screen saver file, and the key structure for the Registry's **scrfile** subkey. The menu shows **C_o_nfigure** and **T_e_st** options because C&onfigure and T&est appear in the Data column of the **config** and **open** subkeys, respectively, where the ampersand specifies that the letter following it is to be underlined. If either text string were deleted from the Data column, then the Context menu option would revert to the name of the subkey, with the first letter underlined by default, as, for example, the **C_o_nfig** and **I_n_stall** options on the small Context menu excerpt in the same figure.

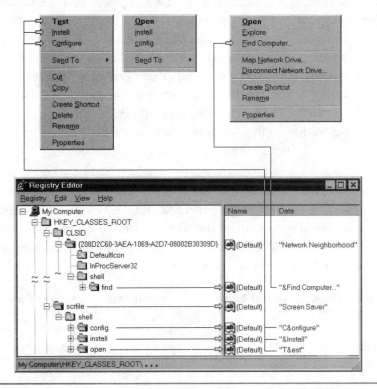

Figure 5.13 *The appearance of the first three options on the screen-saver Context menu is determined by the Contents Pane Data entries seen at the bottom of the illustration. The small menu to the immediate right shows the effect of deleting the* T&est *entry from the Data column. The* **Find Computer** *option on the Network Neighborhood's Context menu is also specified in the* **find** *key's Data column. If erased, the option would revert to* **Find.**

Sometimes the first letter on the menu is uppercase, although it may be lowercase in the actual subkey name. This is because, in the absence of a string in the appropriate Data column, the menu option name is taken from the **SHELL32.DLL** file instead of from the subkey name. This is shown in Figure 5.13 by the menu's **T̲est** option, which becomes **O̲pen** if T&est is deleted from the Contents pane, even though the key itself is labeled *open*.

The **P̲rint** and **F̲ind...** options are also read from **SHELL32.DLL**. For example, Figure 5.13 also shows the CLSID key structure for the Network Neighborhood. By default, the Data column for the **find** (note lowercase *f*) subkey shows &Find Computer. . . and therefore the Context menu shows F̲ind Computer. . .. However, if this Data column entry is deleted, the menu option becomes **F̲ind...** (note uppercase *F*), because this unique string is embedded in, and read from, the **SHELL32.DLL** file. The **O̲pen** and **P̲rint** menu options are likewise read from this file, which accounts for why they always appear with the first letter in uppercase and underlined.

Table 5.3 lists several subkeys in which a text string in the Contents Pane Data column supersedes a menu option taken from a subkey name or from the **SHELL32.DLL** file. To summarize the use of an ampersand in the Data column, it specifies the underlined letter. If omitted, no letter will be underlined, as shown by these **edit** subkey examples:

Contents Pane	Context Menu	Contents Pane	Context Menu
" "	e̲dit	e&Dit	eD̲it
&edit	e̲dit	&Edit	E̲dit
edit	edit	Edit	Edit

Table 5.4 *Use of Data Column to specify a Context Menu Option*

HKCR Subkey	\shell Subkey	Contents Pane Data Column Shows:	Context Menu Option: (Default)	(Other) *
.pps	open	S&how	Show	Open ‡
{208D2C60... †	find	&Find Computer...	Find Computer...	Find... ‡
AVIFile	play	Play	Play	play
cplfile	cplopen	Open with Control Panel	(same)	cplopen
midfile, mplayer	play	Play	Play	play
Office.Binder.95	new	New	New	new
Power.Point.Show.7	show	S&how	Show	show
regfile	open	Mer&ge	Merge	Open ‡
scrfile	config	C&onfigure	Configure	config
	install	&Install	Install	install
	open	T&est	Test	Open ‡
Unknown	openas	(value not set)	Open With...	Open With...‡
(*various*)	print	(value not set)	Print	Print ‡

* Context menu option reverts to this string if string in Data column is deleted.

† CLSID number is for Network Neighborhood.

‡ Context menu shows this text string taken from **SHELL32.DLL** file *unless* an alternate phrase appears in Data column.

Context Menu Modifications

This section describes several modifications that can be made to any Context menu.

CHANGE OPTION NAME AND/OR UNDERLINED LETTER

The first few menu options are the names of actions that appear under various **Shell** subkeys under the **FileType** or **Program Identifier** key located under the HKCR key. For example, Figure 5.14 shows the **batfile** key and the three action subkeys that appear within its **Shell** key structure. The Figure inset shows how these commands appear as Context menu options if any file with a **BAT** extension is selected. (The **Add to Zip** option is discussed separately, later.)

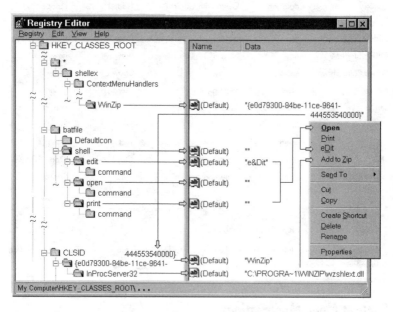

Figure 5.14 *This **batfile** key structure offers another example of how entries in the Contents Pane Data column appear on the Context menu. The **Add to Zip** option is supported by the file specified in the **InProcServer32** subkey seen at the bottom of the figure.*

Note that although the following three Registry subkey names appear on the Context menu, the menu's capitalization and sequence do not match that shown under the **Shell** key, as summarized here:

Subkey Name	Contents Pane	Context Menu	Actual Sequence
edit	e&Dit	e<u>D</u>it	*(default option)*
open	*" "*	<u>O</u>pen	*(other options, as*
print	*" "*	<u>P</u>rint	*described later)*

In this example, the **Edit** option has been edited to display the unique capitalization shown on the Context menu, and the **Open** and **Print** options show an underlined uppercase first letter for the reasons described earlier. On the menu, the action subkeys under the **Shell** key appear after the default option in the sequence in which they were added or edited in the Registry. These options are followed by other options added by the **Asterisk** key, QuickView, and other utilities. Thus, if an original Context menu sequence was **Open, Print, edit, Add to Zip,** and the **Print** subkey was subsequently edited, the new sequence would be **Open, edit, Print, Add to Zip.**

CHANGE DEFAULT OPTION

As just noted, the default action is always the first option listed on the Context menu, where it appears in boldface type (usually, as **Open**). The safest way to specify some other action as the default is to open Explorer's View menu, select **Options**, and click on the **File Types** tab. Scroll down the list of Registered file types, highlight the desired file type, and click the **Edit** button. Note the action listed in boldface type, which is the current default. To make some other action the default, highlight it and click on the **Set default** button.

It's often faster to accomplish the same task via the Registry, especially if the desired file type is not easy to find. For example, a batch file appears in the list of Registered File types under *M* for *MS-DOS Batch File.* A Word document appears under the same letter, but this time it's for *Microsoft Word Document.* To save a bit of time searching a long list of *M*-words, you can directly edit the Registry. To do so, open a subkey such as

batfile, then open the **Shell** subkey below it and edit its Contents Pane's (Default) Data column. Type in the name of any subkey action that appears below the **Shell** key (**edit** or **print,** for example) and then click the **OK** button. That action will now become the default action, and it will appear at the top of the Context menu.

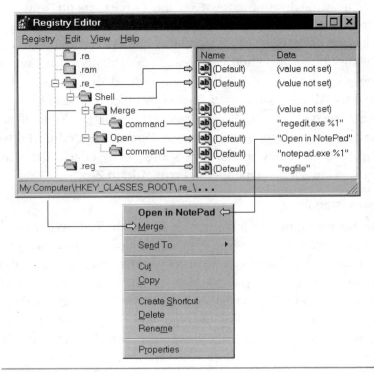

Figure 5.15 The **Merge** *and* **Open in NotePad** *options on this custom subkey's Context menu offer some protection against accidentally merging a critical Registry file with an extension of* **.re_** *instead of the customary* **.reg.** *The default option has been renamed* **Open in NotePad,** *and* **Merge** *is available as a nondefault option.*

ADD MERGE OPTION

If you decide to name potentially dangerous registry files with an extension of say, *re_* instead of the customary *reg*, you can add a **Merge** option to the file type's Context menu, as shown in Figure 5.15. With the new **.reg** subkey structure added beneath the **HKCR** key, the resultant Context menu shown in the figure will be displayed for any file with that extension. The default action is **Open**, and the Context menu shows **Open in NotePad** as a reminder. Select the **Merge** option whenever you really do want to merge the file into the existing Registry. In either case, the **command** subkey executes either **REGEDIT.EXE** or **NOTEPAD.EXE**, as indicated in the Data column. This procedure prevents a critical file (with an *re_* extension) from being accidentally merged into the Registry by double-clicking on it.

ADD PRINTTO OPTION

In at least one circumstance, an action key located under a **FileType** key's **Shell** subkey does not appear on the Context menu. Using **Printto** as an example, this section shows how to force a missing action key to appear on the menu. For the purposes of this illustration, it is assumed that the **Printto** and **Printto\command** subkeys are present and in good working order. The same general procedure described here should be valid for any other action key that is missing from the Context menu.

If a document file icon is dragged to a printer icon and dropped there, the print job will be handled by one of two subkeys in the Registry. If the appropriate **FileType** key contains a **Printto** subkey, then its **command** subkey handles the job. Otherwise, the regular **Print** subkey does the job. Assuming there is a **Printto** subkey for the file type, there's rarely a point to having a **Printto** option on the Context menu, because by definition **Printto** is reserved for drag-and-drop operations. If the file is to be printed via the Context menu, then that menu's regular **Print** option is used, and the appearance of a **Printto** option would be redundant.

However, if you specify that a file is to be drag-and-drop printed using a different application than the default (see "Drag-and-Drop Printing"), then you may want **Printto** available on the Context menu for use when actual drag-and-drop printing is inconvenient.

To place the **Printto** option on the menu, open the **Printto** subkey and type **Printto** in the Contents Pane's Data column, with an ampersand inserted immediately before the letter that is to be underlined, as for example, **P_rintto**. This simple action places the option on the menu, with the letter _r_ underlined. In fact, you may even enter **&Printto** to force the use of an underlined _P_ for this option. However, because this letter is already used for the **Print** option, you may prefer to select another letter instead.

ADD OTHER MISSING OPTIONS

If an unrecognized file type's Context menu is opened and its **Open With...** option is selected, the user can specify the program to open the selected file. As noted in Chapter 2, if the **Always use this program to open this file** box is checked, then the next time a file with the same extension is selected, the Context menu will display the usual **Open** option instead of the **Open With...** option. However, other options appropriate to the same program may not appear on the Context menu.

To verify this, copy a short text file to the Desktop and rename it as, say, **TEXTFILE.XYZ**. Then open its Context menu, select the **Open With . . .** option, put a check in **Always use**

this program... box, and associate the file with the NotePad applet. The next time you open the **TEXTFILE.XYZ** file's Context menu, the **Open** option appears, but the expected **Print** option does not. To find out why, open the **.xyz** subkey and note the entry in the Data column, which probably reads **xyz_auto_file.**

You'll also find a new **xyz_auto_file** subkey under the **HKCR** key, and its **Shell** subkey leads to an **open\command** subkey, but not to an equivalent subkey for **Print.** To resolve the problem, simply erase the entire **xyz_auto_file** subkey structure (which won't be needed), then reopen the **.xyz** subkey and change **xyz_auto_file** to **txtfile.** The next time you select any file with that extension, its Context menu will display the same options available to files with **.txt** and other extensions associated with NotePad.

Use the same general procedure to correct any other new file type whose Context menu does not list all the desired options.

THE ADD TO ZIP OPTION

This Context menu option is added via the **WinZip** subkey and its associated **{CLSID}** key, as was illustrated in Figure 5.14. Because the **WinZip** subkey appears under the **Asterisk** key's **ContextMenuHandlers** subkey, it appears on the Context menu of any file that can be written into a compressed (zipped) archive file. In this specific example, the key was added by WinZip 6.1 from Nico Mak Computing, Inc.

Delete Options. In certain cases, one or more options can be deleted from a Context menu for some default Desktop objects. Refer to the Attributes Flags section earlier in the chapter for instructions on how to do so.

Cascading Menus

If a menu option with a solid black right-pointing arrow is highlighted, a cascading menu appears to its immediate right. Under default conditions, the menu appears or disappears one-half second (500 milliseconds) after the highlight is applied or removed. This interval may be adjusted by adding a MenuShowDelay line to the Contents pane of the subkey listed here:

HKEY_CURRENT_USER\Control Panel\desktop

Name	Data	
MenuShowDelay	"xxxx"	xxxx = delay time, in milliseconds
MenuDropAlignment	"1"	1 = right alignment (described below)

By setting the delay time to say, 2000, a cascading menu will not appear until a menu option remains highlighted for 2 seconds. If the highlight is subsequently moved to another menu option after a cascading menu appears, the present menu will continue to be displayed for another 2 seconds. Some users prefer a delay time of 1 second or more, to prevent cascading menus from popping up on screen as the mouse pointer slowly moves across a menu. Also, the delay time permits the mouse pointer to move diagonally from a highlighted option to a cascading menu option without having the latter disappear if the pointer isn't moved fast enough. Or, set the delay time to zero for instant menu access.

Menu Alignment

The drop-down menus that appear within any Explorer window are by default aligned with the left edge of the selected menu name on the Menu bar. To align these menus with the right edge instead, add the MenuDropAlignment line shown above. If the open window is positioned so that part of the menu would now be offscreen to the left, the menu shifts to the right by whatever it takes to keep the entire menu onscreen. To restore the default alignment, either delete the line or reset the Data value to 0.

The Desktop New Menu

Two of the options on the Desktop's New menu—**Folder** and **Shortcut**—are hard coded into the **SHELL32.DLL** file in **C:\Windows\System** and are therefore not a function of the Registry. During the Windows 95 setup procedure, Registry entries for three other options—**Bitmap Image**, **Text Document**, and **Wave Sound**—are taken from the **SHELL.INF** file, and the **Briefcase** option is taken from the **NET.INF** file (in each case, assuming the associated applet is installed during setup). Additional options may be placed on the New menu as various Windows 95 applets and applications are installed.

New Menu Modifications

Options may be added to or removed from the New menu as described here.

ADD MENU OPTION

In order to successfully add an option to the New menu, make sure a valid **File Extension** subkey exists and is associated with a Registered file type. For example, to add a **Custom Document** option to the New menu, open Explorer's View menu, select **Options**, click on the **File Types** tab, and then click on the **New Type** button. Enter the following information:

Description of Data—Custom Document

Associated extension—jmw (or any other new extension)

Actions—Click New button and enter name of action and executable application name (for example, Open, and C:\WINWORD\WINWORD.EXE /n "%1", respectively)

NOTE

The "%1" parameter shown here may be required in order for Microsoft Word to recognize long filenames containing spaces.

Once this is done, the **HKCR** key should show new **.jmw** and **jmwfile** subkeys. The latter contains a **Shell\open\command** subkey with the path and name of the executable file cited earlier. Now complete the following steps to add **Custom Document** to the New menu:

1.   Highlight the **File Extension** subkey (**.jmw** in this example), open the Edit menu, and select the **New Key** option.

2.   Type **ShellNew** in the NewKey #1 box and press the **Enter** key.

3.   Open the Edit menu and select the **New String Value** option.

4.   Create one (only) of the following String value entries in the Contents Pane:

Name	Data
NullFile	" "
FileName	winword.jmw (or similar, assuming file exists)

Refer to "The ShellNew Key" in Chapter 2 for additional details about each of the entries listed.

To put a **MIDI sequence** option on the New menu list, add a **ShellNew** subkey under the **HKCR\.mid** subkey with the following binary value in the Contents Pane:

Name	Data
Data	4D 54 68 64 00 00 00 06 00 00 00 01 01 E0 4D 54 72 6B

This is the MIDI header data described in Chapter 2 and illustrated in Figure 2.11, and should only exist if a Windows 95 MIDI recorder application is installed. It is shown here simply to illustrate how such an application might modify the Registry.

DELETE MENU OPTION

By comparison with the preceding, this is quite easy: just delete the **ShellNew** subkey under the appropriate **File Extension** key and the option will disappear from the New menu.

The Start Menu

There are several way to customize the Start menu, which may or may not require Registry editing as described here.

Add Menu Option

The fastest way to add an option to the Start menu is to open Explorer, find the desired folder, application, or shortcut, and drag it to the Start menu button on the Taskbar. For example, if any icon in the Explorer's Folders Pane is dragged to the Start button, it will appear on the Start menu, as shown in Figure 5.16. To create a cascading menu option, open the Registry Editor and find the **{CLSID}** key for the desired object. For example, search the Data column for Control Panel and copy its **{21EC2020...** number. Then open the **C:\Windows\Start Menu** folder and create a new folder with the following name: **Control Panel.{21EC2020-3AEA-1069-A2DD-08002B30309D}**.

This places a cascading **Control Panel** option on the Start menu, as also shown in Figure 5.16. Although there's probably not much point in having two **Control Panel** options on the same menu, the figure shows that it can be done. However, the same general procedure can be used to add various other cascading menu options to the menu.

Figure 5.16 *This customized Start menu shows the effect of dragging various Explorer icons onto the Start button. In addition, the cascading **Control Panel** option at the top of the list was installed by creating a new folder named **Control Panel.{21EC2020...** as described in the text.*

Delete Documents List

The Start menu's cascading Documents menu lists the last 15 documents that were edited, as shown in Figure 5.17. Although the icon next to each document does not show the customary shortcut arrow, each item on the list represents a shortcut file stored in the **C:\Windows\Recent** folder, and the same list is also maintained in the Registry.

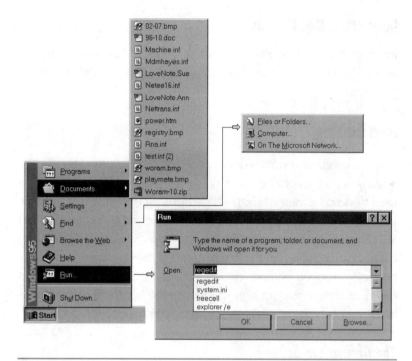

Figure 5.17 *The Start menu's* ***Documents*** *and* ***Run*** *options let you (or anyone else) review what you've done lately. The* ***Find*** *option will also show a list of files, folders, and computers that you've recently looked at.*

This document history list may be convenient on a single-user system, because it permits the user to simply double-click on any list item to open the associated application and load the document for review or further editing. However, the list also lets snoopers know what the user has been doing lately, which may or may not be a diplomatic problem. If it is, refer to the "INF File as a Registry Editor" section earlier in this chapter for detailed instructions on how to erase this and other history lists whenever it becomes necessary (or advisable) to hide evidence.

Delete Find, Run Options

Refer to the "System Policy Editor" section earlier in this chapter and to Table 5.1 for details on removing these options from the Start menu.

Icon Editing

In this section, *icon editing* does not describe any method to alter the actual internal graphic content of an icon file. Instead, the term is used to describe various methods of replacing one icon with another. For any icon that appears on the Desktop or elsewhere within Windows 95, there are several ways to do this. Some, but not all, icon changes are recorded in the Registry, and of those that are, some may be easily changed without directly editing the Registry. This section describes how to find an icon specified in the Registry and then looks at the various ways in which some other icon may be selected.

The DefaultIcon Subkey

Many Windows 95 icons are specified in a **DefaultIcon** subkey located under a **{CLSID}** or other Registry key. The **DefaultIcon** subkey's Contents Pane resembles the following entry:

Name	Data
(Default)	"C:\WINDOWS\SYSTEM\SHELL32.DLL, 12"

The actual path, filename, and icon number will vary to indicate the actual source of the icon. To change that source, simply double-click on the small **ab** icon to the left of the Name column's (Default) entry. Then edit the Value data box as required to specify the desired icon source.

If no effect is noted, then it's quite likely that a default icon specified under a **{CLSID}** key is superseded by another icon specified elsewhere. If this is the case, refer to "DefaultIcon Precedence" in Chapter 2 for help in locating the currently active icon. Then change that icon using the procedure just described.

DefaultIcon Search Procedure

If you're not sure of the location of the appropriate **DefaultIcon** subkey, or even if such a subkey exists for the icon you want to change, then make a note of the appropriate object type. If necessary, open Explorer's View menu, select **Options**, and then select the **File Types** tab. Highlight the desired file type and note the extension listed. Then search **HKEY_CLASSES_ROOT** for a subkey with that extension name. Open the subkey, note the **Filetype** that appears in the (Default) item's Data column, and then find the subkey with that name. Finally, open the **DefaultIcon** subkey underneath that key.

If the object is not a file type (Recycle Bin, The Microsoft Network, for example), then follow the same procedure anyway, which will probably lead to a **CLSID** key. Open that subkey and then locate and open the **DefaultIcon** subkey beneath it.

If this general procedure does not locate the desired **DefaultIcon** subkey, then there's a good possibility that such a key does not exist for this object, as might be the case under either of the following conditions:

■ The default icon may be embedded in the executable file associated with that file type. To verify this, highlight the Registered file type (as earlier), click on the **Edit** button, and then click on the **Change Icon** button. (If necessary, refer to the "Edit Flags" section in this chapter if one of these buttons is disabled.) Change the icon to anything else, then back again to the original icon and click on the **OK** button. This action should force a **DefaultIcon** subkey to be written into the Registry.

- Some icons are not specified in the Registry, or the Registry entry may not be immediately obvious. In this case, refer to the "Shell Icons Key" section later.

In a few cases, a partial icon change may be noted. For example, if the default icon for the **Drive** or the **Folder** key is changed, the new icon appears only in the Registered file types list: drive and folder icons elsewhere retain their original appearance. In cases such as this, refer to one of the following sections.

Negative Icon Number

In most cases, the **DefaultIcon** subkey's Contents Pane refers to an icon source file in which the icon is specified by its position within the file. For example, the My Computer's **SHELL32.DLL, 15** or **EXPLORER.EXE**, 0 clearly indicates that the icon is at position 15 or 0. Sometimes, however, a negative number is given, as in the **DefaultIcon** key for Control Panel (−137), Printers (−138), and a few others. Each such negative number is an icon resource identifier, which locates the icon without regard to its physical position in the file. Thus, if a new version of the file containing that icon were installed and the icon was now at a different position, Windows 95 would still find it.

The Shell Icons Key

In some cases, there is no **DefaultIcon** key for an object. Typical examples are the default icons on the Start menu, various diskette and other drive icons, and the Share and Shortcut overlay icons. This may suggest that these icons are unchangeable, but in fact Windows 95 does permit most such icons to be changed, via a **Shell Icons** subkey. Although not written into the Registry as part of the standard Windows 95 setup procedure, the key is added to the Registry by the Microsoft Plus! Companion for Windows 95 software. If MS Plus! is not installed, the subkey can be added by the user and then used to change various Desktop and Explorer icons. Its location is given here:

```
HKLM\SOFTWARE\Microsoft\Windows\CurrentVersion\Shell Icons
```

Figure 5.18 shows the Contents Pane for a typical **Show Icons** subkey after MS Plus! has been installed. Each number in the Name column is associated with a specific object, and the information in the Data column identifies the icon that now supersedes the default icon for that object. Table 5.5 lists various Windows 95 objects that can be specified by a number in the **Shell Icons** key's Name column. For each number listed in the table's Name column, the **SHELL32.DLL** and **COOL.DLL** columns list the number of the default icon associated with that object before and after MS Plus! is installed.

Table 5.5 *HKLM\SOFTWARE\Microsoft\Windows\CurrentVersion\ explorer\Shell Icons Subkey*

Object	Number in Name Column *	Icon Number in SHELL32.DLL	Icon Number in COOL.DLL
Generic (unknown format) doc file †	0	0	37
MSN, other document files †	1	1	—
Application • †	2	2	—
Folder, closed §	3	3	11
Folder, open §	4	4	18
Drive, 5.25" diskette §	5	5	9
Drive, 3.5" diskette §	6	6	8
Drive, removable §	7	7	—
Drive, hard §	8	8	0
Drive, network §	9	9	1
Drive, network, offline §	10	10	29
Drive, CD-ROM §	11	11	10
Drive, RAM §	12	12	—
Network, entire §	13	13	13
My Computer †	15	15	28
Printer §	16	16	22

Object	Number in Name Column *	Icon Number in SHELL32.DLL	Icon Number in COOL.DLL
Network Neighborhood †	17	17	17
Network, workgroup †	18	18	—
Start Menu, Programs §	19	19	4
Start Menu, Documents §	20	20	2
Start Menu, Settings §	21	21	6
Start Menu, Find §	22	22	3
Start Menu, Help §	23	23	15
Start Menu, Run §	24	24	5
Start Menu, Suspend §	25	25	33
Start Menu, Eject PC (undock) §	26	26	32
Start Menu, Shut Down §	27	27	7
Share (hand overlay) †	28	28	34
Shortcut (arrow overlay) †	29	29	—
Recycle Bin, empty ‡	31	31	20
Recycle Bin, full ‡	32	32	21
Folder, Dial-Up Networking ‡	33	33	27
Folder, Desktop (Explorer root) §	34	34	—
Settings Menu, Control Panel icon †	35	35	12
Folder, Program Group §	36	36	24
Settings Menu, Printers icon †	37	37	—
Folder, Fonts §	38	38	14
Settings Menu, Taskbar icon †	39	39	—
Audio CD †	40	40	26
Folder, Control Panel ‡	(–137)	46	12 ‡
Folder, Printers ‡	(–138)	47	19 ‡

*Number does not appear in **Shell Icons** subkey if device is not installed.

–No icon in **COOL.DLL** file for this object.

†No **Shell Icons** entry required if default icon is used. Otherwise, **Shell Icons** entry supersedes default icon.

‡**Shell Icons** entry has no effect. Icon specified in **DefaultIcon** subkey for this object.

§Registry does not contain a **DefaultIcon** subkey for this object. Use **Shell Icons** subkey to specify nondefault icon.

(–xxx) Negative number indicates icon resource identifier (see "Negative Icon Number" in text).

•Application defined here as any **.com** file, plus any DOS **.exe** file (Windows 95 **.exe** file has its own icon).

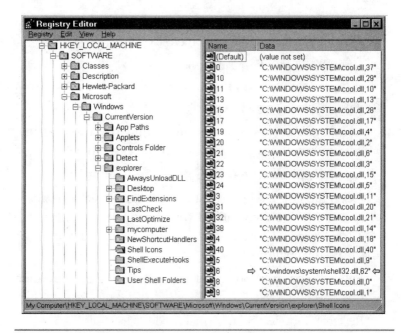

Figure 5.18 The **Shell Icons** *subkey displays a list of icons currently assigned to objects associated with the numbers in the Name column (as listed in Table 5.5). Note that object 6 (Drive, 3.5" diskette) has been assigned icon 62 in the* **SHELL32.DLL** *file, which is a document page with the letter A on it.*

If the **Shell Icons** entry for a Start menu icon or any other object *not* also represented by a **DefaultIcon** subkey is removed, then the icon for that object reverts to the former **SHELL32.DLL** default icon. There is no obvious effect though, because the two default icons are identical.

To select some other icon, first make sure there is no **DefaultIcons** key for that object. If there is such a key, then refer to "The DefaultIcon Subkey" section instead. Otherwise, open the **Shell Icons** subkey or create a new subkey with this name if it does not already exist. Then use the following procedure to make the change:

1. Make a note of the path, source file, and icon number that you want to use as a replacement icon.

2. Open Windows 95 in safe mode.

3. Erase the hidden **ShellIconCache** file (described later) in the **C:\Windows\System** folder.

4. Using Table 5.5 as a reference, find the number that corresponds to the object whose icon you want to replace.

5. Open the **Shell Icons** subkey.

6. Open the Edit menu, select the **New\String value** options, and overtype **New Value #1** with the number found in step 3 (this step is not necessary if that number already exists in the **Name** column).

7. Enter the information found in step 1 into the **Value data** box and click **OK**.

8. Restart Windows 95 in Normal mode.

The ShellIconCache File

The hidden **ShellIconCache** file (note, no extension) contains copies of currently used icons, and this file restores Desktop and Explorer icons every time Windows 95 starts. After erasing the file (step 3, earlier), Windows 95 will need a bit of extra time to restart as it rebuilds the file. However, the icon change(s) made earlier will be written into that file, subsequent restarts will not be delayed, and the changes will be permanent—until you decide to make further changes. Figure 5.19 is a typical before-and-after view of the Start menu showing the effect of customization.

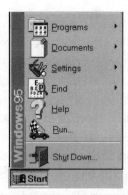

Figure 5.19 *A before-and-after look at the Start menu showing how each of its icons can be customized to suit personal preference.*

*If the hard drive icon is changed by editing the **Shell Icons** subkey, that change is applied to all hard drives on the system. To change the icon for a single hard drive only, refer to "Hard Drive" in the "Drive Media Icons" section later.*

N O T E

Some Superfluous Shell Icons Key Entries

Some **Shell Icons** listings are redundant and can be erased without having any effect. For example, both **Recycle Bin** icons are always written into the Recycle Bin's **DefaultIcon** subkey under the {645FF040... key. The MS Plus! setup procedure changes the **DefaultIcon** source file from **SHELL32.DLL** to **COOL.DLL**, and the icon numbers from 31 and 32 to 20 and 21, and it inserts the following lines in the **Shell Icons** Contents Pane to record the change:

Name	Data
31	C:\WINDOWS\SYSTEM\cool.dll, 20
32	C:\WINDOWS\SYSTEM\cool.dll, 21

In other words, object 31 (the empty Recycle Bin) is now represented by icon 20 in the **COOL.DLL** file, and object 32 (the full Bin) is icon 20. But now that MS Plus! has made this change, the inclusion of these entries in the **Shell Icons** Contents Pane is not required. In fact, if either Data column entry were removed or changed, it would have no effect because the **DefaultIcon** listing takes precedence.

MS Plus! Desktop Themes

As a further consideration, if one of the MS Plus! Desktop themes is selected, some **DefaultIcon** subkey entries will have been changed to specify the appropriate icons, as in this Recycle Bin example from the Dangerous Creatures theme:

Name	Data
(Default)	"C:\Program Files\Themes\Dangerous Creatures Recycle Full.ico,0
empty	"C:\Program Files\Themes\Dangerous Creatures Recycle Empty.ico,0
full	"C:\Program Files\Themes\Dangerous Creatures Recycle Full.ico,0

Because these lines appear in the Recycle Bin's **DefaultIcon** subkey, they take precedence over the **Recycle Bin** icons (objects 31 and 32 in the **Shell Icons** subkey). If such a Desktop theme is subsequently removed but MS Plus! itself is left in place, then the Recycle Bin's **Default Icon** subkey would once again refer to the **COOL.DLL** or **SHELL32.DLL** icons cited earlier.

Desktop Icons

Some or all of the icons listed in this section are placed on the Desktop during the Windows 95 setup procedure. If an icon cited here does not appear, it represents an object that was not installed, either because it is not supported (Network Neighborhood on a single-user system, for example) or because the user elected not to install it (My Briefcase, for example). For future reference, the **CLSID** key for each object is also given.

Object Name	CLSID key
Inbox	{00020D75-0000-0000-C000-000000000046}
My Briefcase	{85BBD920-42A0-1069-A2E4-08002B30309D}
My Computer	{20D04FE0-3AEA-1069-A2D8-08002B30309D}
Network Neighborhood	{208D2C60-3AEA-1069-A2D7-08002B30309D}
Recycle Bin	{645FF040-5081-101B-9F08-00AA002F954E}
The Internet	{FBF23B42-E3F0-101B-8488-00AA003E56F8}
The Microsoft Network	{00028B00-0000-0000-C000-000000000046}

By default, the names of the three objects marked by an asterisk do not appear in the Data column for the associated CLSID key. However, if My Computer or Network Neighborhood is renamed—even if the new name is the same as the old one—then that name will appear in the Data column. If My Briefcase is renamed, its **CLSID** folder's Data column still shows a one-word *Briefcase*, because this key may apply to more than one briefcase icon, regardless of its icon title. The actual icon title for any briefcase icon is stored as a folder name only. Thus, if there are two Briefcase icons on the Desktop, Explorer should show the following two folders:

```
C:\Windows\Desktop\My Briefcase
C:\Windows\Desktop\New Briefcase
```

If either Briefcase is renamed, that name will take the place of My Briefcase or New Briefcase, but the Registry will show no record of this change.

Because of the differences in the way these Desktop objects are recorded in the Registry, it may be more reliable to search for the associated **CLSID** key instead. Once it's found, click on the plus sign next to it and then on the **DefaultIcon** subkey.

Remove Desktop Object and Icon

With a few notable exceptions, most Desktop objects can be deleted via their Context menu's **Delete** option. However, Figure 5.20 shows a few Desktop objects whose Context menus don't support that option. In most cases, the object can be removed by deleting one of the Registry subkeys shown in the same figure. As their names suggest, each subkey is a pointer to the **{CLSID}** key for the object specified in the Data column. By deleting the subkey, the object disappears from the Desktop, yet the actual **{CLSID}** key remains intact under the **HKCR** key.

As always, export a copy of the subkey before you delete it, just in case you decide you'd like to restore the object to the Desktop.

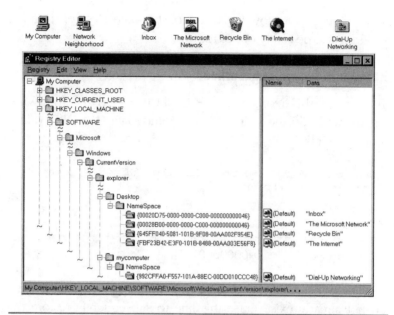

Figure 5.20 *Although the Context menus for the icons shown here do not support the* **Delete** *option, most can be removed from the Desktop by deleting the appropriate* {**CLSID**} *subkey under one of the* **NameSpace** *keys.*

Remove My Computer

If the **HKCR** key's {**20D04FE0...**subkey is deleted, the **My Computer** icon remains on the Desktop but is inoperative and cannot be renamed. If it had been previously renamed, the name reverts to My Computer if the subkey is deleted, and it cannot be renamed again in the absence of the subkey. The icon and its default title seem to be hard-coded into the operating system, and there is no known Registry edit that will remove them from the Desktop. If you must hide this object, rename it as " " and use an icon-edit utility to create a transparent icon for it. Then move the now-invisible icon to some Desktop location where it will be safely out of the way.

Remove Network Neighborhood

To remove this icon from the Desktop, open the following subkey and add the indicated Name and Data (DWORD value) to its Contents Pane:

```
HKEY_CURRENT_USER\Software\Microsoft\Windows\CurrentVers
ion\ Policies\Explorer
```

Name	Data
NoNetHood	0x00000001 (1)

If necessary, create the **Policies** and **Explorer** subkeys if they do not already exist. Erase this line to subsequently restore the Network Neighborhood to the Desktop. In either case, the change will take effect the next time Windows 95 is opened. Refer to "The System Policy Editor" in this chapter for additional information about the **Policies** subkey.

Remove Dial-Up Networking Icon

Figure 5.20 also shows the **NameSpace** subkey under the **mycomputer** key. This icon appears in the My Computer window, and as described earlier, it can be removed by deleting the {**992CFFA0...** subkey shown at the bottom of the figure.

Drive Icons

Windows 95 reads the CMOS configuration to determine the diskette drive configuration (**A:** = 3.5, **B:** = 5.25, and so on) and then uses the appropriate icon for each such drive, as was shown in Figure 2.12 in Chapter 2. To change either icon, refer to the "Shell Icons" section earlier, and to Table 5.5. Refer to the same section and table to change the icon assigned to any other drive type (CD-ROM, hard drive, etc.).

In addition to these icon changes, a custom icon can be assigned to any removable medium or hard drive partition, as described next.

Drive Media Icons

Most Windows 95 CD-ROMs contain an **AUTORUN.INF** file in the root directory, as described in the "AutoRun" section of Chapter 2. To briefly review here, the **AUTORUN.INF** file contains an Icon= line that specifies the icon to be displayed when that disc is inserted in the CD-ROM drive.

By default, Windows 95 is configured to recognize an **AUTORUN.INF** file on various media and to ignore it on others, based on the Registry key shown here. The default Data entry also shown here can be revised as desired:

```
HKEY_CURRENT_USER\Software\Microsoft\Windows\CurrentVersion\
Policies\Explorer
```

Name	Data
NoDriveTypeAutoRun	95 00 00 00

The first Data byte (95 = 1001 0101) is a bit mask in which each bit set to 1 prevents a certain drive type from being recognized, according to the following list.

Bit Drive Type		Bit	Drive Type
0	Unknown	4	remote
1	"NO_ROOT_DIR" *	5	CD-ROM
2	Removable	6	RAM
3	hard drive	7	reserved

*Microsoft documentation gives no clue what this means.

Under default conditions, therefore, the set (underlined) bits prevent unknown, removable, and remote drives from using the AutoPlay mode and the **AUTORUN.INF** file.

To enable any diskette to display its own custom icon, change the Data entry to clear the removable-drive bit (91 = 1001 0001). Then write an **AUTORUN.INF** file on every diskette that you would like to identify with its own icon, as shown here:

```
[autorun]
icon=CUSTOM.ICO (or, C:\WINDOWS\SYSTEM\SHELL32.DLL, xx,
or similar)
```

If the diskette containing the **AUTORUN.INF** file is in a drive prior to opening Explorer, its icon will be displayed when the Explorer window is opened. If a diskette is inserted after Explorer opens, highlight the drive and press **F5** to refresh the display.

Hard Drive

Under default conditions, all hard drives are represented by the same icon (**SHELL32.DLL**, **9**, or **COOL.DLL**, **0** if MS Plus! is installed). To use a different icon for one hard drive only, write the two-line **AUTORUN.INF** file shown earlier and place it in the root directory of that drive. Highlight the drive and press **F5** to display the new icon, which takes precedence over any other icon change made via the **Shell Icons** subkey described earlier. Because the hard drive bit (3) is cleared by default, there is no need to edit the Registry to enable this feature.

Other Editing Techniques

The concluding section of this chapter describes a few additional Registry edits that may be used to further customize the Windows 95 configuration.

Animated Window

When a window is minimized or restored, the transition in its size may take place in one of the two ways described here. In either case, the effect is controlled by a MinAnimate entry in the Contents Pane of the following key:

```
HKEY_CURRENT_USER\ControlPanel\desktop\WindowMetrics
```

Onscreen Effect of Window Transition	Name	Data
Disappears/reappears instantaneously	MinAnimate	"0"
Gradually collapses/expands	MinAnimate	"1"

Edit the Data column as desired to change from one mode to the other. The change will not be noted, however, until Windows 95 is closed and reopened.

Bitmap Thumbnail Icons

The **HKCR\Paint.Picture\DefaultIcon** subkey specifies the icon that appears next to every bitmap file (BMP extension), as shown by the first (Default) line below:

Name	Data
(Default)	"C:\Program Files\Accessories\MSPAINT.EXE,1"
(Default)	""%1"" (note two quotation marks on either side of the %1)

If the Data entry is rewritten as shown in the second (Default) line, each bitmap file will display its own icon, which will be a thumbnail version of the actual graphic file image. In making the edit in the Value data box, include a quotation mark on either side of the %1 parameter, so that it will be enclosed in two sets as shown. This is so that the replaceable parameter will recognize a long filename with a space in it.

Note, however, that this option will considerably slow down an Explorer window with bitmaps in its Contents Pane, because the distinctive thumbnail icon for each such file must be created separately as the window opens. If you like the feature enough to stick it out, you may want to make a point of keeping all bitmap files in a separate **C:\BITMAPS** (or similar) folder. That way Explorer won't be detained unless you specifically want to view your bitmap collection.

Control Panel Applet Access

The usual method to access a Control Panel applet is to open the Start menu, select the **Settings** option, select the **Control Panel** folder icon, then double-click on the desired icon. For faster access, open the **HKCR\cplfile\shell** key and rename the **cplopen** key to **open.** To open a Control Panel applet, select the Start menu's **Run** option and type the name of its CPL file into the Open box. Table 5.6 lists various applets and their associated CPL files.

Table 5.6 *Control Panel Access via Start Menu's Run Command* *

Control Panel Applet	Run Command
Accessibility Options	ACCESS.CPL
Add/Remove Programs	APPWIZ.CPL
Date/Time	TIMEDATE.CPL
Desktop Themes (*MS Plus!*)	THEMES.CPL
Display	DESK.CPL
Find Fast	FINDFAST.CPL
Hewlett-Packard JetAdmin	JETADMIN.CPL

Control Panel Applet	Run Command
Internet	INETCPL.CPL
Joy Stick	JOY.CPL
Messaging Settings	MLCFG32.CPL
Modem	MODEM.CPL
Mouse	MAIN.CPL
Multimedia	MMSYS.CPL
Network	NETCPL.CPL
Password	PASSWORD.CPL
System	SYSDM.CPL
Tweak UI	TWEAKUI.CPL
Workgroup Post Office Admin	WGPOCPL.CPL

* Indicated file must be present in **C:\Windows\System** folder.

Drag-and-Drop Print Editing

As noted in Chapter 2, drag-and-drop printing is handled by the **Printto** subkey or, in its absence, by the **Print** subkey, and under most circumstances there would be little reason to change such settings. However, if you regularly use the NotePad applet to print **TXT** files, you may not care for its habit of printing the name of the file at the top of the page and the page number at the bottom. If so, try the following procedure to use the WordPad applet instead.

Open the **HKCR\txtfile\shell** subkey and create new **Printto** and **Printto\command** subkeys. In the latter's (Default) Data column, enter the command line copied from the **Printto\command** subkey found under the **Wrifile\Shell** subkey. After doing this, any **TXT** file dragged to a printer icon will be opened and printed via the WordPad applet, thus eliminating NotePad's printed header and footer. When you do want NotePad's header and footer to appear on the printed page, use the Context menu's regular **Print** option instead of the drag-and-drop method.

Refer to "Add Missing Option" in the "Context Menu" section earlier for information about adding this option to the menu.

Internet Explorer Start Page

After a successful Internet logon, the Microsoft Internet Explorer displays the page specified in the following subkey's Contents pane, as shown here:

HKEY_CURRENT_USER\Software\Microsoft\Internet Explorer\Main

Name	Data
StartPage	"http://www.msn.com"
(or)	"http://www.home.msn.com"

To specify some other default page, edit the Data column entry as required.

MS Plus! Features

If MS Plus! is installed, some of its features may be temporarily disabled as described here.

Remove Plus! Tab

To prevent compulsive Desktop decorators from making various icon and visual setting changes, search the **HKCR\CLSID** key section for **plustab.dll** in the Data column. Export the {41E300E0... key and then delete it from the Registry. This action removes the **Plus!** tab, which ordinarily appears on the Display Properties sheet. To make subsequent revisions, import the key back into the Registry.

Drag Full Windows Feature

A **Show window contents while dragging** option is available in the Visual settings area of the **Plus!** tab described earlier. If its box is checked, the full content of a Desktop window is seen as the window is dragged across the screen, and the following entry appears in the indicated Registry key:

```
HKEY_CURRENT_USER\Control Panel\desktop
```

Name	Data
DragfullWindows	"1"

In some early beta versions of Windows 95, the entry was all that was required to implement this feature, which was, however, disabled in the retail version. Now, the feature requires the presence of the MS Plus! **COOL.DLL** file in the **C:\Windows\System** folder and the following additional entry, which is written into the Registry as MS Plus! is installed.

```
HKEY_LOCAL_MACHINE\SOFTWARE\Microsoft\Plus!\Setup
```

Name	Data
cool.dll	""

If either the file or this entry is missing, the DragFullWindows entry has no effect, which may explain why it won't work unless MS Plus! is installed.

"My Computer" Label in Registry

As shown in Figure 5.21 (and in many other illustrations throughout the book), the six Registry Hkeys appear beneath a computer icon labeled **My Computer,** and that phrase also appears in the Status Bar at the bottom of the Registry Editor window.

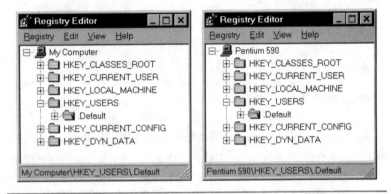

Figure 5.21 *The "My Computer" label at the top of the* **HKEY** *tree can be revised by editing the* **REGEDIT.EXE** *file.*

Because this label is embedded in the **REGEDIT.EXE** file, you'll need to edit that file if you want to change My Computer to something more descriptive of your own system. If so, make a copy of **REGEDIT.EXE** and then search for the phrase, which begins at either byte 0001A3BA (original version of Windows 95) or 00016C1A (some OEM versions). In either case, it is written in Unicode format as shown here:

```
M.y. .C.o.m.p.u.t.e.r.    4D 00 79 00 20 00 43 00 6F 00 6D 00 70 00 75 00
                          74 00 65 00 72 00
```

Note that each letter is followed by a null character (ASCII 00), and that style must be preserved when changing My Computer to a new label.

WARNING

This edit serves no purpose other than cosmetic and should only be attempted by the user who is comfortable editing a binary file. The hexadecimal addresses cited have been observed on several systems, but are subject to change.

Numeric Tails

Although Windows 95 supports long filenames, it always creates a conventional, or "8.3," filename for the sake of backward compatibility. The 8.3 name consists of the first six letters of the long filename, a tilde character, a number, the period separator, and the first three characters of the extension, as shown by these few examples:

Long Filename	8.3 Filename	"Friendly" 8.3 Filename
RatherLongLetter.Document	RATHER~1.DOC	RATHERLO.DOC
RatherEXTENDED.Doc	RATHER~2.DOC	RATHEREX.DOC
RatherLongmemo.txt1	RATHER~1.TXT	RATHERLO.TXT
RatherLongmemo.txt2	RATHER~2.TXT	RATHER~1.TXT
RatherLongmemo.txtfile	RATHER~3.TXT	RATHER~2.TXT

As the second column shows, a numeric tail (~1, ~2, etc.) is used to truncate a long filename to 8.3 format, even if the first eight characters of that name would be sufficient to distinguish one file from another.

An optional "friendly" naming convention may be used instead, in which the "~1" numeric tail is not used for the *first* occurrence of a long filename. Instead, the 8.3 name simply takes the first eight characters of the long filename, as shown by the examples in the third column. However, if the first eight characters are not sufficient to distinguish one name from another, then a "~1" tail is applied to the second file, a "~2" to the third, and so on.

To enable this feature, add the following entry as a binary value to the **control** subkey's Contents Pane.

HKEY_LOCAL_MACHINE subkey	Name	Data
System\CurrentControlSet\control	NameNumericTail	0

WARNING

In practice, this function may be more of a bug than a feature, because some Windows 95 applications will not recognize a long folder or filename created without the "~x" tail. Also, the numeric tail serves as an obvious visual clue that a long filename exists.

ScanDisk Bad-Cluster Check

If a cluster had been marked as bad, ScanDisk for Windows 95 makes no attempt to repair it. The procedure described here forces ScanDisk to test and attempt to repair such clusters, although there is some risk in doing so. For example, some applications mark a cluster as bad even if it is not, in order to prevent other applications from accessing those clusters. Or a marginal cluster may have been marked as bad by some other utility, yet a ScanDisk test might not detect the same problem. In these or similar cases, if ScanDisk reset the bad-cluster mark, there could be subsequent problems with data corruption. However, if there is a valid reason for forcing ScanDisk to retest bad clusters, you can force it to do so by opening the following Registry key to display the Contents Pane entry, which is also listed here:

```
HKEY_CURRENT_USER\Software\Microsoft\Windows\CurrentVers
ion\Applets\Check Drive
```

Name	Data	
Change:	Settings	*aa bb cc* 00
To read:	Settings	*aa bb cc* 04

By changing the final hexadecimal value from 00 to 04, ScanDisk will retest all clusters formerly marked as bad. If an apparently good cluster is discovered, ScanDisk will offer three options: leave it as is, mark it as good, or retest it. In case of doubt, choose the latter option. If the retest passes, the cluster is probably good.

CHAPTER 6

Backup, Restore, and Compare

There are quite a few methods that can be used to back up the Registry files and then restore them later. To present a reasonably concise (and consecutive) overview of the options available, backup procedures are described first, followed by a companion section in which the associated restore procedures are described. In a few cases, a section may visit, or revisit, information found in other chapters. However, this chapter reviews only those aspects relevant to backup and restore procedures. The chapter concludes with a description of various techniques that can be used to compare any two Registry files.

Registry Backup Procedures

Keep in mind that even the finest Registry backup is only as good as the day on which it was made. It's therefore worthwhile to make a complete Registry backup by whatever means is most convenient immediately before doing anything serious to the Registry.

Table 6.1 lists the files associated with some of the backup utilities described in this section.

Table 6.1 *Name and Location of Registry Backup Utility Files*

Application and Files	Location *	Purpose
Registry Editor		
REGEDIT.EXE	C:\Windows	executable file
SYSTEM.DA0 †	C:\Windows	SYSTEM.DAT backup
USER.DA0 †	C:\Windows	USER.DAT backup
Configuration Backup Utility		
CFGBACK.EXE	x:\other\Misc\Cfgback	executable file
REGBACKx.RBK	C:\Windows	full Registry backup ‡
REGBACK.INI	C:\Windows	backup file record
Emergency Recovery Utility		
ERU.EXE	x:\other\Misc\Eru	executable file
SYSTEM.D_T	A: or C:\ERD	SYSTEM.DAT backup
USER.D_T	A: or C:\ERD	USER.DAT backup

* x:= CD-ROM drive letter.

†Created as part of normal Windows 95 startup (not by **REGEDIT.EXE**).

‡Compressed file contains complete **SYSTEM.DAT** and **USER.DAT**.

The Backup .DA0 Registry Files

As noted in Chapter 4 and elsewhere, Windows 95 makes its own Registry backup files, which it names **SYSTEM.DA0** and **USER.DA0**. The files are used by Windows 95 itself if the associated **SYSTEM.DAT** and **USER.DAT** files require replacement and are rarely needed by the user. Nevertheless, they can be copied by the user during a restore operation, as described in the "Restore" section later in this chapter.

Real-Mode Registry Editor

The use of the Registry Editor for real-mode troubleshooting is covered in some detail in Chapter 7. However, beyond its use as a troubleshooting device, it can also be used for routine Registry backups, as described here. For example, exit Windows 95 and type one of the following lines at the MS-DOS prompt to back up all or part of the Registry to a file named *filename*.**REG**:

```
REGEDIT /E filename.REG
REGEDIT /E filename.REG   HKEY_CLASSES_ROOT
REGEDIT /E filename.REG   HKEY_CLASSES_ROOT\batfile
```

In each case, the specified key and all its subkeys are backed up to the *filename*.**REG** file. If no **HKEY** is specified, the entire contents of the Registry are backed up.

The Registry Editor's Export Option

This is perhaps the simplest of all backup procedures. Just highlight any element in the Registry Editor's Key Pane, open the Registry menu, select **Export Registry File**, give the file a name, and click the **Save** button to complete the backup. For example, highlight one of the following Key Pane items to back up the indicated section of the Registry:

Highlight:	To backup:
My Computer	The full Registry
HKEY_CLASSES_ROOT	**HKEY_CLASSES_ROOT** and its subkeys only
HKEY_USERS\.Default\AppEvents	The **AppEvents** subkey and its subkeys only

Don't forget to use this convenient backup medium to save a copy of any key structure before editing it.

Configuration Backup Utility

There is a Registry backup and restore utility in the **Other\Misc\Cfgback** folder on the Windows 95 CD-ROM (**CFGBACK.EXE** and **CFGBACK.HLP**).

Double-click on the file to open the Microsoft Configuration Backup window shown in Figure 6.1, then click the **Continue** button to read each of three informational screens. (The **Close** button in the upper right-hand corner has no effect on these screens.) Figure 6.2 shows the Configuration Backup dialog box, which appears next (the **Close** button is once again enabled). Give the proposed backup a distinctive name and click the **Backup** button to begin the process. To make sure you're really serious about all this, the confirmation box shown in the figure inset appears. Click **Yes** to begin the backup. The two Working... and Configuration Backup windows shown in Figure 6.3 report the status of the procedure.

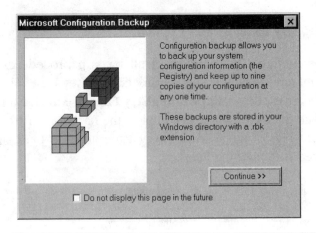

Figure 6.1 *One of several informational screens that introduce the Microsoft Configuration Backup utility. If the **Do not display** box is checked, a* Show=0 *line in the* [StartWizard] *section of **REGBACK.INI** disables these screens.*

The Configuration backup utility creates a single **C:\Windows\ REGBACK***x***.RBK** file, where *x* is the number of the backup. The file contains a complete compressed copy of the current **SYSTEM.DAT** and **USER.DAT** files. In addition, a **C:\Windows\REGBACK.INI** file records the following information for up to nine backup files (and at the same time, proves that Windows 95 *does* use **INI** files):

REGBACK.INI	**Comments**
[File1]	
FileDescription=Backup-1	selected Backup Name (Figure 6.2)
Date=9/22/96	date of first backup
[File2]	
FileDescription=Backup-2	
Date=9/25/96	date of second backup
...and so on, through [File9]	
[StartWizard]	
Show=1	1 = display opening windows (Figure 6.1)

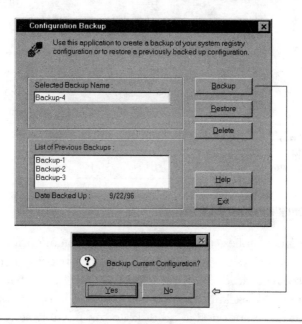

Figure 6.2 *The Configuration Backup dialog box is used to back up and restore the Registry. Enter an appropriate name in the Selected Backup Name box and click the **Backup** button to display the confirmation dialog box seen in the inset. The **Restore** and **Delete** buttons are enabled if a backup listed at the bottom of the screen is highlighted. An erroneous check box (not seen here) may appear next to the backup date; if so, just ignore it.*

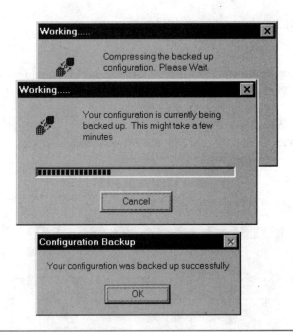

Figure 6.3 *These two Working dialog boxes report the progress of the backup procedure. The Configuration Backup box appears if the backup concludes successfully.*

Emergency Recovery Utility

As its name implies, the utility is primarily intended for use in restoring your system configuration should it become necessary to do so. The accompanying **ERU.TXT** file states that "...the recommended [backup] location is a bootable floppy in drive A" but does not point out that no diskette can possibly store all the files that need to be saved. For example, Figure 6.4 shows a typical list of files to be saved; you may notice that the critical **SYSTEM.DAT** file is missing. Click the **Custom** button to find out why. As shown in Figure 6.5, there is not enough room on the diskette to store all the files, and therefore **SYSTEM.DAT** has been omitted from the check list. In order to check its box, some other files will have to be unchecked to make room for it.

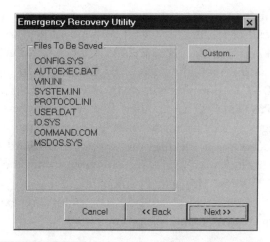

Figure 6.4 *If the Emergency Recovery Utility is used to create a recovery diskette, the list of saved files probably does not include the* **SYSTEM.DAT** *file due to space limitations on the diskette.*

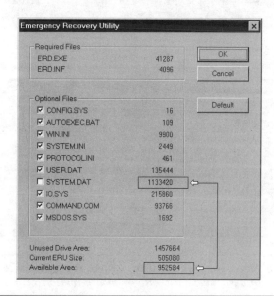

Figure 6.5 *Under default conditions, the Optional Files check list usually precludes the inclusion of* **SYSTEM.DAT**, *because its file size exceeds the diskette's available space.*

You may therefore prefer to back up all the files to a **C:\ERD** folder instead of to diskette. Or for subsequent Registry recovery only, back up just the **SYSTEM.DAT** and **USER.DAT** files to diskette. As another alternative, back up everything except **SYSTEM.DAT** to one diskette, then rerun the applet and back up only **SYSTEM.DAT** to another diskette. In any case, one of the messages shown in Figure 6.6 will appear at the conclusion of the procedure. If the files are saved to the hard disk, the message concludes with "It is not advisable to run the recovery while in Windows." (It's actually impossible.) If you try to do so, a message directs you to "re-boot computer and execute the program from a command-line prompt."

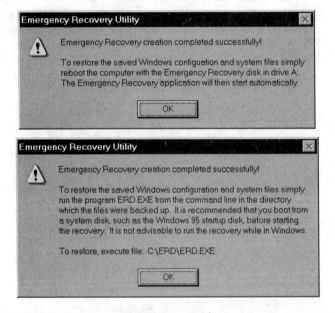

Figure 6.6 *Messages seen at the completion of the successful completion of a recovery diskette or of a backup to a folder on the hard drive.*

Figure 6.7 shows a typical directory listing if an incomplete file set is saved to a diskette in drive **A**. Refer to "Emergency Recovery Utility" in the "Recovery" section later for information about restoring the Registry files from the recovery diskette or hard drive folder.

```
A:dir

 Volume in drive A has no label
 Volume Serial Number is 1E48-9241
 Directory of A:\par
AUTOEXEC BAT          7  07-23-95 12:05p AUTOEXEC.BAT
AUTOEXEC B_T        109  06-05-95  5:23p AUTOEXEC.B_T
COMMAND  C_M     93,766  05-22-96  9:35p COMMAND.C_M
CONFIG   S_S         16  06-16-96  2:45p CONFIG.S_S
ERD      EXE     41,287  05-22-96  8:38p ERD.EXE
ERD      INF        333  07-23-95 12:06p ERD.INF
IO       S_S    215,860  05-22-96  9:34p IO.S_S
MSDOS    S_S      1,692  07-19-95  4:41p MSDOS.S_S
PROTOCOL I_I        461  07-19-95  4:41p PROTOCOL.I_I
SYSTEM   I_I      2,449  07-23-95 12:04p SYSTEM.I_I
USER     D_T    135,444  07-23-95 12:04p USER.D_T
WIN      I_I      9,900  07-22-95  6:28p WIN.I_I
        12 file(s)       501,324 bytes
         0 dir(s)        952,832 bytes free
```

Figure 6.7 *A typical directory listing from an emergency recovery diskette.*

Third-Party Backup Utilities

In case of doubt, check the User's Guide (if any) for specific information about how the utility handles Registry backup issues. Because there are about as many variations in this procedure as there are software packages, this aspect of Registry backups is not covered in this book. In most cases, though, one of the backup procedures described here should do the job if the third-party utility doesn't.

Print (Hard-Copy) Backups

A paper copy of a Registry key structure is often handy for reference purposes, but remember that the size of a complete **HKEY** printout may range from about 50 pages to more than 1000. You may therefore want to print out only that portion of the Registry that contains the key structure you want to examine closely. In any case, refer to "Registry Print Jobs" in Chapter 4 and Table 4.3 in the same chapter, before hitting the **Print** button. For comparison purposes, Table 6.2 shows the format of a Registry subkey printed to a **PRN** file and as exported to a Registry (**REG**) file.

Table 6.2 *Comparison of Registry Editor and Registry Files* *

TestKey in Registry Editor window

Name column	Data column
(Default) †	(value not set)
NumericData 1	34 45.62 23 21 57 40
NumericData 2	0x0045da9f (4577951)
SampleText	"This is a sample."
SampleWithNumbers	"3.14 + 2"

TestKey printed to TESTKEY.PRN file

[HKEY_USERS\TestKey] ‡
SampleText=This is a sample.
NumericData 1=34,45,62,23,21,57,40
SampleWithNumbers=3.14 + 2
NumericData 2=9f,da,45,00 §

TestKey exported to TESTKEY.REG file

REGEDIT4

[HKEY_USERS\TestKey] ‡
"SampleText"="This is a sample."
"NumericData 1"=hex:34,45,62,23,57,40
"SampleWithNumbers"="3.14 + 2"
"NumericData 2"=dword:0045da9f

*See Figure 4.9 for another comparison.

†Lines following (Default) listed alphabetically.

‡Line sequence indicates order in which entries were made.

§Note reverse order of hexadecimal number sequence.

Registry Restore Procedures

After using any of the backup procedures just described, refer to the appropriate procedure in this section for information about restoring the backed up data.

The Backup .DA0 Registry Files

In most cases, there is no reason for the user to access the hidden **SYSTEM.DA0** and **USER.DA0** files in the **C:\Windows** folder, as these files are reserved for use by Windows 95 itself if it becomes necessary to perform an automatic Registry restore operation as part of system startup. Because both files are rewritten every time Windows 95 successfully opens, they represent the last configuration known to be good.

If something unfortunate happens during the current session and you suspect that the current Registry has been damaged, you may want to exit Windows 95 to the MS-DOS mode, erase the current Registry files, and replace them with copies of the **DA0** backups. Doing so obviates depending on Windows 95 to take care of this the next time it opens. Although Windows 95 usually gets it right, there are times when a minor Registry problem can escape notice, in which case the slightly defective files would be copied to their **DA0** backups. If you think this is a possibility, use the procedure given here to restore the Registry from the backup files. At the MS-DOS command prompt, type the following lines:

DOS command	Comments
`attrib -s -h -r *.da?`	Clear attributes from Registry files
`erase SYSTEM.DAT`	Erase suspected bad **SYSTEM.DAT**
`erase USER.DAT`	Erase suspected bad **USER.DAT**
`copy SYSTEM.DA0 SYSTEM.DAT`	Create new **SYSTEM.DAT** from backup
`copy USER.DA0 USER.DAT`	Create new **USER.DAT** from backup
`attrib +s +h +r SYSTEM.DA?`	Reset **SYSTEM.DAT**, **SYSTEM.DA0** attributes
`attrib +s +h +r USER.DA?`	Reset **USER.DAT**, **USER,DA0** attributes

Reboot the system to reopen Windows 95 in the last known valid configuration.

Real-Mode Registry Editor

After exiting Windows 95 to the MS-DOS command mode, type one of the following command lines to restore all or part of the Registry:

```
REGEDIT /C filename.REG
REGEDIT filename.REG
```

As will be noted again in Chapter 7, use the **/C** switch with extreme care, because it replaces the entire current Registry with the backup version in the *filename.***REG** file. If that file is indeed a valid version of the full Registry, no harm is done. Otherwise, you're in trouble.

If **REGEDIT** is followed by the name of a file and no command-line switches, then the subkeys specified in *filename*.**REG** are imported without affecting any other part of the Registry.

Registry Editor's Import Option

To restore a previously backed up section of the Registry, open the Registry Editor's Registry menu, select **Import Registry File**, enter (or highlight) the filename to be imported, and click the **Open** button to complete the procedure.

Remember that the **Import** option does not necessarily execute a complete replacement of an existing key structure with a new one. Refer to "Import Operations" in Chapter 4 for details about the effect of the **Import** option on the existing key structure.

Configuration Restore Utility

The **CFGBACK.EXE** utility described in the "Configuration Backup Utility" section is also used to restore the Registry from the compressed **REGBACK*x*.RBK** file created during the backup operation. Double-click on the file icon to open the Configuration Backup dialog box shown earlier in Figure 6.2. Then highlight one of the previous backups to enable the **Restore** and **Delete** buttons. Click on the former to begin the restoration, during which the Working... dialog boxes shown in Figure 6.8 appear, followed by this message at the conclusion of a successful operation:

```
Your Configuration has been successfully restored. You
need to shut down and restart the computer for your
changes to take effect. Do you want to restart the
computer now?
```

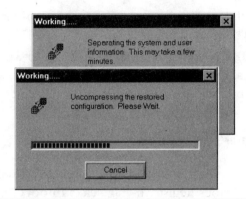

Figure 6.8 *During the Registry restoration process, the* ***REGBACKx***
.RBK file is first uncompressed, and then the ***SYSTEM.DAT*** *and*
USER.DAT *file data are separated so that both files may be created.*

Despite the "shut down" phrase, it is only necessary to exit and
restart Windows 95, which is what happens when you click **Yes**.

Configuration Restore Warning

Pay attention to the following message, which appears before
the restoration begins:

```
WARNING: You have chosen to replace your current
configuration with the backed-up one. Restore Selected
Configuration?
```

As the message points out, the configuration restore operation is in
fact a Registry *replacement* procedure. That is, the current Registry
will be deleted and replaced by the backed-up version, and
therefore key structures that exist in the current Registry but not in
the backup copy will be gone forever. If there is a key structure that
you want to preserve, export it first, do the restore procedure, and
then import the saved key structure back into the new Registry.

Emergency Recovery Utility

If you used the **ERU.EXE** utility described earlier to back up the **SYSTEM.DAT** and **USER.DAT** files, then exit Windows 95 or reboot to a command prompt. Type **ERD** to begin the file restoration. If you've created an emergency recovery diskette, boot the system with it and the **ERD** program (described later) is automatically executed. In either case, the Emergency Recovery screen shown in Figure 6.9 will be displayed. Select the files to be restored, then scroll down to the **Start Recovery** option and press **Enter** to begin the recovery.

If you've used **ERU.EXE** to back up just the **SYSTEM.DAT** and **USER.DAT** files, you may prefer to simply copy those files to the **C:\Windows** folder instead of running the **ERD.EXE** program. If so, note that the files are named **SYSTEM.D_T** and **USER.D_T** on the backup diskette or hard drive directory, and their system, hidden, and read-only attributes are not set. Copy the files into the **C:\Windows** folder, rename them with the correct **DAT** extension, reset the attributes, and then restart Windows 95.

The ERD.E_E File

A file with this name is in the **x:\other\Misc\Eru** folder on the Windows 95 CD-ROM disc, and is transferred to the **C:\Windows** folder along with the **ERU.EXE** file if the accompanying **ERU.INF** file is installed. When the Recovery utility (**ERU.EXE**) is used for the first time to create an emergency recovery (backup) diskette, the file is copied to that diskette (or to the **C:\ERD** folder) and renamed **ERD.EXE**, so it's safe to assume that the three-letter filename stands for *emergency recovery diskette*. Execute this file in MS-DOS mode to begin the Registry (and other) file-recovery operation.

```
Microsoft Emergency Recovery
Recovery Creation Date          Recovery Creation Time
09/26/96                                 13:42:31

        Please Select The Files To Recover

    *      MSDOS.SYS
    *      COMMAND.COM
    *      IO.SYS
    *      SYSTEM.DAT
    *      USER.DAT
    *      PROTOCOL.INI
    *      SYSTEM.INI
    *      WIN.INI
    *      AUTOEXEC.BAT
    *      CONFIG.SYS


    *      Start Recovery
    *      Exit

Use Arrow Keys to Move      SPACE> or <ENTER> to Select
```

Figure 6.9 *The MS-DOS mode Emergency Recovery screen.*

Third-Party Restore Utilities

As previously noted, third-party backup utilities are not discussed
here. And neither, therefore, are the equivalent restore utilities.

Registry Comparison Techniques

It's often useful to compare one version of a Registry file with
another: to discover the effect of a recent configuration change,
as part of a troubleshooting session, to verify that an indirect edit
(via Control Panel, for example) occurs where you think it does,
or simply to get a better understanding of what's going on under
the hood.

Of course, if you know (or think you know) exactly where a
change will take place, then the simplest thing to do is to open

the Registry Editor and check the location before and after the edit takes place. But if you need assistance tracking down the spot at which the action takes place, one or more of the following procedures may be of some assistance.

1.   Export the suspected key structure as **BEFORE.REG** prior to making any changes. If necessary, export an entire **HKEY**, but if possible export the smallest possible key structure to cut down the time it will take to make a post-change comparison.

2.   Take the action whose effect you want to investigate.

3.   Export the same key structure as **AFTER.REG** immediately after making the change.

Compare the size of the two exported files. If they are not identical, proceed to the "Word Processor File Comparison" section, which follows. Otherwise, keep reading here.

MS-DOS fc /B Command

If you suspect some action makes a minor change to the Registry, such as changing a flag from 0 to 1, open an MS-DOS window and type the following line at the command prompt:

```
fc /B BEFORE.REG AFTER.REG
```

This command line executes a binary (byte-by-byte) comparison and displays a list of all differences like that shown here:

```
000005F0: 44 52
000005F1: 6F 65
000005F2: 20 41
000015AA: 59 64
000015AB: 6F 20
000015AC: 75 4D
000026F3: 20 65
```

If the list is small and the file size is 64 Kbytes or less, refer to the "MS-DOS Debug Utility" section, which follows. Otherwise, refer to the "Norton Disk Editor" section later.

MS-DOS Debug Utility

Load either of the files into the debug utility (**C:\Windows\ Command\DEBUG.EXE**) and type the following command at the debug prompt (a hyphen):

```
d cs:xxxx
```

where *xxxx* are the last four digits of the eight-digit number cited earlier, plus hexadecimal 100. The addition is required because the debug utility begins at cs:0100, not CS:0000. Thus, to review the location at which byte 000005F0 changed from 44 to 52, type the following three lines in either column:

```
debug BEFORE.REG    or    debug AFTER.REG
d cs:06F0                 d cs:06F0       (to view byte 000005F0)
q                         q               (to exit Debug)
```

The ASCII text readout on the right-hand side of the Debug screen should reveal enough of the actual Registry content to pin down the location where the change took place. If necessary, press the **d** key one or more times to continue reviewing the Registry until you can make a positive identification. Once that's done, exit Debug, open the Registry, and proceed to the appropriate key to examine the area in context.

Norton Disk Editor

If the file is larger than 64 Kbytes, load it into the Norton Utilities Disk Editor (or similar) and scroll down to the eight-digit number cited earlier, but do not add 100 to it. Again, the right-hand side of the screen displays the ASCII text of the Registry, making it possible to identify the location where the change took place.

Word Processor File Comparison

If the **BEFORE.REG** and **AFTER.REG** files are quite large, of different sizes, or contain many differences (or possibly, all of the above), load either file into any Windows 95 word processor and use that application's **Revisions** option to find the places where it differs from the other one, as illustrated by this Microsoft Word for Windows version 7.0 example.

First, create the following two single-line files:

This is the file, before making a change.   Save as **BEFORE.REG**
This is the ile, after making a change.   Save as **AFTER.REG**

While viewing either file, open the Tools menu, select **Revisions**, and click the **Compare Versions** button. Type the name of the other file in the File name box at the bottom of the Compare Versions window and click the **Open** button. Depending on which file is on-screen, you will see "before" with a line through it (strikethrough font) and "after" as underlined, or vice versa. In either case, the strikethrough font identifies text that does not actually appear in the present file. The underlined text is part of the current file but does not appear in the other file. Figure 6.10 illustrates both examples. Don't forget to erase these test files immediately after you're done; they are not suitable for use in the Registry.

Assuming an actual Registry file is compared with another one, it's likely that the revised section or sections will be several pages into the body of the open document. It is therefore probably necessary to reselect the **Revisions** option on the Tools menu, click the **Review** button, and then click the **Find** button to locate the first revision. Click the **Find** button to move to the next revision, and so on.

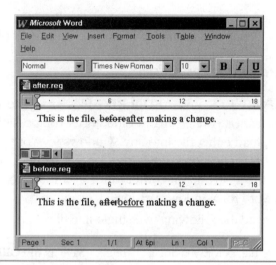

Figure 6.10 *In this much-simplified example of a Registry file comparison, the strikethrough font identifies text not actually present in the open file, while underlined text is present but does not appear in the other file.*

The description given here may vary from one word processor to another, but once you are familiar with specific file-comparison details, the **Revisions** option can be a powerful tool to help you review the differences between two versions of the same Registry key structure.

Word Processor Comparison Warnings

Keep the following points in mind before using a word processor to compare two Registry files:

> **Spell-Check**. As far as any word processor is concerned, a Registry file is just another conventional ASCII text file, with one important distinction: just about every word in it is misspelled. Before comparing Registry files, make sure automatic spell-checking is disabled. Otherwise the word

processor will spend much of its time pointing out all the errors and will probably be unable to complete the file comparison. Disable any other automatic "helpers" that may get in the way of the job at hand.

Comparison Time. If the Registry files are large, it may take several minutes to complete a comparison. Comparison time will also increase if a fairly large key structure has been inserted in—or removed from—one of the files, because the routine must compensate for the significant content shift.

File Save. Don't do it. As you exit the word processor, it will offer to save the compared files. If it does so, both may contain the strikethrough/underlined text, which renders the files useless for further Registry use. No harm is done if you plan to discard the files anyway, but otherwise make sure you exit without saving.

File Compare Utilities

The Norton Utilities File Compare applet (or similar) can also be used to compare two versions of an exported Registry file, as shown in Figure 6.11. In most cases, the files are displayed in separate windows for side-by-side comparison, with differences highlighted in a distinctive color. An optional ìShow Differences Onlyî mode may display only those lines that differ between files, but not lines unique to one file only. An additional option may summarize lines added, moved and deleted, and also identify which file is the newest.

Registry File Comparison Notes

Keep the following points in mind when comparing any two Registry files, regardless of the means used to make the comparison.

File Size Differences

If a Registry key structure is exported immediately before and after running a hardware or software setup procedure, there will be a significant difference in the before-and-after file sizes, due to the addition, revision, and possible deletion of various key structures. Although such a comparison is valuable to learn the precise effect of the setup procedure on the Registry, it will take a bit longer than a comparison made after a minor status change that does not effect the length of the exported section(s).

Irrelevant Revisions

Keep in mind that a file comparison may turn up revisions not directly related to the Registry action you are investigating. For example, if the same key is exported twice within a short interval of time, revisions will be found in subkeys like the two listed here:

Hkey and Subkeys	Changed subkey	Contents Pane
HKCU\Software\...	RecentDocs	MRUList=
HKLM\SOFTWARE\...	UuidPersistentData	"LastTimeAllocated"=

These revisions have nothing to do with a before-and-after Registry file comparison and should be ignored.

Word Processor vs. File Compare Utility

Since a good file-comparison utility is a single-purpose applet, it should be significantly faster than a word-processor in making Registry file comparisons. However, if a word-processor comparison reveals a difference between such files, it's reasonably easy to make a direct edit to the highlighted data, as required. By contrast, a file-comparison utility's Edit mode may load the file into Notepad or WordPad, and the user will then have to scroll through the file to find once again the spot that needs to be edited. It's not impossible to do that, but the word processor does make the job a bit easier. On the other hand, a differences-only display mode is usually unique to a file-comparison utility.

The serious Registry tweaker will probably want to use both methods of file comparison, due to their alternate manner of displaying the desired information.

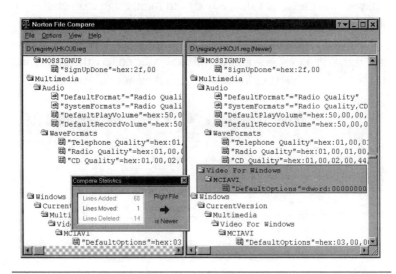

Figure 6.11 *In the Norton Utilities for Windows 95, version 2.0, the File Compare applet displays side-by-side comparisons of Registry (or other) files. In an actual File Compare pane, the area shown here in a shaded box would be displayed in a distinctive color. The* floating *Compare Statistics box summarizes the differences between the compared files.*

Registry Tracker Applet

As a variation on the Registry file comparison techniques described above, an applet such as the Norton Utilities Registry Tracker can display a detailed view of recent modifications to the Registry. For example, Figure 6.12 shows a conventional Registry Editor view of an Edit/command subkey under the

HKCR\htmfile key. Although the experienced user may recognize this as a non-default key structure, the Editor gives no evidence of when the key was added. By contrast, the Norton Registry Tracker window in Figure 6.13 shows two *snapshot* views of the same key. In the lower snapshot, each document icon with a plus sign indicates a new entry, while the icon with a minus sign indicates the previous value. Since both minus-sign icon entries are blank, the Edit and command key were apparently added shortly before the indicated date/time stamp. The upper snapshot shows that the Edit key's command subkey was edited the following day, when NOTEPAD.EXE was replaced by WORDPAD.EXE.

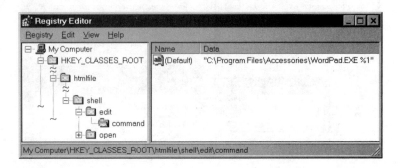

Figure 6.12 *This conventional view of a Registry subkey displays the current contents, but gives no indication of the key's recent history.*

The history record shown in the figure is maintained separately from the Registry itself, in a TRKDB.SDB file in the C:\Program Files\Norton Utilities\RegTrk folder.

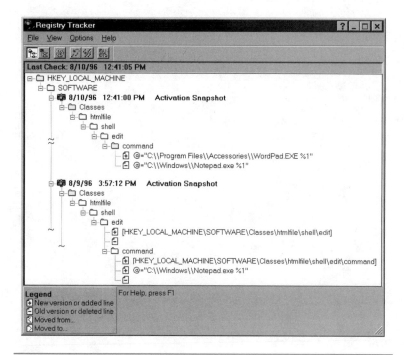

Figure 6.13 In this Norton Registry Tracker applet window, the
snapshot dated 8/9/96 indicates a recent new Edit and
command key structure. The 8/10/96 snapshot reveals that the
former NOTEPAD.EXE file has been replaced by WORDPAD.EXE.
These tracker snapshots retain the upper/lowercase style in
which the user made the edits.

CHAPTER 7

Troubleshooting the Registry

Because anecdotal evidence suggests that the Windows 95 Registry team may have included someone named Edsel Murphy, it is safe to assume that if anything can go wrong here, it will. And although all those anythings have not yet been uncovered, this chapter takes a look at a few that have turned up—often unexpectedly—while writing this opus. The chapter begins with a review of the Registry files and the Registry Editor itself. This is followed by some general problem-solving suggestions, and the chapter concludes with a list (or possibly, a litany) of specific Registry problems.

If a suspected Registry problem announces itself with an error message, you may want to refer to Chapter 8 first to see if that message is listed there. Otherwise, dig in here and look for either a specific solution or a technique that can be modified to resolve the problem.

Registry File Review

The Registry files were described in detail in Chapter 4 and listed in Table 4.1. For help in surviving a Registry troubleshooting session, that information is briefly reviewed here. For more information, refer back to Chapter 4.

File	Location	Attributes	Contents
SYSTEM.DAT	C:\Windows	S H R	**HKEY_LOCAL_MACHINE** key
SYSTEM.DA0	C:\Windows	S H R	Most-recent valid backup of **SYSTEM.DAT**
SYSTEM.1ST	C:\	S H R	**SYSTEM.DAT** copy, created at successful conclusion of initial Windows 95 setup procedure and not updated
USER.DAT *	C:\Windows	S H R	**HKEY_CURRENT_USER** key
USER.DA0 *	C:\Windows	S H R	Most-recent valid backup of **USER.DAT**
USER.1ST	(none)	—	There is no **USER.1ST** equivalent to the **SYSTEM.1ST** file

*On a system configured for multiple users, each **C:\Windows\Profiles\username** folder contains a **USER.DAT** and **USER.DA0** for that user. See Chapter 4 for additional details.

The .DA0 Files

These copies of the equivalent **.DAT** files were made the last time Windows 95 opened successfully and are therefore presumed to be valid replicas of the most-recent Registry.

Additional Backup Files

From time to time, Windows 95 may make its **.DA0** backups from marginal **.DAT** files that contain minor problems. Therefore, before doing any serious Registry troubleshooting, you may wish to make an additional set of backup files with say, **DA1** extensions for use in case the original **DAT** files and the **DA0** backups are both defective. If you follow the Windows 95 naming convention (**.DA1**, **.DA2**, and so on), the file attributes will be set and reset automatically if the **ATTRIBS.BAT** batch file (described later) is used.

The SYSTEM.1ST File

This file contains a copy of the **HKEY_LOCAL_MACHINE** key configuration only and is created as part of the initial Windows

95 setup procedure. The file is a "baseline" reference of the initial hardware configuration, but it is not updated as subsequent changes are made to the system.

File Attributes

Note that all these files have their system, hidden, and read-only attributes set and are therefore not seen in a conventional MS-DOS mode Directory listing.

In any Registry troubleshooting session, it often becomes necessary to copy, rename or erase one or more of these files; in order to do so, these attributes must first be cleared. The most convenient way to do this is in the MS-DOS mode for two reasons:

- After making any change, it will be necessary to restart Windows 95 anyway, so there's no real point to working on the files from within the Windows 95 GUI (graphical user interface).

- Although each file's attributes can be viewed via the file's Properties sheet, the System attribute cannot be cleared, as may be noted by the disabled **System** check box shown in Figure 7.1.

In the following discussion, whenever it is suggested that a certain Registry file be copied, renamed, or deleted, it will be assumed that its attributes have first been cleared so that the operation can be performed and that the attributes will be reset later. To do so, follow the instructions given here.

Clear File Attributes

At the MS-DOS command prompt, type one of the following lines, as appropriate:

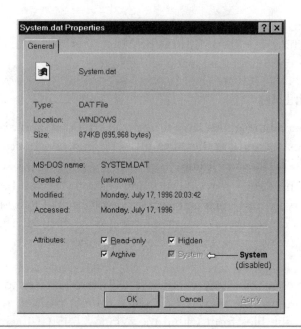

Figure 7.1 The status of the system attribute can be verified but not changed via the General tab on a file Properties sheet. To clear the attribute, type *ATTRIB filename.ext -h* at an MS-DOS command prompt.

Command Line	Clears attributes for:
attrib -s -h -r C:\Windows\SYSTEM.DAT	**SYSTEM.DAT** only
attrib -s -h -r C:\Windows\SYSTEM.DA?	**SYSTEM.DAT** and **SYSTEM.DA0**
attrib -s -h -r C:\Windows\USER.DAT	**USER.DAT** only
attrib -s -h -r C:\Windows\USER.DA?	**USER.DAT** and **USER.DA0**
attrib -s -h -r C:\Windows*.DA?	All files with any three-character extension (**DAT**, **DAO**, possibly others)
attrib -s -h -r C:\SYSTEM.1ST	**SYSTEM.1ST** (in **C:** directory)

Reset File Attributes

To restore the file attributes to their default state, retype the appropriate line, but replace each minus sign with a plus sign, as shown in these two examples:

Command line	Resets attributes for:
`attrib +s +h +r` `C:\Windows\SYSTEM.DA?`	**SYSTEM.DAT** and **SYSTEM.DAO**
`attrib +s +h +r` `C:\Windows\*.DA?`	All files with any three character extension (**DAT**, **DAO**, possibly others)

Use the second line (***.DA?**) with care, though; it will set the attributes for all files with a **DAT** extension, such as **C:\Windows\TTY.DAT** and any other **DAT** file that resides in the same folder.

Attributes Batch File

If you frequently use the **ATTRIB** command to clear and set file attributes, the following batch file automates the process:

ATTRIBS.BAT file	Comments (not part of batch file)
`goto %ATTRIBS%`	Go to :SET or to :CLEAR, as appropriate
`:CLEAR`	Attributes are currently cleared
`attrib +s +h +r C:\Windows\SYSTEM.DA?`	Set **SYSTEM.DA?** attributes
`attrib +s +h +r C:\Windows\User.DA?`	Set **USER.DA?** attributes
`set ATTRIBS=SET`	Set **ATTRIBS** to indicate set attributes
`goto END`	Bypass next section
`:SET`	Attributes are currently set
`attrib -s -h -r C:\Windows\SYSTEM.DA?`	Clear **SYSTEM.DA?** attributes
`attrib -s -h -r C:\Windows\User.DA?`	Clear **USER.DA?** attributes
`set ATTRIBS=CLEAR`	Set **ATTRIBS** to indicate cleared attributes
`:END`	End batch file

Before running the batch file the first time, type **SET ATTRIBS=SET** at the command prompt, assuming the attributes are indeed set. When the batch file is run, the SET environment variable is detected and program execution jumps to the :SET section, where the attributes are cleared and the environment variable is changed to CLEAR to indicate the new status. The next time the file is run, the CLEAR variable is detected and the attributes are again reset. At each subsequent run, the attributes toggle between set and clear.

Registry File Replacement

If there is a problem with the **SYSTEM.DAT** file, Windows 95 usually creates a new version by copying the backup **SYSTEM.DA0** file that, as noted earlier, was created at the conclusion of the most-recent successful startup and should therefore be the best-available recovery medium. There are times, however, when it copies the **SYSTEM.1ST** file instead, as, for example, if both **SYSTEM.DAT** and **USER.DAT** are corrupt. Although there is no explicit warning that **SYSTEM.1ST** has been used, the opening Desktop will revert to its original appearance, and some shortcuts may not function.

The general appearance of the Desktop should be sufficient warning that things are not quite the way they should be. But to verify the problem, exit Windows 95 and compare the size of the **SYSTEM.DAT** file with the **SYSTEM.1ST** file in the **C:** (root) directory.

On a typical system, the normal **SYSTEM.DAT** file is two to five times the size of the **SYSTEM.1ST** file. If, however, **SYSTEM.DAT** is very close in size to **SYSTEM.1ST**, that's a definite clue that it was recently reconstructed from **SYSTEM.1ST**. If you have a recent valid backup copy of your previous **SYSTEM.DAT** file on hand, you may want to erase this newly created copy and replace it with the backup version.

Although there is no equivalent **USER.1ST** file, it's a pretty safe bet that the existing **USER.DAT** file is also not up-to-date, and it should be replaced with a valid backup version.

Registry File Comparison

If a Registry key structure is suspected of being incomplete, damaged, or otherwise invalid, it may be worthwhile to check the same key on another system known to be in good working order. Depending on the specific key, it may be possible to export the valid key from machine A and then erase the invalid key on machine B and import the machine A version. Or course, this will not work if the key is associated with a specific hardware or software configuration that is not identical on both systems.

Other File Replacement

If any file cited in the Registry is damaged or missing, that file must be replaced with a valid copy. In the case of Window 95, MS Plus!, and many other applications distributed on CD-ROM, such files are compressed in one of the **CAB** (cabinet) files on the CD-ROM, so the file must first be found and then extracted, as briefly summarized here.

File Finding

Because each **CAB** file also contains an uncompressed list of its contents, Explorer can be used to locate the desired **CAB** file. Select the Tool menu's **Find Files** or **Folders** option and enter the following information in the indicated boxes:

Tab	Box	Enter:	Comments
Name & Location	Named:	***.CAB**	Search all **CAB** files
	Look in:	**x:\Win95**	CD-ROM drive letter, path
Advanced	Containing text:	**filename.ext**	name of desired file

Note that although a global file search (***.CAB** = all files with **CAB** extension) is valid, the **Advanced** tab does not support a global *text* search (***.TXT** = all files with **TXT** extension). To find all files with any extension, omit the period and enter the extension only. This finds all occurrences of the search characters, so it may also turn up erroneous hits. In most cases, however, you will be searching for only one specific file, and Explorer's find limitations should not be a problem.

File Extraction

If the Windows 95 PowerToys CabView utility (free download from `http://www.microsoft.com/WINDOWS/software/powertoy.htm`) has been installed, a **View** option should appear on any **CAB** file's Context menu. If selected, an Explorer window opens to display the compressed files within that **CAB** file. Highlight one or more files, open the Context menu, and select the single **Extract** option. Specify the location in which to expand the files and click **OK** to complete the process. If any selected file already exists in the specified location, it will be overwritten without a warning. You may therefore wish to expand the files into a **C:\TEMP** (or similar) location if you want to compare them with the existing version before making a final replacement.

If CabView is not available, use the Extract utility (**EXTRACT.EXE**) in the **C:\Windows\Command** folder instead. Open an MS-DOS window, type **EXTRACT** for a list of command-line switches, and then type **EXTRACT** again, followed by the necessary switches. For example, type the following line to extract **SHELL32.DLL** from an unknown **CAB** file:

```
EXTRACT  /A  x:\WIN95\WIN95_02.CAB  /E  SHELL32.DLL  /L  C:\TEMP
```

The command line shown here means: sequentially search all (`/A`) **CAB** files, beginning with **x:\WIN95\WIN95_02.CAB**, and extract (`/E`) the **SHELL32.DLL** file into the location (`/L`) **C:\TEMP** (where *x*:**WIN95** is the location of the **CAB** file folder). Each **CAB** file will be opened and searched, the desired file will eventually be found (it's in **WIN95_13.CAB**), and a copy will be extracted into the **C:\TEMP** directory. If the file already exists in the specified location, an "Overwrite?" prompt will appear.

Safe Mode and the CD-ROM Drive

If a troubleshooting session requires you to open Windows 95 in its Safe mode, remember that a minimal set of drivers are loaded and the CD-ROM drive will not be available. Therefore, if you need to run the Policy Editor utility (described in Chapter 5) or extract files from a **CAB** file on the Windows 95 CD-ROM, you'll need to boot with real-mode CD-ROM drive support in your **CONFIG.SYS** and **AUTOEXEC.BAT** files. To obviate the need to do this, copy **POLEDIT.EXE** and **ADMIN.ADM** to a diskette while the CD-ROM drive is available, for use later when it is not.

Registry Editor in Real Mode

The Windows 95 Resource Kit refers to "the Windows-based version of Registry Editor or the real-mode version on the Windows 95 emergency startup disk," which may suggest there is more than one utility with that name. However, the **REGEDIT. EXE** file on the emergency startup diskette is simply a copy of the same file in the **C:\Windows** folder, and either may be used for real-mode editing of the Registry.

To use the Registry Editor in real mode, either reboot the system to the command prompt or select the **Restart the computer in MS-DOS mode** radio button on the Shut Down dialog box. Then type **REGEDIT** at the command prompt. If you type this within an MS-DOS window during a Windows 95 session, the Registry Editor will open in its customary Windows 95 mode.

If a Registry problem prevents Windows 95 from opening in its graphical mode, then there is no alternative, and the real mode is the only way to go. In that case, the **REGEDIT** command-line switches are listed in Figure 7.2 and summarized here. But remember that in its real mode, the Registry Editor is quite fast—and very dangerous. While the correct command sequence can save the day, the wrong one can ruin it—and perhaps the next few days as well.

```
Imports and exports registry files to and from the registry.

REGEDIT [/L:system] [/R:user] filename1
REGEDIT [/L:system] [/R:user] /C filename2
REGEDIT [/L:system] [/R:user] /E filename3 [regpath1]
REGEDIT [/L:system] [/R:user] /D regpath2


  /L:system      Specifies the location of the SYSTEM.DAT file.
  /R:user        Specifies the location of the USER.DAT file.
  filename1      Specifies the file(s) to import into the registry.
  /C filename2   Specifies the file to create the registry from.
  /E filename3   Specifies the file to export the registry to.
  regpath1       Specifies the starting registry key to export from.
                 (Defaults to exporting the entire registry).
  /D regpath2    Specifies the registry key to delete.
```

Figure 7.2 Exit Windows 95 and type **REGEDIT /?** at the command prompt to display a list of switches that may be used with the Registry Editor in real mode. The /D switch is only available on OEM versions of Windows 95.

Real-Mode Command-Line Switches

To review the real-mode Registry Editor switches, type **REGEDIT /?** at the command prompt to display the list shown in Figure 7.2. For future reference, the switches are reviewed here in alphabetical order. In each example, type **REGEDIT** and a space, then replace the italicized *filename* or **HKEY** with the actual filename and/or HKEY and subkey that you want to process. Replace *filename*.**REG** with the complete path and filename, as appropriate.

> *filename*.**REG**—If no switch precedes *filename*.**REG**, that file is imported into the Registry without affecting any other part of the Registry.

> **/C** *filename*.**REG**—Copy. Use with extreme caution. The /c switch replaces the entire existing Registry with the *filename*.**REG** file. If that file is not a full version of a valid Registry backup, the accidental use of this switch can make subsequent repair work even more difficult. The Registry Editor does not check *filename*.**REG** for validity and gives no warning if the new Registry is invalid.

> **/D HKEY*subkey*—Delete. This switch is currently supported only in OEM versions of Windows 95; it can be quite helpful in removing a troublesome Registry subkey. Refer to "Alternate Real-Mode Recovery" for a typical example of its use.

> **/E** *filename*.**REG**—Export. There's no danger here. The /E switch simply exports the entire existing Registry into a file named *filename*.**REG**.

> **/E** *filename*.**REG** **HKEY\subkey**—Export. In this example, the export begins at the specified **HKEY** or **HKEY*subkey*.

> **/L:C:\\<*path*>\SYSTEM.DAT**—Location. Specifies the location of the **SYSTEM.DAT** file, but only if it is not in the **C:\Windows** directory.

> **/R:C:\\<*path*>\USER.DAT—USER.DAT** location. Specifies the location of the **USER.DAT** file, but only if it is not in the **C:\Windows** directory.

Attribute Reset. If any Registry file attribute was cleared prior to using the editor in real mode, be aware that REGEDIT resets the attribute(s) whenever it is executed. This point is mentioned here to avert the possibility of panic if it appears that the Editor has wiped out the editee.

The Windows 95 Resource Kit

The online version of the Resource Kit (in the **\admin\Reskit\ Helpfile** folder on the Windows 95 CD-ROM) may be some help in Registry troubleshooting sessions and is of course useful for problems not related to the Registry. For convenience, you may want to copy the **WIN95RK.HLP** and **WIN95RK.CNT** files into the **C:\Windows \Help** folder to make them available at all times.

Figure 7.3 shows the Find Setup Wizard dialog box that appears the first time the Find tab is selected. Note that **Minimize database size (recommended)** is enabled and—unless changed—will be applied when the **Next** and **Finish** buttons are clicked to create a **WIN95RK.FTS** (full-text search) file of slightly less than 1 Mbyte. If you subsequently need a more-comprehensive search database, click the **Rebuild** button and select one of the other options shown in the figure. The **Customize** button allows each of the following options to be enabled or disabled:

Include untitled topics   Display matching phrases

Include phrase searching   Support similarity searches

The new **WIN95RK.FTS** file will be almost 4 Mbytes in size; searches will take longer but be more comprehensive. If you decide searches are now too long or too comprehensive, click the **Rebuild** button again and restore the minimal database.

The **Find** tab is not always the most-reliable way to find something, though, due to its case-sensitivity. For example, a search for "HK" finds **HKEY_Current_User**, **HKLM**, and **HKR** and seven topics only, while "Hk" or "hk" finds all six **HKEYs** and 52 topics. Therefore, if you can't find a topic that should be in the Resource Kit, try entering it in all lowercase characters.

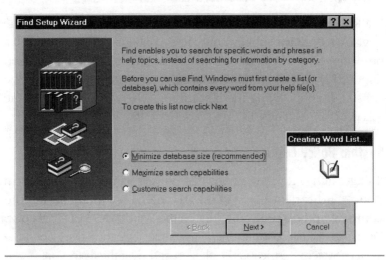

Figure 7.3 The Find Setup Wizard proposes a minimum size database. Accept or change the option, then click the **Next** and **Finish** (not shown) buttons to complete the operations. The Creating Word List... status window shown in the inset appears while the STF file is being created.

General Troubleshooting Techniques

This section describes some procedures that may be useful during a troubleshooting session, regardless of the specific nature of the problem.

If there's a Registry problem of uncertain origin on a system configured for multiple users, it may be worthwhile to exit and ask some other user to log on and check for the same problem. If it no longer exists, it is probably confined to the **HKEY_CURRENT_**

USER section of the Registry, which is different for each user. However, if the problem is common to other users too, then it may be traced to **HKEY_LOCAL_MACHINE** instead.

Restriction Recovery Procedure

If a Restrictions message precludes a certain operation, one of the Registry's **Policies** subkeys probably contains an entry that must be removed to clear the restriction. If this restriction has been imposed by a system administrator, then that person should be consulted about lifting the restriction. Otherwise, try one of the following procedures, listed in order of difficulty (easiest first).

System Policy Editor

If there are no Run restrictions that prevent its use, run the System Policy Editor utility (**POLEDIT.EXE**), which is in the **admin\Apptools\Poledit** folder on the Windows 95 CD-ROM disc. Or use a diskette copy if one is available. In either case, open the Shell or System Restrictions book icon and clear the restriction(s).

If you can't run the Policy Editor utility to remove the restriction, try the following procedures in the order listed here.

RECOVER.INF File. Create the **RECOVER.INF** file shown here:

```
[version]
signature="$CHICAGO$"

[DefaultInstall]
DelReg=Recover

[Recover]
HKCU, Software\Microsoft\Windows\CurrentVersion\Policies,
HKCU, Software\Microsoft\Windows\CurrentVersion\Policies\System,
HKCU, Software\Microsoft\Windows\CurrentVersion\Policies\Explorer, NoRun,
```

The three lines shown in the [Recover] section will do the following:

1. Delete the **Policies** key and all its subkeys, thereby lifting all restrictions.

2. Delete the **System** subkey under the **Policies** key to re-enable the Registry Editor.

3. Delete the NoRun restriction only (remove the **Run** command).

Write one of these lines (or similar) into the [Recover] section and then save the file as **RECOVER.INF**. Open its Context menu and select the **Install** option, which will delete the specified subkey or individual restriction.

If a restriction prevents you from following this procedure, then continue reading here.

Real-Mode Recovery

Create the following Registry file, whose two DWORD:00000000 lines will remove the restriction on running applications and re-enable the Registry Editor (RestrictRun and DisableRegistryTools, respectively).

```
REGEDIT4

[HKEY_CURRENT_USER\Software\Microsoft\Windows\CurrentVersion\Policies\Explorer]
"RestrictRun"=dword:00000000

[HKEY_CURRENT_USER\Software\Microsoft\Windows\CurrentVersion\Policies\System]
"DisableRegistryTools"=dword:00000000
```

Save the file as **RECOVER.REG**, restart Windows 95 in MS-DOS mode (reboot if necessary), log onto the **C:\Windows** directory, and type the following command line:

```
REGEDIT RECOVER.REG
```

This command imports the Registry file and clears the restrictions cited earlier. You can now open Windows 95 and run the Policy Editor or the Registry Editor to clear any other restrictions that are still in place.

Alternate Real-Mode Recovery

If your version of the real-mode Registry Editor supports the /D switch (see "Real-Mode Command Line Switches"), the following command line will delete the entire **Policies** key structure, thus removing all restrictions:

```
REGEDIT /d HKEY_CURRENT_USER\Software\Microsoft\Windows\
CurrentVersion\Policies
```

Safe-Mode Recovery

As one more alternative, if the Registry Editor itself has not been restricted by a DisableRegistryTools line, open Windows 95 in safe mode and run the Registry Editor to clear some or all restrictions.

Recovery on multi-user System. On a system configured for multiple users, each user's custom USER.DAT file is located in the C:\Windows\Profiles\ *UserName* folder, as described in the *Custom Profiles* section of Chapter 4. Therefore, if restrictions have been imposed on a specific user, those restrictions are written into that user's own USER.DAT file, not into the one residing in the C:\Windows folder. Although this file can be edited as described above, there are additional factors to be taken into consideration, as described here.

The System Policy File. On a multi-user system, user-specific restrictions are written into a system policy file, whose path and filename are probably similar to that shown here:

```
C:\Windows\CONFIG.POL
```

When the user logs on, the restrictions in **CONFIG.POL** are written into the Registry, thus resetting any restrictions that were lifted by editing the user's **USER.DAT** file during or after the previous Windows 95 session. Therefore, restriction recovery is a three-step process, as summarized here:

1.   Remove current restrictions from the **USER.DAT** file.

2.   Disable **CONFIG.POL**, so restrictions are not reset when user logs on.·

3.   Re-enable and edit **CONFIG.POL**, to permanently remove restrictions.

The following sections give more details about each step listed above.

1.   **Remove Current Restrictions.** Exit Windows 95 to MS-DOS mode—by rebooting if necessary. Log onto the appropriate **C:\Windows\Profiles*UserName*** directory, clear the USER.DAT file's system, hidden, and read-only attributes and copy it to the **C:** (root) directory (not into the **C:\Windows** directory). This is necessary so that the command described here will not exceed the 128-character limit. Then type the following as one continuous line at the command prompt:

```
REGEDIT /R:C:\USER.DAT /E C:\FIXIT.REG

HKEY_USERS\Software\Microsoft\Windows\CurrentVersion\Policies
```

The command tells **REGEDIT** that (/R) the **USER.DAT** file is in the **C:** directory, that part of it is to be exported (/**E**) into a new file named **FIXIT.REG**, and the specific key to be exported is **HKEY_USERS\...\Policies**. See *Real-Mode Command-line Switches* above for more details on these switches, and note that the *UserName*, which usually appears in the key path—**HKEY-USERS\John\Software\...**, for example—is omitted here.

Having done that, open **FIXIT.REG** in any ASCII text editor to review the Policies key and the subkeys which contain the current restrictions. Find the restriction(s) you wish to lift and change the expression following the equal sign from dword:00000001 to dword:00000000—or do a global search-and-replace if you want to clean the entire set of restrictions. Now type the following line at the command prompt to import the edited **FIXIT.REG** back into the **USER.DAT** file, thus clearing the restriction(s).

```
REGEDIT /R:C:\USER.DAT C:\FIXIT.REG
```

The **C:\USER.DAT** file is now clear of restrictions and ready to be copied back into its original location. To do so, clear its attributes and copy it into your **C:\Windows\Profiles\ UserName** directory where it overwrites the original version, then reset the attributes and erase the version in the **C:** directory (or not, if you think you might need it again sometime).

2. Disable **CONFIG.POL.** Temporarily rename the **CONFIG.POL** file as **CONFIG.OLD** to prevent the restrictions from being reimposed, and log on with your user name and password. Ignore the *Unable to update configuration* message and Windows 95 should open without the previous restrictions.

3. **Re-enable and Edit CONFIG.POL.** Rename **CONFIG.OLD** back to its original **CONFIG.POL** name. Since the file still contains the old restrictions, run the System Policy Editor to remove them, and thus prevent history from repeating itself.

DLL File Check

If you suspect a problem related to a **DLL** file, open the following Registry key and check the subkeys listed here:

```
HKEY_LOCAL_MACHINE\System\CurrentControlSet\control\
SessionManager
    CheckVerDLLs        KnownDLLs
    Known16DLLs         WarnVerDLLS
```

As noted in Chapter 3, a Windows 95 application is supposed to check its own **DLL** files against those listed here, but it (or you) may have accidentally replaced a valid **DLL** file with another version, usually—but not always—older. If you find a suspect **DLL** file listed in one of the keys, check the version, date, and location of the file on your system against the same file in the appropriate Windows 95 **CAB** file. If the latter is a later version, rename the current **DLL** file as *filename*.**OLD** and extract a fresh copy of the **CAB** file version into the same location, which is probably **C:\Windows\System**. Also review "Known16DLLs" in Chapter 3 for information about how Windows 95 searches for 16-bit **DLL** files.

Specific TroubleShooting Procedures

Each heading in this section describes a specific Registry problem and offers suggestions for resolving it. If you can't find the exact problem you've encountered, it's probably worth scanning the other problems listed because the same general solution may be appropriate for a related Registry problem.

Connect Remote Registry Option Launches Microsoft Network Sign-In Window

As noted in Chapter 4, the **Connect Remote Registry** option requires an NT or NetWare server to function. If you nevertheless attempt to use it on a Windows 95–only network system, and **Dial-Up Networking** is enabled, the action may open the Microsoft Network's Sign In window (assuming it's installed). When you click the **Cancel** button, an *Unable to connect* message appears. Click the **OK** button to clear the message, and don't try this again.

Contents Pane Headings Missing

If either the Name or Data heading is missing, it's probably off-screen to the left or right. If the Name column is visible and a horizontal scroll bar appears at the bottom of the Contents Pane, scroll to the right until the Data heading comes into view. Then drag that heading to the left until both Name and Data can be seen. If neither the Name nor the Data heading is visible, place the mouse pointer in the blank Title Bar and move it slowly to the left until a double-arrow pointer appears. Drag the pointer to the right and release it. The Data heading should now appear. Repeat the procedure to bring the Name column back in view.

As an alternative, close and reopen the Registry Editor. This should display "N..." and "D ..." in the Title bar. Drag the vertical lines next to each fragment to the right to display the complete heading.

Device Usage Section Does Not Appear on General Tab

If a hardware device is highlighted in Device Manager and the **Properties** button is clicked, the Device Usage section near the bottom of the **General** tab lists the available configurations. However, this section does not appear if the highlighted device is connected to a SCSI or other controller. If you want to edit a hardware profile to add or remove a device and its controller, highlight the controller and try again. Refer to "Hardware Profile Editing" in Chapter 5 if you need help doing so or if you want to remove one device from a specific hardware profile while leaving the controller itself enabled.

Desktop Object Won't Open

If a Desktop icon is present but double-clicking it has no effect, it's possible that the associated {**CLSID**} key or in-process server file is either missing or damaged. To verify this, find the object in

Table 7.1 and check the **HKEY_CLASSES_ROOT** key's **CLSID** key for the existence of the **{CLSID}** subkey listed in the table. Assuming the key itself is present, open its **InProcServer32** subkey and verify the filename for the **.DLL** file, which should agree with that given in the table. The file itself should be in the **C:\Windows\System** folder unless otherwise specified.

Table 7.1 *Desktop Objects and Associated CLSID Subkeys*

Object *	HKEY_CLASSES_ROOT\CLSID Subkey	InProcServer32
Briefcase, My	{85BBD920-42A0-1069-A2E4-08002B30309D}	SYNCUI.DLL
Computer, My	{20D04FE0-3AEA-1069-A2D8-08002B30309D}	SHELL32.DLL
Control Panel †	{21EC2020-3AEA-1069-A2DD-08002B30309D}	SHELL32.DLL
Dial-Up Networking	{992CFFA0-F557-101A-88EC-00DD010CCC48}	RNAUI.DLL
Printers †	{2227A280-3AEA-1069-A2DE-08002B30309D}	SHELL32.DLL
Inbox	{00020D75-0000-0000-C000-000000000046}	MLSHEXT.DLL
Internet, The	{3DC7A020-0ACD-11CF-A9BB-00AA004AE837}	SHDOCVW.DLL
Microsoft Network	{00028B00-0000-0000-C000-000000000046}	MOSSTUB.DLL
Network Neighborhood	{208D2C60-3AEA-1069-A2D7-08002B30309D}	SHELL32.DLL
Recycle Bin	{645FF040-5081-101B-9F08-00AA002F954E}	SHELL32.DLL

*Indented objects are in My Computer window.

†If **CLSID** key is damaged or missing, object may be accessible via Start menu, **Settings** option.

Expand a fresh copy of the same file from the distribution diskettes or CD-ROM disc into that folder, overwriting the current file if it is present. Then double-click the object again. If it still doesn't open and no other solution is apparent, you may have to uninstall and reinstall the object or rerun the Windows 95 setup procedure.

File Missing Problems

If a folder or file has been renamed or relocated, various "cannot find" messages may appear when an application requiring the renamed or relocated item is executed. Depending on specific circumstances, Windows 95 may be able to find the missing item or it may find the closest (but incorrect) match. If you recall the previous location and or name of the missing item, search the registry for occurrences of that string and make the necessary replacement edits. As an obvious example, if a new drive or partition shifts the CD-ROM drive from drive **D** to drive **E**, search the registry for all occurrences of D:\ and change them to E:\.

HKEY_CLASSES_ROOT Key is Empty

If this key does not show a plus sign next to it and the Contents Pane displays a one-line (Default) (value not set) entry, then the **HKLM\SOFTWARE\Classes** key is likewise empty, and therefore its contents were not copied into **HKCR** when Windows 95 started. To resolve the problem, import a valid copy of the **Classes** key into **HKLM\SOFTWARE**. This should restore the key structure in both locations. If only **HKLM\SOFTWARE\Classes** is restored, close and reopen Windows. Once both key structures are in place, press **F5** (if necessary) to restore all Desktop icons.

Menu Options

Problems related to various Windows 95 menus are described here.

Desktop Context Menu: An Expected Option does Not Appear on the Cascading New Menu

If an option that should appear on the menu is missing, refer to "Add Menu Option" in the "Desktop New Menu" section of Chapter 5 for help in placing that option on the New menu.

Disabled or Missing Option

Various Start menu options may be missing or disabled if certain restrictions have been set by the System Policy Editor. Refer to the "System Policy Editor" section of Chapter 5 if you need help verifying, or lifting, such restrictions.

Duplicate or Erroneous Option

Although possible, it's unlikely that a Windows 95 menu will display options that aren't supposed to be there, and if such options do show up, the most likely cause is an experiment that didn't work out as expected. For example, the source of an **Empty Recycle Bin** option on a bitmap Context menu can be traced to a **ContextMenu Handlers** subkey under the **Paint.Picture** key, as described in the "Context Menu" section of Chapter 5 and illustrated in Figure 5.12. In problems such as this, the solution is obvious: delete the erroneous key structure and the menu option will disappear.

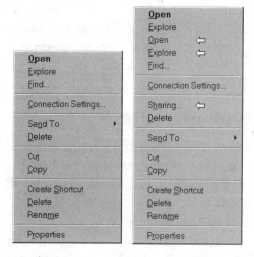

Figure 7.4 *The correct Context menu for the Microsoft Network is shown on the left, while the menu on the right shows duplicate* ***Open*** *and* ***Explore*** *options and an erroneous* ***Sharing*** *option. Such entries may be seen if an object normally associated with the Desktop is re-created in a folder.*

Figure 7.4 illustrates an even more unlikely condition, which at first may not be traceable to a recent customization session. Here, the menu shows duplicate action options (**Open**, **Explore**) appear, as well as a Context menu option (**Sharing**) not appropriate to the object, which in this example is the Microsoft Network.

This problem showed up after a new Microsoft Network icon was placed in a custom folder, as described in Chapter 5, and its {00028B00... subkey was deleted under the **NameSpace** key shown in Figure 5.20. Later, the icon was dragged back to the Desktop, where it now displays its own Context menu options and others associated with any folder, hence the duplicate and erroneous options seen here in Figure 7.4.

To verify and resolve a problem such as this, export the **HKCR\folder** key, then delete it from the Registry and recheck the Context menu. If the options are gone, re-import the deleted key and delete the object on the Desktop. Then re-instate the {00028B00... subkey under the **NameSpace** key and restart Windows 95. The object should again appear on the Desktop—this time with the correct Context menu.

System Policy Editor: File and Edit Menu Options are Disabled

This condition occurs if the System Policy Editor can't find the **ADMIN.ADM** file, which should be written into the **C:\Windows\INF** folder if the utility has been installed from the Windows 95 CD-ROM. If the Open Template File dialog box appears and **ADMIN.ADM** is listed in the File name area, click the **Open** button. Otherwise, click on the **down arrow** next to the Look In bar immediately below the Title Bar. Select the **C:\Windows\Inf** folder and highlight the **ADMIN.ADM** file if it is present. Otherwise, copy the file from the CD-ROM and try again. Or, if you want to run the Policy Editor from a diskette, make sure **ADMIN.ADM** is also copied to that diskette.

Missing Data after Importing Registry Script File

The most likely culprit is an editing error in the file. For example, if a bracket is missing from any key specification, that key will not be imported into the Registry. Despite the missing information, no error message is displayed, and the import operation concludes with a message that the operation was successful, even though it wasn't.

If you determine that a line is missing, either edit the appropriate line in the Registry script file to correct it or simply edit the Registry directly to fill in the missing information. Once that's done, re-export the corrected key if you think you might need it again in the future.

Missing Subkey or File Specified by Subkey

If a subkey and/or file specified in the Registry is missing but the function that one would associate with the missing element appears to be in good working order, that function is currently handled by some other means, and the "missing" element is simply a pointer to a file that may be installed in the future by an application or perhaps a Windows 95 upgrade. Refer to "{D3B1DE00...(Tools tab)" in the "HKCR\Drive" section of Chapter 2 for a specific example.

Post-Installation Problems

If any problem occurs immediately after installing some new software or hardware, and can't be resolved by non-Registry troubleshooting, it may be worthwhile to find the new device's **INF** file, which should be in the **C:\Windows\Inf** folder. If you're not sure of its name, the same file may be on the distribution diskette(s) or CD-ROM. Open the file for editing, find

the [Install] or [DefaultInstall] section and look for a DelReg=
line (if necessary, look for DelReg= in other sections too). Note the
name of the sections listed on every DelReg= line, and then review
those sections to see what Registry keys were removed when the
device was installed.

Properties Sheet Problems

If there is a problem with a Context menu's **Properties** option,
you may see an error message when that option is selected, or the
Properties sheet may open but be missing some tabs. In either
case, the problem can usually be traced to either a missing subkey
or a missing file. Follow the procedures described here to identify
the missing element; once you know what it is, either edit the
Registry to restore the key structure or expand a fresh copy of the
missing file.

Error Message

If a Properties not available message appears when you select the
Properties option, the culprit is a missing subkey related to the
object or a **DLL** or **CPL** file that supports the properties sheet
under a **Property SheetHandlers** key. To verify this, make a
note of the object whose properties are not available and then
find the **CLSID** key for that object.

For example, if the message appears when you attempt to
view the properties for any file with a certain extension, search the
HKCR key for the subkey with that extension name, open it, and
note the FileType listed in the (Default) entry's Data column. Now
search for that key. If you already know the FileType, proceed
directly to that key instead. Open the key and then open the
shellex key beneath it. This should lead in turn to a
PropertySheetHandlers subkey. If that key's Contents Pane
shows a text string in the (Default) entry's Data column, then a
subkey with that name should appear immediately below the

PropertySheetHandlers subkey and its Contents Pane will specify a **{CLSID}** subkey. Or if the Data column shows either (value not set) or an empty ("") string, then the subkey itself should be labeled with the **{CLSID}** subkey name instead. (See Figure 2.7 for examples of both subkey formats.)

Once you know the correct **{CLSID}** number, find the subkey whose name is that number, under the **HKCR\CLSID** key. That key's own **InProcServer32** (or similar) subkey will indicate the **DLL** or **CPL** file that supports the missing Properties sheet(s).

Find the **CLSID** key for that object. For example, if the message appears when you attempt to view the Recycle Bin properties, search the **HKCR** key Data column for **Recycle Bin,** and then open its **{645FF040...CLSID** key in the Key Pane. Open the **Shellex\PropertySheetHandlers** key and look for a subkey with the same **{645FF040...** name as the Recycle Bin itself. If any subkey in this structure is missing, write a new subkey to replace it.

Missing Properties Tab(s)

If only a **General** tab appears when a Context menu's **Properties** option is selected and no error message is displayed, there are two possibilities: either there are no other properties for the selected object, or a **PropertySheetHandlers** key or subkey is missing. In case of doubt, try to verify that a Properties tab is indeed missing. If it is, search for the **{CLSID}** key associated with the object and then for the **PropertySheetHandlers** subkey. If that key's Contents Pane shows a text string in the (Default) entry's Data column, then a subkey with that name should appear immediately below the **PropertySheetHandlers** subkey, and its Contents Pane will specify a **{CLSID}** subkey. Or if the Data column shows either (value not set) or an empty ("") string, then the subkey itself should be labeled with the **{CLSID}** subkey name instead. (See Figure 2.7 for examples of both subkey formats.)

Once you know the correct **{CLSID}** number, find the subkey whose name is that number, under the **HKCR\CLSID** key. That key's own **InProcServer32** (or similar) subkey will indicate the **DLL** or **CPL** file that supports the missing Properties sheet(s).

Erroneous Tabs

Figure 7.5 shows a valid Property sheet and the same sheet with erroneous **General** and **Sharing** tabs on it. Because the problem and its solution are described in "Duplicate or Erroneous Option" in the "Menu Option" section of this chapter, refer to that discussion for help resolving the problem.

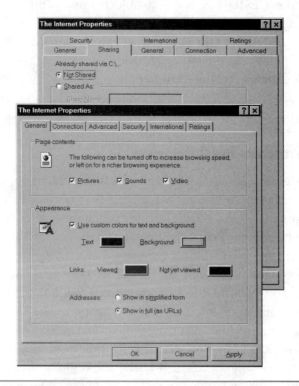

***Figure 7.5** The correct Internet Properties sheet appears in the foreground, while the sheet behind it shows a duplicate (and erroneous) **General** tab and a **Sharing** tab that does not belong here. Note that the **Sharing** tab displays conflicting information: that the Internet object is already shared (correct) and that it is not shared (incorrect).*

Recycle Bin Icons are Reversed

Windows 95 sometimes gets confused when a Desktop theme is changed. For example, if an MS Plus! theme is removed in favor of the Windows 95 default, you may see an empty icon when the Recycle Bin is not empty and vice versa. To correct this reversal, open the Registry Editor's Edit menu, select the **Find** option, check the **Data** box, and then search for **Recycle Bin**. In the Key Pane, click the **plus** sign next to the {**645FF040...** key and then open the **DefaultIcon** subkey that appears beneath it. Note the empty and full data entries, and swap the icon numbers at the end of each line. Or if a different file is used for each icon (**...Empty.ico, 0** and **...Full.ico, 0** for example), then swap the filenames too.

Registry Editor: Recent Edit Lost when Windows 95 Restarts.

As noted in Chapter 1 (*Contents Pane - INI File Comparisons*), some Registry configuration data may also be retained in an old **INI** file, which in most cases should be automatically re-written to track a Registry change. However, this may not happen if the Registry is directly edited by the user, in which case the entry in **WIN.INI** (typically) may be re-written into the Registry the next time Windows 95 starts, thereby nullifying the recent edit. If you suspect this is happening, re-edit the Registry, and then look in **WIN.INI** for a line that specifies the same item. If one exists, edit it to agree with the Registry entry. If necessary, search other **INI** files if **WIN.INI** itself is not the problem.

Registry Editor: Import Problem in Real Mode

If an error message indicates an unsuccessful import operation, there may not be enough conventional memory available for the Registry Editor to import a very large file into the existing Registry. If it's possible to do so, open Windows 95 and retry the operation. If the nature of the problem prevents the graphical user interface from opening, you may be able to edit the file you want to import, to cut it into smaller segments that can be imported sequentially. Or rename the existing **SYSTEM.DA?** and **USER.DA?** files, so that Windows 95 won't find them, and be forced to rebuild the Registry from the **C:\SYSTEM.1ST** file. Once the Windows 95 GUI successfully opens, use the Registry Editor's **Import** option to import the file into the Registry.

Registry Editor: Incomplete Command line in Real Mode.

If the REGEDIT command followed by various switches, paths and filenames exceeds 128 characters, it will not be possible to write the entire command. This might happen if you try to edit a USER.DAT file in a non-default location, as shown in this example:

```
REGEDIT /R:C:\Windows\Profiles\username\USER.DAT (and so on).
```

In this case, temporarily move **USER.DAT** into the **C:** (root) directory, and do the same for any file to be imported/exported, which should enable the command to be written in less than 128 characters. Move all files back to their proper locations after the operation is successfully completed.

Shortcuts Don't Work

If only one shortcut doesn't work, the problem is probably related to the shortcut itself and not to the Registry. However, if many shortcuts do not function properly, then follow the appropriate procedure given here to resolve the problem.

Dos Application Shortcuts Only

If every MS-DOS shortcut opens an Open with dialog box but other shortcuts continue to function properly, the problem is probably related to the **piffile** subkey. To verify this, select the Start menu's **Shut Down** option and select **Restart the**

computer in MS-DOS mode. If the Open with dialog box appears, then the **piffile** subkey is either missing or corrupt, and a valid version will have to be imported into the Registry.

Windows 95 Shortcuts Only

If DOS shortcuts continue to work but every Windows 95 shortcut doesn't, refer to one of the following procedures.

Shortcut Icon Opens an Open with Dialog Box

The most likely culprit is a missing or corrupt **HKCR\lnkfile** subkey. In case of doubt, exit and restart Windows 95. If there is a **lnkfile** problem there may be several Open with dialog boxes on the Desktop—one for each Windows 95 shortcut in the StartUp group. In addition, each such shortcut in that group will appear with a generic Microsoft document icon, and icon titles on the Desktop may show a **lnk** extension.

To resolve the problem, import a valid copy of the **lnkfile** key back into the Registry. Then place the mouse pointer on any clear Desktop area and press **F5** to refresh the Desktop and restore the shortcut icons to their previous condition.

Shortcut Icon Has No Effect

If nothing happens when a Windows 95 shortcut is double-clicked, then the problem is probably with the **Shortcut CLSID** key, which is {00021401-0000-0000-C000-000000000046}. In this case, no Open with dialog boxes appear when Windows 95 restarts, and the shortcut icons remain correct though still inoperative. In this case, import a valid copy of the **CLSID** key into the Registry.

All Shortcuts

If all shortcuts are inoperative, press **F5** to refresh the Desktop. Chances are, *all* document icons will change to the generic Windows 95 document icon, and the Recycle Bin and Network objects will display unlabeled folder icons. This indicates a larger problem with the entire **HKCR** key structure, which can be verified by attempting to restart the computer in MS-DOS mode.

Status Bar is Missing

The most likely reason is that it has been disabled. To restore it, either open the View menu and put a check next to **Status Bar** or press **Alt+V, B** (hold down **Alt+V** and repeatedly press **B** to toggle the Status Bar on and off).

System Policy Editor: Menu Options Disabled

Refer to "System Policy Editor" in the "Menu Options" section earlier.

Uninstall Problem

The list of Windows 95 software that can be uninstalled is displayed on the **Install/Uninstall** tab, and is maintained in the Registry as shown in Figure 7.6. In most cases, the **Uninstall** subkey key name bears a close resemblance to the name on the list. If not, a DisplayName entry in the subkey's Contents Pane will show the list name, as shown by the inset in Figure 7.6.

If a well-behaved (and listed) device is uninstalled, it should restore anything removed during its own setup procedure; if it doesn't, a general awareness of what's missing may help in the recovery procedure. If necessary, refer to the "Post-Install Problems" section earlier for help in reviewing the **INF** file associated with the uninstalled device.

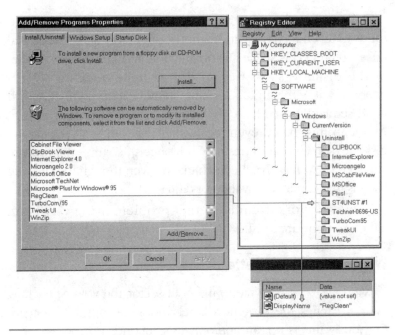

Figure 7.6 *The list of software that can be uninstalled is maintained in the Registry, where there is an* **Uninstall** *subkey for each item listed on the* **Install/Uninstall** *tab. In most cases, the tab name is reasonably close to the equivalent subkey name. The inset at the bottom of the illustration shows the Contents Pane for the uninformative* **ST4UNST #1** *key, which reveals its true identity.*

Volume-Tracking Problem

Occasionally, an application diskette will function properly at first, but later an error message warns that the diskette is invalid. Or there will be a prompt to insert the correct diskette, even though that diskette is in the drive and appears to be in good order. The problem may be caused by the Windows 95 volume-tracking system, which is briefly reviewed here.

When Windows 95 first accesses a diskette, it writes data into the 8-byte OEM field within the boot sector, at hexadecimal offsets 03-0A. This space customarily identifies the OEM supplier of the diskette software, but the volume-tracking system overwrites it with a unique volume identification number, which is subsequently used to verify that the current diskette is correct. Although this may prevent accidental disk writes to the wrong diskette, some applications may no longer recognize the diskette after the OEM field has been changed, even though the diskette itself is in fact neither invalid nor damaged.

Several workarounds to this problem are given here, although none are satisfactory for all situations.

Write-Protect the Diskette

If Windows 95 can't write to the boot sector, the volume-tracking system caches the diskette's label and serial number instead. Obviously this is not an appropriate solution if it is necessary to write to the diskette during normal operations. However, it is generally good operating procedure to write-protect any new application diskette, especially before running an install or setup procedure from that diskette. If it turns out to be necessary to write to that diskette, a message will let you know about it. In that case, you may want to review the rest of this section before continuing.

Edit the NoVolTrack Subkey

Figure 7.7 shows the Contents Pane for the **HKLM\System\CurrentControlSet\control\FileSystem\NoVolTrack** key, in which each entry shows a 10-byte hexadecimal string in the Data column. The first two bytes (underlined in the figure) are the offset at which the OEM field begins, which is usually at byte 3, or 03 00 in the reverse notation shown in the figure. The final eight bytes are the OEM field itself.

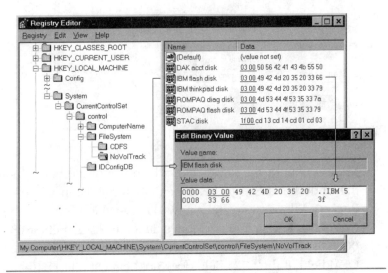

***Figure* 7.7** *The Windows 95 volume-tracking system will not overwrite a diskette's OEM field if that field is listed in the **NoVolTrack** key's Contents Pane. The underlined bytes indicate the file offset where the OEM field is located.*

When a diskette is first accessed, its OEM field is compared with those listed in the **NoVolTrack** key's Contents Pane. If a match is found, the field will not be overwritten by the volume-tracking system. Therefore, a diskette can be protected against a volume-tracking overwrite by writing its OEM field into the Registry *before* Windows 95 gets the chance to write to that diskette. If this is a consideration, use the following procedure to accomplish this:

1. Temporarily write-protect the diskette.

2. Use the Debug utility to view its boot sector. Assuming the diskette is in drive **A**, open a DOS window and type the boldface portions of the following lines:

```
C:\WINDOWS>debug            (to run the Debug utility in the
                             C:\Windows\Command folder)

-L CS:0100 0 0 1            (to load the boot sector from the
                             diskette in drive A)

-D CS:0100 010F             (to display the first 16 bytes)


0F64:0100  EB 3C 90 4D 53 44 4F 53-34 2E 30 00 02 01 01 00    .<.MSDOS4.0.....


-Q                          (to exit the Debug utility)
```

3. Make a note of the OEM field, which is indicated here by
    the underlined 8-byte hexadecimal string. Then use the
    Registry Editor to create a new binary-value entry in the
    NoVolTrack key. Use any convenient name, then enter **03
    00** in the Data column, followed by the eight bytes from the
    OEM field. If the OEM field does not begin at offset 3, then
    revise the first two hexadecimal characters as appropriate.

4. Close and reopen Windows 95.

5. Remove the diskette's write protection.

From now on, the diskette can be used for normal read/write
operations, and the volume-tracking system will not overwrite
the OEM field.

Get a New Diskette

The edit procedure just described won't work if the volume-
tracking system has already overwritten the OEM field. Assuming
you know what that field was, you could always restore it and
then edit the Registry, but who reads OEM fields before the fact?
The more likely resolution is to contact the software supplier and
get a new diskette. Or, depending on how alert their technical
support is, you might try asking for the OEM field over the phone.

CHAPTER 8

Registry Error Messages

This chapter lists some of the error messages that may be encountered as a result of problems related to the Registry, the Registry Editor, and the System Policies Editor. In most cases the message is accompanied by whatever information is needed to verify the source of the problem. A reference is frequently made to a troubleshooting section in Chapter 7, which may be consulted if additional information is needed to help resolve the problem.

The error messages listed in this chapter are organized into the following four sections:

Section	Error Message Seen:
Edit Session	When opening the Registry Editor, during an edit session, or when using the Configuration Backup/Restore utility.
Real Mode	When using the Registry Editor in real mode.
Startup and Exit	As Windows 95 opens or closes after an edit session.
Other	During session not related to the Registry, but nevertheless traceable to a Registry problem.

To help avoid wading through irrelevant messages, refer to the appropriate section for assistance in resolving the problem. However, if a message can't be found where you would expect it to be, try looking through the other sections before abandoning hope.

Because many messages begin with the magic word "Windows" followed by a rambling phrase, some messages have been edited here to focus on the subject of the error and not the perpetrator, as shown by these examples:

Windows cannot find ...	Cannot find ...
Windows encountered an error accessing ...	Error accessing...
Windows has detected a registry/configuration error.	Registry/configuration error.

In troubleshooting some of the error messages given here, don't forget to back up (export) a key before deleting it, unless you are certain it is no longer needed. By so doing, the key can be imported back into the Registry if required. Keep this suggestion in mind before reaching for the **Delete** option.

Remember that the **SYSTEM.DAT** and **USER.DAT** files and the **.DA0** backups have their hidden, system, and read-only attributes set. In order to copy, rename, or erase these files, the attributes must first be cleared. Refer to Chapter 7 if you need assistance doing so.

Edit Session Messages

The messages in this section may be seen only when the Registry Editor is in use or when using the Configuration Backup utility. If a Registry-related error message occurs at any other time, refer to one of the other sections of this chapter for assistance.

Backup cannot find this file (during a file comparison after backup). Refer to the "Errors occurred during this operation" message.

Cannot create key: Error while opening the key My Computer. This message indicates that attempting to create a new key immediately beneath "My Computer" at the top of the Registry Editor window is illegal.

Cannot edit (*Name entry in any Contents Pane*): Error reading the value's contents. If the Device Manager and Registry Editor are both open, this message may appear if you double-click on an item whose **Resources** tab is displayed by the Device Manager. To resolve the problem, toggle to a higher-level subkey and then back again. If necessary, select the View menu's **Refresh** option, and then try again. To avoid the problem in the future, close the Device Manager before trying to edit the Registry.

Cannot edit *name entry*. Error writing the value's new contents. If this message appears while editing Contents Pane data within the **HKDD** section, remember that this data is maintained dynamically and cannot be edited via the Registry Editor.

Cannot import *path \filename*.REG: ... Note the rest of the message and refer to the appropriate message continuation listed here.

Error accessing the registry. The most likely problem is the specific **HKEY** into which the specified file should be imported. In the specific case of the **HKEY_DYN_DATA** key, the message shown in Figure 8.1 serves as a reminder that its data is maintained dynamically by the system and cannot be imported by the user. For any other key, you might want to delete the existing key and then try the import procedure again.

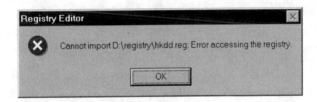

Figure 8.1 *This message warns that data cannot be imported into the **HKEY_DYN_DATA** key, which is dynamically maintained by Windows 95.*

The specified file is not a registry script. You can import only registry files. If you accidentally tried to import a nonvalid Registry file, that's the reason for the message. However, if the file is believed to be a valid registry script file (*filename*.**REG**), then perhaps it's damaged. Refer to "Creating a Registry Script File for Importing" and "REGEDIT4 File Header" in Chapter 4, then open the file in an ASCII text editor and make sure the file header is correctly written, and the general file format is correct. Edit the file as required (the most likely culprit is the file header), and then try again.

Cannot open DefaultIcon: Error while opening key. If this message appears during an attempt to view a **DefaultIcon** subkey under any **HKCR\AutoRun\x** key (where *x* is a number corresponding to a drive letter), there is probably no icon specified in the **AUTORUN.INF** file on the CD-ROM disc currently in the drive. To verify this, open the Registry Editor's View menu and select the **Refresh** option. The **DefaultIcon** subkey should no longer appear under the numbered key.

Cannot open HKEY_CLASSES_ROOT: Error while opening key. Open the View menu and select the **Refresh** option. If the plus sign next to the **HKCR** key disappears, then the **Classes** subkey under **HKEY_LOCAL_MACHINE\SOFTWARE** is probably missing or corrupt. To verify this, open **HKLM\SOFTWARE** and check for the existence of the **Classes** subkey. If it exists and appears to be in good order, then exit Windows 95 via the Shut Down menu's **Restart the Computer** option. The **Restart the computer in MS-DOS mode** option probably won't work.

If the **HKLM\SOFTWARE\Classes** key structure does not exist, then import a valid copy of this key into the Registry before restarting. In either case, the **HKCR** key should be rebuilt from the valid **HKLM\SOFTWARE\Classes** key when Windows restarts.

Cannot rename *keyname:* ... Note the rest of the message and refer to the appropriate message continuation listed here.

Error while renaming key (*or* value). If this message appears while editing a subkey in the **HKEY_DYN_DATA** section, it is because these keys cannot be edited via the Registry Editor.

The specified key name already exists. Type another name and try again. This one should be self-explanatory. If not, it's time for a break.

The specified key name contains illegal characters. The only illegal character seems to be the backslash (\). Try some other character instead.

The specified key name is too long. Type a shorter name and try again. The maximum length for a key name is 255 characters. If you need more space to express yourself, you should think about writing a book.

Errors occurred during this operation. Do you want to view them now? (Error log reports Microsoft Backup cannot find this file for files named **HKLMBACK** and **HKUBACK**). If the Microsoft backup utility is configured for full backup, these two temporary files are created in the **C:\Windows** folder, backed up along with everything else, then used during a restore procedure to rebuild the Registry. Because the files have no other purpose, they are erased from the **C:\Windows** folder when the Backup utility is exited. Therefore the error message will be seen if the utility is subsequently reopened for file comparison, because the files are no longer available for comparison. This is part of the normal backup/restore operation, and if no other cannot find message is seen, the backup set is presumed to be good.

HKEY_DYN_DATA Error Messages. If any message appears while editing this **HKEY**, the problem is related to memory—yours. That is, you forgot that this key should not be edited. The **HKDD** key information is dynamically written and continuously refreshed by the system and cannot be changed via editing.

Registry Editor: Registry editing has been disabled by your administrator. The message indicates that the **Disable Registry editing tools** restriction is enabled. Refer to "Restriction Recovery Procedure" in Chapter 7 if you need to re-enable this feature.

Registry 'Replace' function failed internally. Look for any hidden files. The Configuration Backup utility creates hidden files and subsequently erases them at the conclusion of the backup procedure. This message may occur during a restore operation if the files were not erased at the conclusion of the last backup. If so, use Explorer's **Find** option to search the **C:\Windows** folder for all ***.~~R** files and erase them. Or open an MS-DOS window and type the following commands:

```
attrib -h *.~~R      (to unhide the hidden temporary files)
erase *.~~R          (to erase them)
```

Now try the restore operation again.

Topic does not exist. Contact your application vendor for an updated Help file (129). On some OEM versions, the Configuration Backup utility's Help Topics window displays a **Contents** tab that leads to a Troubleshooting book icon. The message appears if the **Registry restore fails with an error** document icon is selected. To access the topic (which is *not* missing), select the **Find** tab and type **Registry** in the box at the top of the window. Then check the **Registry restore fails with an error** topic below and click the **Display** button. Or refer to the "Registry 'Replace' function failed" message earlier, which covers the same ground.

Unable to delete all specified values. This message shown in Figure 8.2 appears if you attempt to delete the (Default) entry on the first line of any Contents Pane. If this is the sole remaining entry in a subkey that is no longer needed, delete the subkey itself.

Figure 8.2 *The usual cause of this message is an attempt to delete a (Default) line in the Contents Pane or other item that cannot be removed.*

The message is also seen if you try to delete any Contents Pane entry in an **HKDD\Config Manager\Enum** subkey. These entries cannot be deleted or edited by the user.

Note: You have chosen to replace your current configuration with the backed-up one. Restore Selected Configuration? Assuming that's exactly what you want to do, then the correct answer is of course, Yes. In case of doubt about the implications, refer to Configuration Restore Warning in Chapter 6 before proceeding.

You are about to backup over a previous backup. Do you want to proceed? If the message appears during a Restore operation, you have just discovered another Windows 95 buglet. Just ignore it and click on the **Yes** button to begin the restoration.

Real-Mode Error Messages

As described in Chapter 7, the Registry Editor can also be run in real mode; that is, from an MS-DOS command prompt before opening or after closing the Windows 95 GUI. Real-mode operations will not function in a DOS window within Windows 95 itself.

Cannot export <*path>filename.ext:... Note the rest of the message and refer to the appropriate message continuation listed here.

Error creating the file. Most likely, the *<path>filename.ext* format was not typed correctly. Make sure the specified path exists and that *filename.ext* does not. If it does, it will be erased without warning.

The specified key name does not exist. The message appears if you try to export a nonexistent key to a file named *<path>filename.ext*.

Cannot open *filename.ext:* **Error opening the file. The previous registry has been restored.** There may in fact be a problem with the cited file, or that file may not exist. In any case, **REGEDIT** has copied the backup **.DA0** files to create a new Registry.

Error accessing the registry: The file may not be complete. This message may appear if you try to import a very large file into the Registry, because there is not enough conventional memory available. You may want to try rebooting in a configuration that will free up as much conventional memory as possible. Or refer to "Registry Editor: Import Problem in Real Mode" in Chapter 7.

Invalid switch. Type **REGEDIT /?** to review the list of valid switches.

Parameter format not correct. Probably one of the switches typed on the **REGEDIT** command line is in error. If necessary, type **REGEDIT /?** and review the correct syntax. Or refer to the "Real Mode Registry Editor" section of Chapter 7 for assistance.

Too many parameters. Either that, or information that must follow a parameter (actually, a switch) was accidentally omitted.

Unable to open registry (14) – System.dat. See "Error accessing the registry," which describes the same problem.

Unable to open registry (1,016) – <*path>filename.ext.* The message really means that **REGEDIT** could not find the specified Registry file, and therefore no action was taken. The number 1,016 may be significant, but on the other hand, it may not.

Startup and Exit Error Messages

Some messages listed here are probably erroneous if seen during a system restart after editing the Registry or after using the System Policy Editor utility. Such messages are often part of a sequence of error messages, including one or more pertaining to the Registry itself. For example, a message reporting insufficient memory or an incorrect display is clearly erroneous if the memory and/or display functioned properly before editing the Registry. As a general rule, just ignore any message that seems to have nothing to do with the Registry and resolve the immediate Registry problem first. Once the Registry itself is in good shape, the non-Registry message may no longer be seen. If a message does persist though, then there is a problem not related to the Registry, which will have to be resolved.

If a command-line message appears and is immediately replaced by the Windows 95 opening splash screen, press the **Escape** and **Pause** keys. This clears the splash screen and halts the startup procedure so that you can read the message. Once you've seen it, press any key to resume the startup.

Cannot find a device file that may be needed to run Windows. The windows registry or SYSTEM.INI file refers to this device file, but the device no longer exists. If you deleted . . . This message may conclude as shown by these two examples. Follow the directions given here, as appropriate.

*filename.*vxd (*followed by*) **Press any key to continue.** If you're not sure why this message appears, check the [386Enh] section of **SYSTEM.INI** for a device=filename.vxd line. If that line exists, then the cited file was probably erased from the **C:\Windows\System** folder, either by accident or on purpose. If in doubt, place a semicolon at the beginning of the line to disable it. If some application subsequently displays a "cannot find *filename*.vxd" message, then you can probably find a copy of the missing file in that application's distribution diskettes. If so, expand it into the folder and re-enable the **SYSTEM.INI** line.

If the cited device line is not in **SYSTEM.INI**, open the Registry and highlight the **HKLM\System\Current ControlSet\Services\VxD** key. Open the View menu, select the **Find** option, and search the Data column for *filename*.vxd. If you know the **open** subkey under the **VxD** key is no longer needed, highlight it and delete it. If you're not sure, export the key first and then delete it. As earlier, an error message will inform you if any application needs the missing file. If so, restore it to the **C:\Windows\System** folder and import the key back into the Registry.

Press any key to continue. (No device file is listed, and Windows 95 opens properly when any key is pressed.) Because no file is specified, the problem is in the Registry, not in **SYSTEM.INI**. Highlight the **HKLM** key cited earlier, but this time search the Values column for StaticVxD, which will be found in almost every subkey. As each one is highlighted by the search process, watch the Data column for an empty ("") entry. If one is found, then delete the **open** subkey.

Connecting X: to \ \\(*computer name*) \ (*folder or filename*). In most cases, this is simply an informational message seen briefly as Windows 95 opens. If the connection fails, however, it will be followed by an error message. Refer to that message here for assistance.

Display: There is a problem with your display settings. The adapter type is incorrect, or the current settings do not work with your hardware. If this message appears after editing the Registry and re-opening Windows 95, just ignore it and resolve the Registry problem.

Display: Your display adapter is not configured properly. To correct the problem, click OK to start the Hardware Installation wizard. Due to a Registry corruption problem, Windows 95 probably created a new **SYSTEM.DAT** file based on the contents of the **SYSTEM.1ST** file. Although you can correct the immediate problem by clicking the OK button, this does not resolve any other issues related to the original problem. Refer to "Registry File Recovery Techniques" in Chapter 7 for additional information.

Error accessing the system registry. You should restore the Registry now and restart your computer. (See Figure 8.3 for the complete message.) Note that the button at the bottom of the message window is labeled **Restore From Backup and Restart,** and no other alternative is available. Furthermore, the Close button in the upper right-hand corner of the window has no effect. Just click the **Restore** button and restart the computer when prompted to do so. If Windows 95 is able to restore the Registry from its backup files, no further messages will appear.

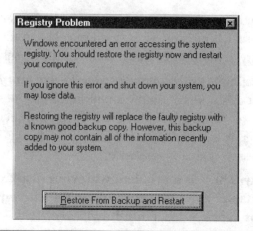

Figure 8.3 *This message implies that you actually have a choice. Click the **Restore** button and hope for the best.*

Error in *filename.ext*. Missing entry: (*or similar explanation*). If the message context in unclear (after all, this *is* Windows 95), and the filename does not suggest anything that loads via the **StartUp** folder or **WIN.INI**'s `load=` or `run=` lines, open the following Registry key:

```
HKEY_LOCAL_MACHINE\SOFTWARE\Microsoft\Window\CurrentVersion\Run
```

Search the Data column for an entry in which the cited filename appears. Chances are, a switch or parameter on that line is invalid. If necessary, uninstall the application and then re-install it.

MS-DOS Prompt. One or more programs did not close. Quit your other programs, and then try again. If no MS-DOS programs are in fact open, the message is probably erroneous, as sometimes happens when shutting down Windows 95 after using the Registry Editor or the System Policies Editor. Just ignore the message and try the shutdown procedure again. If the problem persists, open the **C:\Windows\Start Menu\Programs\StartUp** folder and examine various MS-DOS shortcut icons. Make sure each one is set to close on exit.

Networking: The following error occurred while reconnecting *X:* **to** *(network computer name)**(share name)*. **The share name was not found. Be sure you typed it correctly. Do you want to restore this connection the next time you log on?** A subkey under the **HKCU\Network\Persistent** key refers to a network share name (network drive, folder, or file) that is not currently available. If you click on **Yes**, the contents of the subkey will be deleted and the message will not appear again the next time Windows 95 opens. Click **No** if you believe the problem is temporary and you want to re-attempt the same connection the next time Windows 95 opens.

New Hardware Found. Various erroneous new hardware messages may appear during startup if there is a Registry problem. Just click the **Cancel** button as often as required. Click the **Yes** button when prompted to restart the computer.

REGEDIT.EXE is not a valid Win32 application. This unlikely news is probably the result of damage to the file header. Rename the file **REGEDIT.OLD** and expand a fresh copy into the **C:\Windows** folder. Once the Registry Editor is back in operation, discard the damaged **REGEDIT.OLD** file.

Registry/configuration error. Choose Safe mode, to start Windows with a minimal set of drivers. Windows 95 may choose the Safe mode for you and continue to load itself without giving you the option to intervene. If a Registry Problem message such as that seen in Figure 8.3 appears, refer to that message in this section. If Windows 95 eventually opens in Safe mode, exit Windows 95 and restart the system. If the same message sequence repeats and backup Registry files are not available, Windows 95 will have to be re-installed.

Registry File was not found. Registry services may be inoperative for this session. (This message may be followed by a full-screen MS-DOS command prompt.) This message is usually attributable to a **SYSTEM.DAT** problem that Windows 95 did not resolve by using the backup **SYSTEM.DA0** file. Rename the existing **SYSTEM.DAT SYSTEM.OLD** (or similar), make a copy of **SYSTEM.DA0** as **SYSTEM.DAT**, and reboot the system. If that does not resolve the problem, rerun the Windows 95 setup procedure.

Registry Problem. If this phrase appears in the message window's Title Bar, the accompanying text gives specific details, as shown by the examples in Figures 8.3 and 8.4. Refer to those messages here for further assistance.

Figure 8.4 *This is another no-choice message. Like the message in Figure 8.3, the* ***Close*** *button in the upper right-hand corner does nothing except decorate the window.*

Restrictions: This operation has been canceled due to restrictions in effect on this computer. Please contact your system administrator. If this message is seen one or more times as Windows 95 opens, a Registry restriction prevents various programs in the **StartUp** folder from being executed. If you need to verify this, restart Windows 95 and hold down the **Control** key to bypass these programs. Refer to this message in the "Other Messages" section for additional details.

Sharing. There are *x* user(s) connected to your computer. Shutting down your computer will disconnect them. Do you want to continue? If this message appears when you attempt a shutdown after using the Policy Editor, it may be erroneous. If you're sure no users are connected, click the **Yes** button to continue. Otherwise, click **No** and use the Net Watcher applet to verify connections. If there are none, ignore the message and shut down the system. The message may be followed by an erroneous MS-DOS prompt or other message.

Shortcut, Problem with: (*followed by explanatory message*). If some shortcuts don't work after restarting Windows 95, the **SYSTEM.DAT** file may be corrupted, and Windows 95 may have created a new version based on the **SYSTEM.1ST** file in the **C:** (root) folder, rather then the **SYSTEM.DA0** file. To verify this, refer to "Registry File Recovery Techniques" in Chapter 7.

System Error: Windows cannot read from drive A: If this is a network drive, make sure the network is working. If it is a local drive, check the disk. If it's neither, the message doesn't make sense. It may be seen, however, if the Registry files are severely damaged. If so, clicking the **Cancel** button leads directly to the Windows 95 Setup Wizard's User information screen. If valid backup Registry files are available, exit the setup procedure, replace the current **SYSTEM.DAT** and **USER.DAT** files with the valid backup versions, and restart the system. Otherwise, you may have to complete the setup procedure to restore the Registry.

System Settings Change: To finish restoring your registry, you must restart your computer. Do you want

to restart your computer now? This is usually the final message after one or more other messages about a Registry problem. If you click the **Yes** button, the system should restart with no further problems noted. It *should*, but if it doesn't, it may return to a previously seen Registry Problem message. If valid backup Registry files are available, replace the current **SYSTEM.DAT** and **USER.DAT** files with the valid backup versions and restart the system. Otherwise, you may have to complete the setup procedure to restore the Registry.

If you click the **No** button in the System Settings Change box, the message loop may repeat, display a "Windows is running in safe mode" message, and then repeat the message cycle.

There is not enough memory to load the registry, or the registry is corrupted. Some devices may not function properly (DOS screen). If this message appears when Windows 95 starts or restarts after editing the Registry, it's likely the problem has nothing to do with memory. If a password prompt appears shortly after the message is seen, it will probably be followed by an erroneous *You have not logged on at this computer before* message. If so, click the **No** button to continue and resolve any other error messages that appear.

Windows could not restore your registry. Either a disk error occurred, or no valid backup copy of the registry exists. Use a utility such as ScanDisk to check your hard disk for errors, and then reinstall Windows. If you continue without reinstalling, you may lose data. If there is indeed a problem with the hard disk, follow the advice given in this message. However, if the message appears after editing the Registry and restarting the system, the more likely problem is that a valid copy of the hidden backup **SYSTEM.DA0** and/or **USER.DA0** files could not be found in the **C:\WINDOWS** folder. If you have backup copies located elsewhere, move them into the folder and try again.

If you previously used the Registry Editor's **Export** option to save a full copy of the registry into a *filename*.**REG** file, reboot the system to a command prompt and use the **REGEDIT** utility in its DOS mode to restore the Registry. If you need help with this, refer to the "Restore Procedures" section of Chapter 6 for detailed instructions. However, if you do not have a full backup file available, you'll have to re-install Windows 95.

The button at the bottom of the message window is labeled **Shutdown Windows Now**, no other choice is available, and the **Close** button in the upper right-hand corner has no effect. Press the **Shutdown** button and the System Settings Change window appears. Refer to that message for additional details.

Windows encountered an error while backing up the system registry. Make sure you have enough space on the drive for three copies of the file C:\WINDOWS\ SYSTEM.DAT [or USER.DAT]. This error should not cause any loss of information, but if space is not made on the drive you may experience additional problems. Please fix the problem, and then restart your computer. Assuming "the problem" is indeed limited space, you'll have to free up some space by moving or deleting some files. However, the message may also be related to a defective driver loaded by the **CONFIG.SYS** or **AUTOEXEC.BAT** file. If this is a possibility, reboot the system and bypass any such drivers. If that resolves the problem, determine which driver is causing the problem and replace it.

When you press **OK**, if the Desktop reverts to its initial appearance when Windows 95 was first installed, the current **SYSTEM.DAT** file was probably just copied from the early **SYSTEM.1ST** file in the **C:** (root) directory. In that case, this message will probably appear every time you open Windows 95. If so, refer to "Registry File Replacement" in Chapter 7 for assistance.

You have not logged on at this computer before. Would you like this computer to retain your individual settings for use when you log on here in the future? If this message appears after editing the Registry, it is probably erroneous. Assuming you *have* logged on previously, click **No** to continue. In fact, do so even if you have not logged on here before, and resolve the Registry problem first.

Other Error Messages

These few messages may not seem directly related to the Registry. However, the Registry edits listed here may resolve the problem that caused the message to appear.

Error occurred while trying to remove *application name*. Uninstallation has been canceled. If this message appears when you try to use Control Panel's Add/Remove Programs applet to remove an application, then that application may have already been removed manually. However, its presence on the Install/Uninstall list indicates that remnants remain in the Registry. Refer to "Uninstall Problems" in Chapter 7 for assistance in removing the application from this list and cleaning up any other lingering Registry references.

Fatal exception 0E has occurred at 0028:*xxxxxxxx* in VxD VMM(06) + *xxxxxxxx*. Fatal exception messages may be generated by a variety of causes, but this one is usually the result of a damaged Registry file. If a fatal exception message repeats after restoring the Registry from valid backup files, try to isolate it to the specific application event that causes it. In this case, however, the solution may not be related to the Registry.

Invalid (*or* damaged, unrecognizable, etc.) diskette. Windows 95 overwrites the OEM name field on a diskette as part of its volume-tracking system. As a result, some applications may no longer recognize the diskette, and an error message appears the next time it is accessed, even though it is in fact neither invalid nor damaged. Unfortunately, the only workaround is to use the Debug utility (or similar) to restore the original OEM name field, providing you know what it is. If not, contact the diskette supplier for the necessary information or a replacement diskette.

Refer to "Volume-Tracking Problems" in Chapter 7 for more information about this "feature" and for ways to protect yourself against it.

Modem is Busy or Not Responding. If this problem cannot be resolved by other means, open the following Registry key and look for the Contents Pane entries listed here:

```
HKEY_LOCAL_MACHINE\System\CurrentControlSet\Services\
Class\Modem\0000\Settings
```

Name	Data (Original)	Data (Revised)
FlowControl_Hard	"\Q3"	""
InactivityTimeout	"\T<#>"	""
SpeedNegotiationOn	"N1"	""

Double-click on each Name entry and delete the highlighted string in the Value Data box. Data strings will vary from those shown here depending on your specific hardware configuration, but should be deleted. However, do not delete the Name entry itself. In case of doubt, open the **0000** key one level above **Settings** and make sure the DriverDesc entry agrees with the modem that is actually installed.

Program Not Found: Windows cannot find *filename*.EXE. This program is needed for opening files of type '(*type description*).' If this message box appears after double-clicking on a document file with a certain extension, then either the executable program required to open that file is missing or the record of its location in the Registry is incorrect. There are several methods to resolve the problem, as described here:

Enter path... to the *filename*.EXE file. If you enter the correct path to the specified file, Windows 95 writes that information into the [programs] section of **WIN.INI**, and it takes precedence over the Registry entry, which is presumably obsolete. Although this is the fastest resolution to the immediate problem, it works by bypassing the Registry instead of fixing it. If you need to resume operations quickly, you may want to use this method and repair the Registry later, when you have more time, by following the procedure given next.

Find the... *filename*.EXE file. If necessary, use Explorer to find or verify the location of the *filename*.EXE file. If the file cannot be found, you'll need to expand a fresh copy into the appropriate folder. Refer to "File Finding Techniques" in Chapter 7 if you need help locating a missing file.

Repair the... Registry Data. Open the Registry's **HKCR** folder and highlight the *.ext* subkey, where *.ext* is the extension of the document file. In the (Default) row, make a note of the string in the Data column, then search **HKCR** for the subkey with that name and open its **Shell\Open\command** subkey. The (Default) Data string indicates the path where the executable file should be located. If necessary, change the path to indicate the correct location. If the path is correct, note the name of the executable file and expand a fresh copy of that file into the indicated location.

If you enter a new path in response to the "Cannot find" message, that path will be written into the [programs] *section of WIN.INI, and the information in the Registry will remain unchanged.*

NOTE

Properties for this item are not available. If this message is seen when a Context menu's **Properties** option is selected, the most likely culprits are a missing subkey related to the object or a **DLL** or **CPL** file that supports the Properties sheet. If you need help locating the missing element, refer to "Property Sheet Problems" in Chapter 7.

A less-likely suspect is an erroneous Attributes entry in a ShellFolder subkey. If this key exists, and bit 30 is set, then the Properties option appears on the Context menu where, presumably, it belongs. However, if the bit is set to 1 when it should be 0, then the option is erroneous and this error message will appear if it is selected. Refer to *Attribute Flags* and Table 5.3 in Chapter 5 for additional details.

Restrictions: This operation has been canceled due to restrictions in effect on this computer. Please contact your system administrator. Assuming this message is valid, contact your administrator if there is some reason to remove the restriction. If the restriction is accidental, refer to "Restriction Recovery Procedure" in Chapter 7 for help in removing it.

Setup cannot find the files on 'X:\' from which you originally installed the product. If this is a network server, make sure that the server is still available. This message may appear if you try to uninstall a Windows 95 application via Control Panel's Add/Remove Programs applet. If the problem is not related to a server, the most likely culprit is a recent drive letter change, as might happen if a newly installed drive pushed the CD-ROM drive letter from say, **D** to **E**, and the application had been installed from a CD-ROM prior to the change. If possible, temporarily uninstall the new drive so that the CD-ROM can fall back to its original drive letter and then try again.

It that's not possible, refer to "Uninstall Problems" in Chapter 7 for assistance in cleaning up the Registry.

Setup Error 544: Setup is unable to open the data file *<path>filename*.STF; run Setup again from where you originally ran it. This is another Uninstall error message. The cited path and filename are listed in a Registry **Uninstall** subkey, and the file contains the information needed to complete the uninstall procedure. When you click **OK**, the following messages may appear in succession:

```
Setup Error 723: The processing of top-level
information has failed.
Setup was not completed successfully.
```

Ignore them and refer to "Uninstall Problems" in Chapter 7 for furthe\r assistance.

Unable to determine your network address. The UUID generated is unique to this computer only. It should not be used on another computer. This message appears if the CLSID Generator utility (described in Chapter 5) is run on a machine that lacks a network card. The last six bytes of the CLSID number are therefore randomly generated, and apparently the odds are not as favorable that the entire number will be unique within the universe as we know it.

Index